The Wardle Family and its Circle

THE WARDLE FAMILY

AND ITS CIRCLE

Textile Production in the Arts and Crafts Era

Brenda M. King

THE BOYDELL PRESS

First published 2019
The Boydell Press, Woodbridge

ISBN 978 1 78327 395 9

The Boydell Press is an imprint of Boydell & Brewer Ltd
PO Box 9, Woodbridge, Suffolk IP12 3DF, UK
and of Boydell & Brewer Inc.
668 Mt Hope Avenue, Rochester, NY 14620–2731, USA
website: www.boydellandbrewer.com

A catalogue record for this book is available
from the British Library

The publisher has no responsibility for the continued existence or accuracy of URLs for
external or third-party internet websites referred to in this book, and does not guarantee that
any content on such websites is, or will remain, accurate or appropriate

Typeset by BBR Design, Sheffield

For my family

'When the history of decorative art in Europe came to be written, Leek would occupy a very high position' due to 'the Leek School of Embroidery, for the highly artistic work that had been produced by them.'

'Thanks to Mr Wardle, England was beginning to see the beauty of Indian dyes when applied to tussur silks, in which their great bloom and beauty were admirably retained.'

Oscar Wilde, 25 February 1884, Leek, Staffordshire

CONTENTS

ILLUSTRATIONS

Plates

Figures

A note on copyright

The author and publisher are grateful to all the institutions and individuals listed for permission to reproduce the materials in which they hold copyright. Every effort has been made to trace the copyright holders; apologies are offered for any omission, and the publisher will be pleased to add any necessary acknowledgement in subsequent editions.

PREFACE

The driving force behind this book was the desire to find out more about the remarkable Wardle family, the outstanding textiles they produced and why they produced them.[1] Certain family members were influential people who had valuable, interdependent exchanges of ideas and sharing of skills with prominent, creative individuals. Although they were acclaimed in their lifetime, footnotes in histories of the Arts and Crafts movement and Aestheticism have never done them justice.[2] When the first wave of Arts and Crafts history was written the Wardles were overlooked for the most part and slipped from view. Sometimes only the expanse of time can give us the true extent of someone's achievement and new evidence has brought them back into focus. Once again they can be understood as the widespread cultural force they once were. Knowing more about the beautiful things they made tells us more about Leek, the place where they were produced, and where that fits into the wider textile sector during a particularly influential, extensive and creative era.

Leek, in north Staffordshire, where the family lived and worked, was no backwater. It was a globally connected and culturally refined centre in the late nineteenth century. What might appear initially as English local history was a complex balance of national and international factors dependent on numerous symbiotic international networks and a coalescence of many different cultures there. This wider context, including a strong engagement with architectural history, evokes correspondences between architects and the local community and thus between public and private lives, bringing textiles to life in numerous revealing ways. Three members of the Wardle family were nationally significant figures for a variety of reasons. Their stories bring to light little-known aspects of the lives of their eminent friends and colleagues, including the world's pre-eminent designers and architects. It was with William Morris that Thomas Wardle was most closely associated, but there were many other eminent figures who had reason to be grateful for his knowledge.[3] Biographies of Morris, Walter Crane, Lewis Foreman Day, Arthur Lasenby Liberty, John Dando Sedding, Richard Norman Shaw, George Gilbert Scott Jnr and Charles F.A. Voysey are illustrated with images of their textiles produced in Leek. To date, however, no publication has fully explored what the Wardles themselves achieved and their subsequent widespread influence. The broad range and fine quality of the textiles that the family developed fed into the Arts and Crafts movement, Gothic Revivalism, Art Needlework, Aestheticism and trade with India. By the 1870s the town of Leek was known as a centre of inventive textile activity in a number of spheres during a nationwide period of immense creativity that is still not fully understood. Yet the significance of the town and the variety of beautiful and useful things created there seems to have gone largely unnoticed. That story will be told here, in the process uniting a number of artistic movements that are often treated independently.

This publication places the Wardle family and its work into its original context. To achieve this, fresh evidence had to be recovered to broaden out what little we knew about a creative dynasty and its global contacts.[4] The research process was not easy, as many vital records have not survived. Proof in the form of documents and objects was widely scattered. Over time, however, and by digging deeper, new material was uncovered. The outcome is this book, the first to focus in depth on the remarkable Leek Embroidery Society and its international impact. An extensive chapter is devoted to an extraordinary range of embroidery designs by the most eminent Gothic Revival architects.

Opulent silk textiles contributed to the strong sense of place that pervades Leek's history. This book explores the broad context of their production, as silk acted as a link between architects, community, commerce and creativity. Surviving pieces reveal a refinement of technical skill and remarkable aesthetic judgement as silk was transformed by architecture and vice versa into a visual metaphor. Unearthing more about these objects rediscovered a community of skilled craftworkers, giving some insight into their lives, about which little was known. The extensive use of wild silks, dyes and designs from India, most particularly in churches at the hub of a north Staffordshire community, was a revelation.

Through new evidence, we now know more of the time when crucial aspects of the international silk trade were transformed through Thomas Wardle's significant research and development. As a pioneering dye chemist his manifold achievements were important to craft workers in England, Europe and America, and silk producers in India, and are still celebrated on the subcontinent.[5] What has often been overlooked is that Wardle's research outcomes allowed not only his family to produce their own work of superior quality but also many others to realise their creative ambitions by using his fine-quality goods in homes and workshops. These revelations allow us to understand just what was lost when the family and the town were despatched to the margins of textile history. It is reasonable to ask why, if this is such a significant history, it has not been fully explored before? One likely reason was the difficulty of locating enough primary evidence to produce a credible account. Surprisingly little proof has remained, so that even quite simple details relating to Wardle organisations active over 160 years are missing. Regrettably, there is no comprehensive archive in one convenient location; the thousands of corporate documents, working drawings and photographs, carved printing blocks, and dyed, printed and stitched textile samples that would have been a fundamental part of daily life have mostly vanished. What little there is – even the most tangential material – gives us some idea of what has been discarded. The pattern-book collection in the Whitworth Art Gallery, Manchester, has yielded a great deal of information on designs printed in Leek, and the famous series of business letters from Morris to Wardle has been well scrutinised, although we know of their alliance wholly from Morris's perspective. There is no hoard of letters to or from Elizabeth Wardle, although there is a small batch of letters to and from members of the royal family who were given woven silks and embroidery by the Wardles. Neither Thomas nor Elizabeth wrote a memoir and if they kept diaries none have surfaced. Thomas published over fifty learned papers; Elizabeth produced just two publications, although others wrote of her achievements. Her *Guide to the Bayeux Tapestry* (1886), while short, is well written and informative about the extraordinary facsimile that she initiated. Her *366 Easy Dinners Arranged for Young Housekeepers* (1891), with a recipe for every day of the year, is full of practical facts, and allows us to see just how knowledgeable she was about food. She knew exactly how a kitchen catering for a large family worked in practice; other aspects of her character, unfortunately, remain inscrutable.

Surviving handmade objects can have a neutral objectivity, as they unarguably demonstrate technically exacting craftsmanship, with its attendant values of luxury, beauty and skill. The intrinsic qualities of the materials alone demonstrate economic and social factors that were important to the market for luxury silk goods. They required innovation, refined designs and the acquisition of demanding techniques if they were to be valued in significant settings.[6] Many costly items produced in Leek were designed to be highly visible, particularly those made for ecclesiastical purposes. As many remain in use today, we can see that both material and emblematic elements were relevant. They added a sense of rootedness to important events in people's lives. They also reveal that both Thomas and Elizabeth Wardle put their ideas into their practice.

As research for this book progressed, an unexpected number of fine embroideries and designs on paper that had not been previously documented were rediscovered. Found in the backs of drawers, literally under beds, or in museums across Britain and India, they have been scrutinised over many years. As the ownership of some items is known, they are able to be directly connected to different aspects of Leek's community. Surviving pieces reveal a wide range of textiles produced for a variety of clients. They were, by widespread agreement, some of the finest produced in the Arts and Crafts era. Details of their textures, colours and designs evoke the lost world of a remarkable tight-knit community with strong local values and fine skills.

Despite long-term, focused searches, much remained unknowable until a large stash of critical evidence was stumbled upon in India in 2009.[7] This important find bears witness to years of intensive research by Thomas Wardle. While some of this history was known it was only with the discovery of thousands of dye samples prepared in Leek that the full magnitude of his study of India's raw materials could be grasped. His investigations into the wild silks and indigenous dyestuffs of the subcontinent still inspire makers in India today. Wardle published a detailed summary of his research findings that is a model of scholarship and intense dedication, yet these significant samples were not rediscovered in India for over 120 years. By reconnecting these finds with other data it has been possible to construct a clearer account of an impressive life.

Over years each item has been inspected from every angle for their influences, which were embedded in the physical and social fabric of the community that created them. The backs and fronts of large, site-specific embroidered pieces in major buildings, individual threads, even lining materials, and a multilayered visual language have all been examined in order to extract as much information as possible in an attempt to reconnect histories that have been treated separately. In the process new ways of looking at old evidence emerged. As the realities of everyday life in Leek encompassed trade, politics, consumerism, aesthetics and the impact that re-evaluating old evidence had on the local community, even familiar pieces have been reassessed as fresh evidence from different sources came to light. One completely unexpected item appeared in an exhibition devoted to Oscar Wilde at the Petit Palace in Paris in 2016. It was a printed leaflet advertising 'The House Beautiful', a lecture given by Wilde in Leek in 1884.

Curating exhibitions over the past ten years was a crucial part of the research process. Bringing previously scattered items together allowed historic items to be positioned side by side for the first time, revealing similarities and reinforcing physical aspects of quality and techniques passed down verbally through families and workshops as a continuous way of life. Such aspects were embedded in pieces alongside more intangible elements relating to beauty, luxury, empire and women's lives.

The landscape was a crucial element that was clearly relevant to this history of things. Local craftworkers needed the river. It shaped their lives, as it provided employment for dyers and printers of cloth, who needed water for the many processes that transformed raw materials into glorious textiles. As a result of the Wardles' influence, the name of Leek itself carried meanings that are complex and often related to a sense of place and shared cultural characteristics that also allowed creativity in the region to flourish.

Although the Arts and Crafts movement is difficult to define clearly, it is generally agreed that the Wardle family fits the criteria and objectives even though individuals operated according to their own motivations and family history rather than simply following movements led by others. The text below explores elements of the Arts and Crafts movement, along with Art Needlework, the Aesthetic movement, Gothic Revivalism, the Anglo-Indian silk trade, technical developments, architectural changes, and aspects of women's lives, all of which are relevant. Experts agree that these various interconnected movements were inspired by a range of historically or culturally different objects, from Pugin's and Ruskin's medievalism to ceramics from Japan. Although versions of Art Needlework[8] and Gothic Revivalism occurred elsewhere, Leek had its own particular set of circumstances that set it apart. As a result of this research we can now add India to this list as it provides a vital international backstory to many relevant events.

Today it is accepted that the ideal of the artisan–craftsman as the epitome of the independent, creative maker almost never happened. It was generally the case that designers such as Morris or architects such as Shaw designed work for others to make.[9] The exhibition 'Architect–Designers: Pugin to Mackintosh', held in London in 1981, demonstrated that many of the finest objects were designed by architects.[10] What was not explored fully, though, was that the spread of Gothic Revival architecture across Britain had many links with ecclesiastical needlework. While this was a countrywide phenomenon, involving nationally renowned figures, the focus within is on the enormous impact this had in north Staffordshire. Throughout this exploration I posed the obvious questions 'why Leek and why then?', 'why did Leek develop so differently from other silk towns in the region' and 'how did it attract the attention of such an extraordinary number of leading figures? The county had the will and ability to fund grand projects and attracted outstanding architects with commissions to work on a variety of schemes, some of which were major ones, at an early stage in their careers. George Frederick Bodley, Augustus Welby Northmore Pugin, George Gilbert Scott Jnr and George Edmund Street, all influential figures greatly interested in the role of elaborate textiles in their ecclesiastical buildings, received important contracts to work in Staffordshire.[11] Prior to the formal development of the Leek Embroidery Society they designed embroideries for their churches that were transformed by local woman who shared an understanding of emblematic aesthetics. Some of their distinguished pupils also built in the region. They, too, became giants of their profession. The connection of Leek's embroidery with architecture creates a strong chapter in this history.

Although they are a crucial element of this story, the architects' lives and buildings are not discussed here, as this task has already been undertaken by eminent architectural historians. Andrew Saint's magnificent work devoted to Shaw has proved indispensable, as have Gavin Stamp's and Michael Hall's publications on Scott Jnr and Bodley, respectively. Michael Fisher's publications on the Gothic Revival in north Staffordshire have a wealth of detail. While the authors may acknowledge embroidery designs, however, by and large they do not explore the finished work or its context. It is the textiles produced for the buildings that are the focus here. Chapter 4 examines the designs and finished embroideries in detail for the first time. As many are still in the churches for which they were made, we have the chance to see the pieces as they were seen originally. They are examples of great individual talents, which gave many people enormous pleasure in their making and using. Approaching the work of so many major architects through the medium of embroidery restores the work of the brilliant Wardle family to a significant position in a number of histories.

In 1886 Elizabeth Wardle produced a facsimile of the famous Bayeux Tapestry. It is now on permanent display in Reading Museum, where it still delights and intrigues visitors. This monumental work deservedly has a chapter to itself. Important new evidence highlights how well the copy was received in America.[12]

The main themes that emerged from the research, and which bind the principal characters together across time and place, can be summarised as: creativity, innovation, transformation, symbolism, collaboration, skills, networks and trade. Different chapters engage with different themes, and explore the borderlands between. It was a challenge to organise the material so that it could be both thematic and chronological and do adequate justice to such varied experiences and the resultant heritage.

Recapturing what happened in late nineteenth-century north Staffordshire still matters. It confirms that it is now necessary to reposition the making of fine textiles there alongside other comprehensive histories to make this important heritage better known. There is another dimension to this. The research at the core of this book also acts as a corrective to some twenty-first-century publications that have detached the Wardle family from its broader context and thus failed to do its achievements justice. Dispelling gendered myths of the stereotypical, money-grubbing manufacturer and the suppressed needlewoman is, therefore, a further ambition of this publication. Some authors have put a distorting theoretical spin on aspects of textile history that was never there originally, while wilfully ignoring what did exist as an inconvenient intrusion, particularly where embroidery is concerned.[13] This is challenged in the

Conclusion. There has been a tendency, incorrectly, to dismiss fine embroidery as simply decorative, merely 'women's work'. In fact, it often had a ritualistic role and engaged with robust topics relating to faith and war as well as fostering a form of social cohesion. Several publications have, nevertheless, miscast Elizabeth Wardle as a marginalised 'every' needlewoman, without agency. Varied horizons are essential in this history if it is to reflect the broader interests that were an essential aspect of the Wardle family's constantly expanding life.

Unpicking this rich and layered history involved intensive searching through local libraries, national archives, museum collections, private homes and churches. Although some embroidery produced in Leek is in national collections, many pieces survive outside the museum sector, with more remaining in the churches for which they were made than was thought. While research in museums and company archives was crucial, fieldwork proved to be essential. Studying textiles in the somewhat sterile atmosphere of a museum does not necessarily reveal their significance to a specific interior or the community that created them. Seeing pieces in the setting for which they were intended often led to unexpected connections and extended the scope of the study. Working in rural churches sometimes meant that previously unrecorded items were 'found', which built up a more complex picture than was previously known. Items have been newly located in Cheshire, Derbyshire, Gloucester, London, Norfolk, Shropshire and Staffordshire. Recording them was fascinating and troubling in equal measure. It sometimes exposed problems, as some pieces are now over 100 years old. Their uncertain future is discussed in the Conclusion.

Linking vital documentary evidence with specific items for the first time brought a particular thrill as unforeseen revelations occurred, adding layers of meaning to the story. In some cases items that had been lying unnoticed for years are now admired once again. Two significant collections of dyed samples and lengths of fabric hand printed in Leek recently emerged in Kolkata (Calcutta) and Rajasthan museums respectively, revealing that Thomas Wardle's exhaustive research was the result of finely calibrated judgements that produced astonishing results.[14] They are discussed in the Conclusion.

Opportunities to view embroideries up close and experience their tactile and visual elements as they would have been known by their makers and others more than a century ago had its own special returns. This, coupled with an element of serendipity, has led to authoritative outcomes that should change how specific aspects of design and craft history are perceived. The in-depth analysis of surviving embroideries from Leek produced between 1864 and 1930 conveys, furthermore, the creative capacity of many remarkable, yet unknown, people. This detail is essential if we are to fully comprehend the scope of various creative networks, including major cultural institutions with which previously unknown people were connected. This will redress the balance and an in-depth analysis of surviving embroideries will make their contribution to an influential period of British history more generally known.

The superior quality of surviving textiles and discoveries relating to significant collaborations clearly indicate that the Leek Embroidery Society and its legacy has claim to its own objective place in a number of important histories. The excellent colours, the result of traditional methods and natural dyes, have remained sound for well over a century. They reveal that the Wardle family was equal to the scale of its ambition. The Embroidery Society can, therefore, be justifiably positioned more firmly in central accounts of an era that produced so many creative, craft-based movements. The revival of demanding textile crafts generally, the enhanced status of Art Needlework and many commissions from leading figures cumulatively raised the profile of the Society, which in turn reinforced the significance of creative embroidery. Without an acknowledgement of what happened in Leek, these histories are skewed. This is important as twenty-first-century developments require us to be knowledgeable about our recent past in order to inform some crucial decision-making.

ACKNOWLEDGEMENTS

My thanks are due to a great many people who have shared their knowledge and expertise with me. I am grateful to Meg Andrews, Jenny Balfour-Paul, Charles Chalcraft, Neil Collingwood, Linda Eaton, Nicholas Gilmour, Pamela Jones, Dr Susan Kay-Williams (Royal School of Needlework), Richard Knisely-Marpole (photographer), Amrita Mukerji, Michael Pollard (photographer), Reading Museum, Linda Schofield for her editorial expertise, the Society of Antiquaries London, Staffordshire Libraries, Staffordshire Moorlands District Council, Eleanor Van Zandt, Cathryn Walton, Isabella Whitworth and all of those who care for the great many unique embroideries in churches across Staffordshire, Cheshire and Derbyshire. I am deeply grateful for all the help and guidance I received from the Editorial and Production teams at Boydell & Brewer. Thank you also to James Helling for the preparation of the index.

INTRODUCTION

… let me express the hope that Leek – which is already deservedly known as a centre of art and science, a patron of culture and beauty, and the home of loving kindness and earnest work, may realise your highest hopes.

John Ruskin, 1897[1]

Today, many travel through the town of Leek on their way to somewhere else, yet those who do stop are quickly rewarded. Once famous for silk production, which has long ceased, Leek retains a strong sense of its past, which is a fascinating blend of global silk history, a glorious architectural heritage and moorland scenery. Although now converted to other functions, several huge mill buildings once used for making yarn and cloth survive alongside a varied and noteworthy range of distinctive buildings built during the Arts and Crafts and Gothic Revival eras. Commercial premises, private houses and a number of fine churches by distinguished architects continue to dominate the townscape, providing a strong sense of continuity.

The town, which still retains its market town status, is set against the rugged landscape of the Staffordshire Moorlands, which provide a water supply and a dramatic backdrop, with miles of meandering drystone walls and a multitude of buildings of weathered local stone. Many of the region's churches, too, are quarried from the landscape, and blend in with the hills and river valleys. They enclose another important heritage, however, that is mainly hidden from sight. Those who know where to look will discover a legacy of the time when richly coloured silks, including fine embroidery, were produced locally. Inside, in calculated contrast to the local stone, can be found embroidered silks designed to stand out as a focal point. The impact they made in the nineteenth century was profound and that effect endures, as the silks are varied and astonishing. Many are decorated with India's timeless patterns and are still radiant with the intense natural colour applied in Leek. Now a valued legacy, they speak of

1

outstanding design and demanding techniques that were once part of daily life in town and village. They are symbolic of the town's relationship with its natural features and specialist skills, which were adapted to serve global demands. They reflect a distinct community structure along with aesthetic, entrepreneurial and spiritual values, and stand today as reminders of the global silk trade and the wider preoccupations of the residents. They are a vivid reminder of the time when numerous creative forces coalesced in this region of north Staffordshire in particularly interesting ways. The neighbouring counties of Cheshire, Derbyshire and Shropshire also have buildings with fine embroideries produced in Leek.

From the 1860s onwards Leek became a place where values embedded in the Arts and Crafts Movement and Gothic Revivalism thrived. As the region prospered it became sufficiently settled and wealthy to attract not one but five major Gothic Revivalist architects to build there in the latter half of the nineteenth century. They were all connected to William Morris, designer and revolutionary, who visited Leek to work with Thomas Wardle. Leek had a lot to offer architects, as it provided the necessary capital along with both a creative community and a positive attitude to new ideas. The building of churches also required different crafts, materials and trades, many of which could be supplied in the town. These architects' buildings were simultaneously places of worship and lavish structures, indicating that the town was a centre of inventive inter-actions, and were sustained by a strong community spirit and the resources of leading citizens, who created a mesh of financial and sympathetic support. A number of the region's churches still contain a range of large, site-specific embroideries designed by the architects for their buildings and stitched by talented local needlewomen, often in their own homes. Further examples are in public collections and are regularly displayed in the town, while others are in private hands, as explored in Chapter 4.

Members of the Wardle family – Thomas, Elizabeth and George Young Wardle – were closely linked to key individuals in the Arts and Crafts Movement at a critical early stage in its development. There is no evidence that they set out to align themselves with Morris and others; rather, they were independently committed to practising their crafts locally, with a comparable ethos. Their aims were remarkably similar to those of leading theorists and makers, although originally for different reasons. Although Thomas and Elizabeth Wardle were always based in north Staffordshire, their reach was international. They maintained strong connections with London, the hub of artistic, scientific and trade activity. Europe, with its many centres of silk excellence, America and India all played significant parts in their lives. They were active during an age that experienced one of the most remarkably innovative periods of British history, as well as the growth and decline of the British Empire.[2] While they thought globally, the Wardle family's impetus came from their

Staffordshire roots. Making fine textiles was a deep-rooted way of life for the majority in Leek and close family ties were important to Leek's strong sense of place. Learning historic textile processes was a hands-on experience in the dye house or workshop, where a skilled family member was often tutor to their own children. Acquiring these skills frequently involved hard physical activity – for the dyers, for example, that could mean regular immersions into cold river water – as well as challenging problem-solving while they developed an understanding of materials.

The story of the Wardle family of Leek is more than a celebration of an arts and crafts community and the worldwide reach of their textile skills. It is also about the wonder of transformation. The family's approach to local occupations expanded traditional, scattered and sometimes isolated craft activity, which created a more buoyant cluster of businesses. Along with technical advances, this strengthened the community's ability to respond readily to new markets as the materials they demanded were perfected by either family members or other local artisans. Thomas Wardle knew that he and other practitioners needed to be open to new methods and to expand their knowledge if they were to survive. Different members of the family explored ways of transforming Britain's and India's fluctuating silk trades, strengthening both creative practice and the home economy in the process, while adding to the subcontinent's export market in raw materials.[3] The launch of the Leek Embroidery Society in 1879/80 took these developments in another direction by adding different historic skills and using one material to enhance another. The Society continued to thrive and produce fine needlework well into the twentieth century.

Although Leek produced a range of extraordinary textiles, remarkably little was known of its products until recently. New information adds a great deal to our understanding of its silk industry, which played a unique role in developing fine-quality commodities for global markets.

Transformation

In the 1830s Leek expanded following a general boom in English silk production. In contrast to the mass production of cotton cloth elsewhere, the silk trades still depended on traditional skills. Leek was part of an east–west dynamic and family firms were necessarily outward-looking and aware of European developments in technology and design, as well as maintaining strong commercial links with London. As a town of trade and commerce it resembled other silk centres that spread across the length and breadth of the ancient silk routes, and developed an integrated, interdependent cluster of small and medium-sized companies; even small silk companies were alert to global market forces, as their raw materials were shipped in from across the developed world. Leek was accessible by rail and canal, which brought in raw materials to be converted into finished goods. Trains and barges then distributed the products across the country.

A rural dye works, a block-printing workshop, a silk-weaving garret or an embroidery workroom relied on the diverse, hands-on skills of a small workforce, some of which related to the domestic sphere, others to the activities of dye houses and workshops. Typically expertise was transferred from one generation of fathers and sons, or mothers and daughters, to another, and was well suited to small-batch production. Macclesfield to the north, Congleton to the west and a number of scattered communities in Derbyshire, to the east of Leek, formed a triangle of silk towns, all of which depended on traditional skills to produce a variety of luxury goods.

From the early nineteenth century, and with increasing diversity, Leek manufactured more specialised products such as hand-woven broadcloth, including serge, sarcenets and damasks, along with a highly specialised chiné silk. Alongside woven, dyed and printed cloth and threads, Leek produced a range of narrow goods, including braids woven from silk, cotton, mohair and worsted. For many years there was an important trade in braid for both women's and men's wear, providing bindings and ornamental trimming for tailoring purposes. A woman's outfit with a long skirt might have several examples of the many varieties, easily reaching a total of more than 45 to 55m (147 to 180 feet). Ribbons, ferrets, bindings, braids, laces and galloons were in constant demand in Europe and beyond.

During the late nineteenth century most activities in the area reflected Leek's established silk industry, although a balance with agriculture was maintained. Producers responded to different markets and ultimately traditional skills existed side by side with mechanisation, complementing and supplying each other.[4] Eventually larger spinning mills increasingly dominated Leek's townscape, as the demands for different threads expanded. By the mid-1880s embroidery and sewing silks, twist, filoselles, crewels and other items for needlework were made there. About fifty large and small manufacturers provided the main sources of employment. In the 1880s the growing use of sewing machines played a major part in the modification of sewing threads, including the production of spun silk. The range of companies involved with different aspects of the silk trade in one modest town meant that the commission, use and support of one person's initiatives could lead to the success of another's enterprise. The continuation of specialist crafts meant that Leek developed a concentrated, connected cluster of small and large traditional businesses that fed into the establishment of an eminent embroidery society, as discussed in Chapters 2, 3 and 4.

Reacting to demand, women, as well as men, acquired skills and prospered from them, increasing their sense of purpose and autonomy. What they created must also have deepened their sense of belonging to a focused community, as the large embroidered pieces that many helped produce were installed in the most prestigious buildings in the region. The transformative impact of architecture spread across the community in a number of ways. The creation of a strong civic identity came through considerable funds that were made available in the town, which, in turn, helped sustain local craft-based businesses that supplied the materials. This reinforced the needlewoman's identity as important to the communal spirit.

While Leek was a typical town in many respects, from the mid-1860s one aspect of town life there was unique. Augmenting that part of its identity shaped by its north Staffordshire context was a huge range of stimuli that came from links with the Anglo-Indian silk trade. As a result, Leek became the only silk town in the region to play a prominent role in the Arts and Crafts Movement, Art Needlework and Gothic Revivalism. The following chapters explore all of these elements in depth.

The Wardle family's multilayered activities reflected the dramatic pace of change in global, material, aesthetic and technical possibilities and thus flourished and attracted attention. Their activities also related to a specific consumer group with high standards and which valued the making of beautiful things. Additional layers of complexity were added through long-standing alliances with leading designers and architects. As Leek became a centre for like-minded and leading figures, so some of the most internationally celebrated textiles of the Arts and Crafts Movement were produced there.

Alongside his involvement in local developments Thomas Wardle simultaneously challenged the international silk trade. As an articulate spokesman for Britain's silk industry, he urged producers to reconsider India's diverse range of wild silks as a newly developed raw material with greater promise than previously thought. Through an intensive programme of research and development he resolved to overcome problems that prevented a widespread use of the wild silks found in abundance across India. The result was an increased range of hand-woven silk cloth and threads, a phenomenon detailed in the following chapters.

A Sense of Place

While a sense of place is important to this history, the founding of the Leek Embroidery Society was not simply the result of an inescapable, insular response to a particular location. Although the relationship between local craftspeople and their environment was important – they had established their trades there because of the character of the natural water supply – other factors were influential. Even though the name of the Society made its geographical setting very clear, that alone did not determine its function. From the outset it was shaped by an acute, outward-looking reaction to national and international factors, and a knowledge of this wider context of the Leek Embroidery Society is essential if we are to gain a full understanding of its relevance on a number of counts. Some previous publications have, however, tended to focus on the provincial nature of the Society and in the process separated it from broader cultural conditions that were vital to its progress. The Society was built partly on Thomas Wardle's research, and its success, in turn, made his other businesses stronger.

Unusually, Leek retained its historic market town status alongside silk production. Living in a long-established market town surrounded by spectacular moorland scenery had specific advantages. Durable family networks in smaller towns meant an increased degree of social cohesion. Although some incomers were attracted to work in Leek's expanding silk industry, many families had deep roots there and knew each other well. It is evident from contemporary Staffordshire newspapers that the town was small enough for residents to feel involved but large enough to sustain a variety of social activities. There evolved a critical mass of shared thought and resources, which enabled, among other things, a series of interesting buildings to be erected in the region. With strong networks and institutions, a good work–life balance was possible for many residents. This included the communal spirit evident in church- and society-related activities such as the making and display of fine embroidery. One result was that religious buildings and their furnishings grew exponentially, to become important elements of Leek life. If they wished it, everyone in the town had access to the finest craft skills and luxurious materials on a regular basis: churchgoing afforded opportunities to experience the best designs realised in wood, glass, metal and paint, as well as silk and gold thread, every day.

The environment in Leek was healthier than that in the polluted major industrial conurbations. The so-called pottery towns, only 21km (13 miles) from Leek, were vividly described by Arnold Bennett as harsh and smoke-blackened. Although they too housed creative, craft-based industries, they were quite different places in which to live and work. Thomas Wardle knew the pottery towns, as the art and technical colleges of Burslem, Fenton, Hanley, Newcastle-under-Lyme, Stoke and Tunstall all invited him to speak to their students and staff. He lectured on the crucial roles that art, craft and design played in local industry. Like Morris, who also lectured in Burslem, on 'Art and Beauty of Earth (1881), he believed that striving for control over materials, the need for precision and self-discipline and a good eye for fine details were universal forces that drove the craftsperson.

Although smaller than any of the pottery towns, Leek was large enough to sustain different types of work and leisure, as intimated above. Its visible trading activities were supported by socio-economic factors including entrepreneurship, wealth and philanthropy; it was these elements that gave the town a particular and lasting identity. Owing to people's interdependence, there was a sense of community and place, and the town was clearly welcoming to talented people, be they industrialists, scientists, craftspeople, designers, architects, retailers or authors. Leek developed sophisticated cultural and educational institutions and societies. The Literary and Mechanics Institute had an extensive library and a reading room with the principal daily papers and journals. The *Staffordshire Sentinel* regularly reported on events in the town (and has been an invaluable source of information for this research). A Free Library, Museum and School of Art were incorporated into the purpose-built Nicholson Institute, which opened in 1884. Designed by a local architectural firm, the Institute still performs its original functions.

Tangible elements merged with intangible factors and brought changes: ecclesiological reform and progress in art, technical and design education directly impacted on daily lives. Leading theorists, galvanised by the work of Morris and Ruskin, passionately promoted the growing use of hand skills in buildings. Ornamental work took on a new significance, as it was increasingly seen as a suitable form of creative expression for men and women where both domestic and church architecture was concerned. As Morris declared, ornament was 'necessary in a work of art'.[5] 'It also ought to have a definite, harmonious, conscious beauty. It ought to be ornamental. It ought to be possible for it to be part of a beautiful whole in a room or church or hall.'[6] All of the above coincided with a boom in church building, changes in fashionable dress and massive growth in the construction of middle-class homes. This combination of factors meant that there were additional opportunities for women to contribute to elaborate domestic and ecclesiastical interiors. Knowledge of these varied perspectives is necessary if we are to understand the circumstances surrounding the development of Art Needlework. Discussions in educational institutions and specialised journals debated the visual changes affecting buildings and interiors, including the stylistic overlaps that occurred as church, home and clothing became more closely linked, possibly owing to the work of specific architects and designers whose influences were strong in both domestic and sacred spheres.

North Staffordshire was and is home to exquisite embroideries and fabrics designed by the most eminent architects. The story of the buildings of Leek and the complex textiles they contain is one of major significance covering seven decades of creative excellence. The local architectural practice, run by the Sugden family, was directly influenced by the architect Richard Norman

Shaw and by Morris, and was responsible for many streets of smart terraced properties, which housed families of textile workers. These impressive buildings, which have survived remarkably well, were the familiar townscape, the daily backdrop to countless people's lives.

When William Morris visited Leek in 1875 it was already a hive of creative activity and renowned for the production of beautiful handmade goods. Its craft skills were vital to Leek's main economy, which revolved around its established silk industry. Although to some extent the Arts and Crafts Movement was built on the lamented decline of craft skills, they had never totally disappeared from Leek. Thomas Wardle had a considerable reputation as the leading dyer working with natural dyes, which is why Morris made several visits to learn the latest advances from him; in Leek, Morris witnessed numerous craft skills practised on a daily basis. Morris and Wardle were well matched in their restless search for almost forgotten techniques and their pursuit of excellence in textile production. Morris brought his designer's genius to Wardle and his persuasive nature turned Wardle into a hand block-printer, bringing new challenges to the dye house for all concerned. Although he had no expertise in the craft of printing, Wardle's willingness to cooperate was life-changing. Theirs was an alliance of like-minded polymaths and, as with many collaborations, it depended on compromise and the willingness to make mistakes for the sake of progress.

Morris's impact on the region took a variety of forms. Many of north Staffordshire's churches have fine stained glass and ornamental features supplied by his firm. He displayed embroideries in Leek in the Exhibition of Modern Embroidery of 1881 and lectured in the town the following year. On his death the first memorial to Morris was in the former Friends Meeting House at Overton Bank, Leek – renamed the William Morris Labour Church by the town's socialists. This unique project, which was intended to create a centre for study, attracted financial and ethical support from notable and principled followers. Walter Crane contributed the mural that was stencilled onto walls lacquered a rich red. Windows were draped in blue velvet printed in Leek with a design by Morris.[7] The talented John Scarrett Rigby of Leek designed a beautiful book-cloth, lettered in the 'Kelmscott' typeface, which was embroidered by a skilled artist on a silk designed by Morris.[8]

The growth of the Arts and Crafts Movement, of which Morris was the celebrated leader, awakened a widespread interest in the handmade. Besides the increasing importance given to the role of appropriate design, handmade objects allowed makers to demonstrate creative expression and flair. The rapid growth of the Art Needlework movement was one manifestation of this way of thinking. As L.F. Day stated, 'The custom has been, since woman learnt to kill time with a needle, to think of embroidery too much as an idle accomplishment.

It is more than that. At the very least it is a handicraft: at the best it is an art.'[9] As a result of Elizabeth Wardle's enterprise, the production of fine embroidery became another skilled activity for which Leek became celebrated.

The actions of Elizabeth and Thomas Wardle were typical of those of other practitioners following an Arts and Crafts philosophy, in that they drew stimulus from pre-industrial practices without simply emulating historic examples. While perfecting traditional techniques, their products were intended for modern markets. Crucially, both Elizabeth and Thomas had a good eye for colour harmony and design, and a number of local, national and international circumstances that coincided with Thomas and Elizabeth Wardle's values fortuitously came together in Leek. While influences had spread far beyond newly created guilds and the metropolitan elite to the provinces, as a complex set of trade, political, artistic and technological factors stimulated activities across the nation, and the Embroidery Society and the small, experimental Hencroft Dye Works had goals similar to those of many craft workshops across Britain, Leek was particularly intriguing, as it supported a wealth of emerging Arts and Crafts activity on the back of its long-established international silk trade. On the one hand there were links between technical innovation, entrepreneurship and international commerce, while on the other certain activities were linked to the Arts and Crafts Movement and hand-making. The catalysts for both were embedded in different members of the Wardle family, who became significant figures in public life.

The Wardle family made major contributions to Arts and Crafts textiles through the goods they produced as well as through the work of other practitioners who used their materials produced in Leek. Aestheticism and the Arts and Crafts Movement had many female followers who excelled in producing fine-quality decorative arts in a range of media. The expansion of Art Needlework was progressive in that it involved many women in creative work. The demand for a greater variety of superior materials was an important factor in the search for greater artistic expression. Newly improved Indian silk threads and cloth, with their rich, deep, natural shades dyed by Wardle & Co., gave needlewomen greater creative scope for collective and individual projects.

Uniquely, the Wardle family used their experience of the European silk trade to promote India's materials. The renowned retailer Arthur Lasenby Liberty turned to Thomas Wardle for his supplies of India's wild silks. Liberty, a crucial figure in the Aesthetic Movement and the Arts and Crafts era, owed a great deal of his initial fame to Wardle's skills. He created ranges of dyed and block-printed textiles for Liberty's London emporium, which opened in 1876. Designs by Lindsay P. Butterfield, Walter Crane, L.F. Day, Thomas Mawson and John Dando Sedding were hand-block printed in Leek for sale on Regent Street. Gorgeous fabrics from Staffordshire filled the London shop's windows, and crowds gazed at the sumptuous displays. Wardle also supplied Liberty with his range of 'Art Fabrics': beautifully coloured, softly draping plain silks popular with followers of the Aesthetic Movement. They were all a critical success when Liberty was building his retail empire.

Embroidery became a highly expressive activity for many women. The Leek School of Embroidery, an integral part of the Society, trained young women in needlework skills. This gave opportunities for income generation through the practice of a refined craft and the joy of innovative expression. The Society, moreover, created an active female community with its own momentum. The rise of art school education as a route into the textile and other creative industries became an increasingly important factor as formalised education gradually replaced the more improvised, domestic system of teaching skills; in Leek both systems coexisted for decades. As in many textile towns, women in north Staffordshire were able to access art- and craft-based courses in local colleges, which may have helped swell the ranks of women employed in Art Needlework, although it was not necessarily a prerequisite. At the same time, demand for embroidered items for both domestic and ecclesiastical interiors grew exponentially, along with stitched accessories and costume adornment.

Ecclesiastical needlework became a major focus of interest for Elizabeth Wardle and others. North Staffordshire patrons had a long history of commissioning leading architects for their churches – George Edmund Street and Augustus Welby Northmore Pugin, important early promoters of Gothic Revival architecture, built some of their best work in the county and both designed textiles for their interiors, as they considered them to be important elements of ritual and of a coherent design scheme. Drawings of medieval examples of textiles made by George Young Wardle were part of this. The following chapters explore these multiple connections in detail.

The Leek Embroidery Society became internationally famous for producing a facsimile of the Bayeux Tapestry, which was and remains displayed in France. Elizabeth Wardle organised local women to stitch the 70m (230-foot) length using yarns dyed by Thomas Wardle. It subsequently toured the world, including a particularly successful trip to America (Chapter 3).

Meanwhile, the expansion of the Garden City Movement provided well-designed homes for fast-growing numbers of middle-class families, which increased demand for aesthetically pleasing fabrics as industrially produced cotton prints were not always thought suitable. In this milieu, Shaw was the leading architect, Morris the foremost designer, Liberty the primary retailer and Thomas Wardle the most notable dyer and printer of textiles.

Chapter 1

THE WARDLE FAMILY
AND ITS CIRCLE

The Manifold is the same river, is it not, which you carried me across on
your back, which situation tickled us so much that, owing to inextinguishable
laughter, you very nearly dropped me in. What pleasant old times those were.
William Morris to Thomas Wardle, 1896[1]

There is a photograph of Thomas Wardle, with ten of his surviving
children, taken around 1879 (Figure 1). The children and their father
are gathered in what seems to be the garden of their home in Leek. The
photographer has captured a sense of family intimacy in a domestic setting,
except that Elizabeth Wardle is conspicuously absent. There are two versions of
this photograph. The other features a large swing on which Margaret Elizabeth
and Frances, two of the children, are seated. Both images project a distinctly
homely atmosphere, reinforced by the various objects that some of the people
featured are holding. They epitomise the great appeal of this family's history,
which lies in each individual's independence as well as a strong history of
collaboration.

If the photographs were taken to mark a special occasion we do not know
what that was. Judging by the nonchalant approach taken, it was clearly nothing
as grand as a wedding. Everyone is wearing warm everyday clothing and sturdy
footwear, and the older sons have their hands in their pockets. The three older
girls are all dressed alike, possibly in a form of school uniform, while the four
older boys have versions of adult suits. Perhaps it was someone's birthday, or
even Christmas, as some children are holding pets and toys. There is a sense of
individuality, even of mischief, in the poses adopted by each child, particularly
the sons. The decision to wear a hat or not, and at what angle, would seem to
be important. Gilbert, the oldest, who must have been about seventeen, has a

Figure 1   T. Wardle and his children. Photographer: P.A. Rayner.
Staffordshire Libraries and Arts Service

strong presence. He is seated on the right of the group in one version, holding a
satchel, and is entirely aware of being observed. He is facing the camera full-on,
while holding a confident, urbane-looking pose. The rakish angle of his bowler
hat – which is even jauntier in the other version, where he is on the left – makes a
drama of the experience. Arthur is carrying his bowler in one version, although
it is missing from the other. Thomas Wardle's embroidered smoking cap, then
fashionable in avant-garde circles, suggests an aesthete rather than a craftsman.
Apart from Frederick and the two older girls, the other siblings are holding an
assortment of objects. Presumably these props are significant. Although they
are everyday items, they might point to some child's passion. At the back of the
group Bernard holds a small rabbit; Tom Jnr, in the centre, then about eight
years old, has a much larger rabbit; young Francis, sitting on his father's knee,
has a small book. The two younger girls are cradling dolls. The tenth surviving
child was born during the period when William Morris was regularly visiting
Leek and staying with the Wardle family in their home between 1875 and 1877.
Although Morris refers to an expected 'master ten' in his correspondence, the
new-born turned out to be a daughter, Elizabeth Leeke. She is seated at the
centre of the front row in both versions and appears to be scowling.

There is no doubt that three generations of the Wardle family were a
dynamic force in the region. They gained huge respect and accolades for

their skills and creativity, which were practised with a passion. While the main focus here is on the work of Thomas and Elizabeth, references to a Wardle dynasty are relevant. Various family members received widespread regard in ways that we are only beginning to understand. Wives, daughters, sisters, nieces, husbands, brothers, sons and nephews all played a part. They were the threads that held this rich, multilayered story together for more than 100 years. Much of what takes place in this global history happens against the backdrop of a busy and demanding family life, particularly where Elizabeth Wardle is concerned. William Morris knew the children, whom he referred to warmly as '"the ruffians", to whom I offer my congratulations on their youth, their holidays and their capacity for noise'.[2]

All of the children who survived into adulthood were successful. Four sons – Arthur, Bernard, Gilbert and Tom Jnr – worked for family firms in different capacities and continued to produce Morris' designs as their father had. Frederick became a solicitor but Francis died aged eleven, when his father was in India. Lydia and Margaret followed their mother and became accomplished embroiderers, while Edith and Elizabeth Leeke had a small input into the facsimile of the Bayeux Tapestry. Other female members of the wider family circle were talented needlewomen.

The photographs, as noted, were taken during a very productive period shortly after Morris had made numerous visits to Wardle's dye works to learn the dyer's craft. Although much has been written about Morris's life, the detailed context of his timely, constructive links with the Wardle family is not widely known. Morris's first biographer, John Mackail, notes that by the time Morris visited Leek Wardle was 'already becoming known as one of the first practical authorities on dye-stuffs and the art of dyeing'.[3] By then Thomas Wardle was already interested in the historical methods practised by his father and was researching a huge range of indigenous dyestuffs that had been shipped to Leek from India.[4] The global recognition Wardle gained was built on his forensic analysis of these indigenous dyestuffs, along with a systematic campaign to better comprehend India's wild silk. His insights made him a world leader in both fields. He was not only a craftsman of the highest order but also a highly motivated businessman who regularly travelled across Europe and had multiple interests outside the workplace. As well as offering Morris technical expertise, he brought a great deal of experience and passion to their shared project. He also had the confidence and vision that came from running a successful company. As Mackail states, the two men restored vegetable dyeing so that it was once again an important industry.[5] An understanding of colour control and how that worked in a complex pattern was always of fundamental importance to Morris. The famous series of textiles designed by him, and block printed by Wardle, was created on the Hencroft site in Leek. What Wardle took from that enterprise changed his working methods considerably, as Morris had persuaded him to become a hand block-printer. It was an ambitious gambit and thereafter Wardle continued to develop strategies to supply different clients' needs. Very rapidly he was providing Arthur Lasenby Liberty with acclaimed dyed and printed materials for his London emporium. Many were designed by leading figures in the Arts and Crafts Movement. He also produced a number of silk ranges for Liberty based on traditional Indian designs, which were often given names evocative of India. Wardle also produced his own block-printed collections with a broad range of cultural references, including velveteens with large-scale patterns. These were named for particular eras or places – a clever marketing device that imparted a cultural value beyond the practical, so encouraging consumers to develop a connection with the product. They were a huge success.

Thomas Wardle was aware that his father and a number of French dyers had tried without success to improve the potential of India's wild silks. Despite this, he was determined and scientific in his attempts to understand and utilise the raw materials that were readily available. Even when his results achieved better outcomes he had to work hard to publicise their potential, cultivate new markets and refine existing ones. This stimulated the production of a wider range of handmade silk goods in Leek, including major embroidery pieces. Conditions in Leek were ripe for expansion and the Wardle family knew exactly how to develop their business so that a great number of residents benefited. The town was the perfect locus for a particular type of textile production, with its abundant water supply, concentration of craft skills and visionary and entrepreneurial people who promoted local industries. The region benefited from the Wardles' global vision, which allowed its historic trades to prosper. By extending the scope of its inhabitants they maintained the skilled structure that was in place and enlarged it. Ultimately the company became the largest family-owned dye and print works in the country, with a variety of clients from Europe and America. Underpinning this success was a considerable work ethic, which meant the company thrived against all odds as mechanised industries threatened to take over so many aspects of textile production. The following chapters reveal how this was accomplished.

By this time Elizabeth Wardle had also developed a reputation as a creative person in her own right. Since 1865, some time before she launched the Leek Embroidery Society in 1879/80, she had worked with a number of eminent architects, transforming their designs on paper into fine embroideries for their churches. Most have survived and are discussed in detail in Chapter 4. The Wardles' genius was to combine the different talents of various family members when they launched the Society. This extended the potential of them all, so that their skills mattered beyond their town as they became known internationally.

George Young Wardle, Elizabeth's brother, also formed a strong and long-lasting alliance with Morris. From 1870 he proved to be an indispensable support to Morris as well as an eloquent observer of the great man and his preoccupations. He became manager of Morris & Co., and was in regular contact with eminent designers and architects. Yet, despite his major role in Morris's success, George Young Wardle never developed a public persona.[6]

Wardle is a common name in north Staffordshire, and it is necessary therefore to clarify what can be a confusing situation. Both Elizabeth Wardle and George Young Wardle were born in Leek to Hugh and Elizabeth Young Wardle, who were from long-established Staffordshire families. Hugh Wardle was a druggist, which suggests that he was involved with dyeing and chemical aspects of the local silk industry. Their mother taught in the family home. At the age of seventeen Elizabeth Jnr was also described as a teacher in the 1851 census.[7] She was twenty-two years old when she married Thomas Wardle in 1857, while he was twenty-six. Elizabeth simply exchanged Miss for Mrs, as her family name remained the same. This situation is compounded by the then common tendency of parents to pass on their first names to their progenies. As a result there is more than one Thomas, at least two Georges and a minimum of three Elizabeth Wardles in this history.

Thomas Wardle, born in Sutton, near Macclesfield in Cheshire, was one of five offspring. His father, Joshua Wardle (1802–1879), initially worked in Macclesfield as a dyer, but moved to Leek when Thomas was a year old. Both Thomas and his younger brother George entered the family firm, while their two sisters, Ann and Martha Phoebe (known as Phoebe), were skilled embroiderers. George and his wife Frances had three daughters, Eleanor, Mildred and Ada, who stitched for the Leek Embroidery Society.

Even though photography was well advanced in the late nineteenth century, few cameras were in private hands. There are some formal individual studio portraits of both Thomas and Elizabeth Wardle taken on the occasion of his knighthood, and a few from family weddings and other group events, yet none that shows just them as a couple. Thomas appears with others in photographs taken during royal visits and on a trip to Kashmir in 1903. To date, not one of George Young Wardle has been traced. Some workaday scenes show men and boys in a dye house, but none are of embroiderers stitching, apart from a studio image of Elizabeth Wardle and Mrs Beatrice Warren.[8]

An Innovative Family

As the Wardle family lived and worked during a period of intense change in a number of respects, no one factor can be isolated as the main stimulus for their activities. As well as reacting to their own ingenuity, family members operated in a constantly evolving environment, responding to a broad range of cultural activities that were local, national and global. These included market changes, government schemes and aesthetically driven movements. This all took place against a backdrop of major social and economic upheaval, when Britain was the textile hub of the industrialising world. Alongside the usual economic considerations related to diversification and supply and demand were other vital factors. It was a time of adjustments and advances that, among other things, affected the global silk industry. The Anglo-Indian silk trade was an ancient web of producers, merchants and clients whose collective skills and demands created and traded sumptuous silks over centuries and nations. The Wardles' multilayered activities increasingly reflected changes in global, material, aesthetic and technical possibilities, which is why they flourished and attracted attention. The spread of commissions for their products was broad and large orders were completed for both individuals and prestigious companies. Ultimately they were widely acknowledged as playing a crucial role in the expansion of India's silk trade.

Three members of the family, Thomas, Elizabeth and George Young Wardle, increasingly moved in varied yet interconnected artistic and commercial circles that linked them to leading figures and institutions. Additional layers of interest were added to their lives by long-standing alliances with influential members of the Arts and Crafts, Gothic Revivalist, Aesthetic and Art Needlework movements. They regularly encountered others working as designers, artists, museum directors, journalists, curators, educators, technologists, retailers and skilled workers of many sorts. As all three were extremely productive it is reasonable to assume that they found pleasure in their work. Everything indicates that it was more than an occupation; it was a way of life. Their work was influenced by market forces, industrial changes, international trade, ecclesiastical demands and Indian government guidelines, and ranged across different sectors, so that at any one time they might have been acting as innovative practitioners, researchers, managers, educators, authors, campaigners, collaborators, retailers or inspiring leaders.

A Creative Couple

Thomas and Elizabeth Wardle made an impact on local life from at least 1864, when they lived at Cheddleton, about 6.5km (four miles) from Leek. From that time they were in regular contact with some of the most famous figures in leading artistic movements, who came to their home town and made their mark. Thereafter, as one important commission followed another, Leek became a place where architect's ideas on paper were transformed into beautiful and desirable embroideries. Elizabeth Wardle took on a number of these challenging projects and her skills were publicly acknowledged early in her needlework career. As many of these fine pieces remain in the buildings for which they were made, we can see today that the Wardle family lived up to its own high ideals. This is explored in detail in Chapter 4, which focuses on the complex embroideries produced for leading architects.

George Young Wardle

George Young Wardle was an intriguing and noteworthy figure in the Arts and Crafts Movement, mainly through his work with Morris. He was an eloquent writer, an efficient manager and a creative craftsman, about whom very little is generally known. This book aims to shed more light on his important contribution and his links to an influential group of characters. After going away to art school George Young Wardle worked as a freelance draughtsman. He made an intensive study of ornamentation in East Anglia's medieval churches in 1865 and 1866, concentrating on the magnificent rood screens in that region. Many of his accomplished measured drawings and letters from the period still survive.[9] He was employed by Morris in various roles from at least 1865, initially on a casual basis, just after the firm moved to Queen Square, London. In 1870 he was promoted, replacing Warrington Taylor as manager of Morris & Co., a position he held for twenty years, during which the company was at the peak of its success.[10]

It is likely that it was George Young Wardle who brought Thomas Wardle and Morris together, as he knew them both independently and would have been aware of their overlapping interests. By 1873 his brother-in-law was already a dyer of international repute and was fast becoming the expert on the wild silks and dyes of India. He frequently visited London and was involved with a number of prestigious institutions. Given their numerous mutual contacts, it is conceivable that they met a decade before Morris's well-documented visit to Wardle's dye house in 1875. Morris and Thomas and Elizabeth Wardle independently collaborated with George Gilbert Scott Jnr on the rebuilding of the parish church at Cheddleton, Staffordshire, in 1865. The different aspects of this significant project are discussed in detail in Chapter 4. Their lives continued to intersect until Morris's death.

The Mystery of Dyeing

Although they had many things in common Thomas Wardle was from an entirely different background to Morris, the son of a London stockbroker. Wardle was the son of a master dyer and the craft of dyeing remained central throughout his long life. His father, Joshua Wardle, had set up a dye house alongside Leek Brook, a tributary of the river Churnet, in north Staffordshire when Thomas was just a year old and thereafter north Staffordshire was his home. Joshua not only continued historic methods but also experimented with raw materials with the aim of developing his craft.[11]

The town of Leek developed in a loop of the river Churnet, which forms a natural boundary around it. This reliable supply of water was crucial to its renown as a centre of dyeing excellence. It was reputed to have some of the best water for dyeing in Europe, possibly due to its mineral content. Good dyeing, like good wine, relies to some extent on the terroir – minerals and trace elements found in the local rivers, the effects of the character of the land on dyers' plants and the particular microclimate – combined with the embedded skills of local workers, whose livelihood often depended on understanding the qualities and consistency of a water supply or a dye vat.

The river Churnet's role in dyeing was well known locally for centuries, although not scientifically understood. Natural dye processes were extremely time-consuming and sometimes unpredictable, but the superior outcomes compared to those of other silk-dyeing towns were thought to be worth the considerable effort involved. A large number of factors affected the quality of the dye, including the temperature of the water, which was tested daily for impurities, and even the mood of the workforce. Over time the river supported many textile activities, including the 'mystery' of dyeing learnt by generation after generation of highly skilled artisans. Unpromising looking powders, rough tree bark, shrivelled roots, dried rinds of fruit, withered berries, dehydrated leaves and desiccated insects were shipped from across the globe and used on a daily basis to transform hanks of dull raw yarn and lengths of 'grey' cloth with deep, unfading colour. A copious amount of clean river water was an essential element in this dramatic change.

Joshua Wardle was renowned beyond Leek as a commission dyer who could achieve a great range of superior, lasting colours for silks, wool and linen, but it was his array of blacks that earned him a widespread reputation. He was known specifically for his 'Raven Black', a blue-black with the sheen of a raven's wing. 'Sulphur Black', which withstood salt spray without fading, was a speciality he developed for the Admiralty. Further variants, which depended on his customers' needs, included 'Napoleon Black', 'Noir', 'Noir Suisse', 'Eugenie' and 'Imperial Black'. Similarly, shades of white included 'White', 'Best White', 'Pure White', 'White Soft', 'Best White Soft', 'Pearl White', 'Lily' and 'Pearl'. Like other dyers, he relied on the 'mystery' of dyeing, an ancient tradition and a practical measure that safeguarded his dye recipes and therefore his trade. Techniques and formulas were kept secret, passed down through generations of the male labour force as inherent knowledge rather than as written records. Joshua also experimented with tussar silk, a wild silk that was abundant across India, but, despite his experience, he failed to overcome its notorious resistance to dyestuffs. His son Thomas later took up this challenge, with spectacular results.

In 1856, Thomas Wardle became a partner in his father's firm, which gave him a solid grounding in historical processes[12] (Figure 2). He belonged to a group of skilled workers who thoroughly understood the nature of the materials they used and who used traditional skills to convert the ordinary into the extraordinary. He was a conscientious, energetic and inventive craftsman who remained passionate about his dyers' heritage and its place in the local and national economy even when he became a figure of global importance.

While Thomas Wardle remained a commission dyer at heart, passionately devoted to understanding his materials and developing techniques, he pursued a life that was quite different from the one led by his father. Rapid changes in

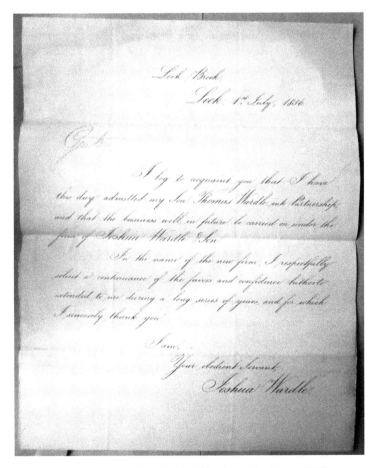

Figure 2   Letter from Joshua Wardle to his clients, 1856.
Courtesy of Charles Chalcraft

the textile sector generally had affected the use of traditional techniques, which were being destroyed elsewhere. Undaunted, he returned to ancient expertise in the face of industrial expansion. He purchased the Hencroft Dye Works in 1872 and brought the few surviving craftsmen with traditional experience back into the business. He revitalised almost forgotten practices and a particular approach to manufacturing that enhanced the value of goods made in Leek. This was not just for financial gain; it was about the survival of tradition. However, by producing objects of beauty that demanded time and skill to create he could reach a specific segment of the international marketplace. Of concern was the need to develop alternative uses for India's traditional raw materials rather than compete with mechanised cotton production. Under his forward-looking direction and pioneering work as a dye chemist the small Hencroft site became a place of research and development into silks and natural dyestuffs. Other family members, meanwhile, continued to work together in the main businesses over three generations.

Even though Thomas Wardle travelled widely across Europe as a businessman, he and his wife Elizabeth remained rooted in their home town. This was something that never held them back. A great deal of evidence confirms that they were collaborative and in tune with the wider world – they had to be if the family companies were to survive. They were members of a national circle of talented individuals with whom they exchanged ideas and shared skills. They must both have had a strong desire to make things and make them well, and expressed themselves through the variety of textiles they produced, which not only were beautiful but also gave pleasure to others. Their abilities and vision enabled many individuals to have their ideas converted into remarkable textiles in Staffordshire. This growth of mutual aspirations and values contributed to an extraordinarily vibrant and creative atmosphere in the town.

It was at the Hencroft site that two major projects took place that changed many aspects of international silk production permanently. From 1872 Thomas Wardle investigated India's wild silks and indigenous dyestuffs there, concentrating on refining them with ancient skills rather than using inferior industrial products. He did not, however, return to tradition at the expense of advancement in modern silk production, as it became a starting point for development. He was clear-sighted and focused in his use of long-established skills as a way of progressing, as the past offered lessons that could be adapted to his current objectives. He sought a better understanding of India's raw materials and, through his growing understanding, historic methods flourished again, being nurtured and expanded in Leek so that they were available for generations of craftworkers to come. It was groundbreaking work which resonated widely. Had Wardle not intervened, generations of dyers' knowledge would

20

have been lost, along with the particular understanding needed to release the beauty locked into dull unprocessed materials.[13]

Thomas Wardle's enquiry into the fundamentals of his materials involved a principled implementation of scientific methods alongside his hands-on experience in the dye house. His research was contingent on his daily environment as it was manifested in his workplace. At the Hencroft site he created a new starting point for traditional dyeing and changed the prospects for wild silks. Wardle's investigations were a bold attempt to find the limits of the raw materials in which he devised a system of testing every known plant and other natural sources of dyestuffs used in India and achieved encouraging results that enlarged the palette of natural colours. Different dye recipes for each plant and type of fibre were tested and the results recorded. Each sample was carefully mounted using a unique system that was revealed only recently.[14] His first success was with more delicate shades, although he soon progressed to deeper tints, over eight years gaining a unique breadth of knowledge and insight into India's dyes.[15] The rich, deep, but softly glowing shades Thomas Wardle obtained were extraordinary and more subtle than the brighter colours of cultivated silks and the harsher tones produced by early man-made dyes. The result was a range of new goods that extended prospects for India's printers and dyers as well as those in Europe, who increasingly imported the raw materials from the subcontinent. Surviving examples reveal that they stood the test of time.[16]

Wardle's concern with achieving good, lasting colour defined the rest of his long working life. His realisation of the potential of the English and Indian silk industries enabled both to offer fresh solutions and varied outcomes. His resolve had its rewards, which were to have a huge effect on his home town's international profile. By introducing new materials he also expanded the range of possibilities and recharged historic artisanal standards, allowing creative integrity to thrive in the workplace and unique pieces to be produced for exhibitions or for his distinguished clients, as required. Because he had a perspective on Leek from both the inside and the outside, he could use his knowledge of ancient practice to critically challenge aspects of contemporary silk production nationally. Crucially, using new evidence, he encouraged debate about sustainability throughout the global silk trade, which retained many of its traditional craft skills, mainly in family-run workshops such as his own. Throughout his life Thomas Wardle retained his extraordinary capacity for hard work and his high-profile involvement in the international silk trade did not wane until six months before his death in 1909.

William Morris's persuasive nature turned Wardle from a dyer into a hand-block printer. Wardle never acted as a mere technician, however, for, as Ray Watkinson states, 'he was a man of stature and force, Morris's equal in many ways'.[17] When working with Wardle, Morris witnessed the trans-formation of wild silks and other natural fibres on a daily basis and realised the importance of the local, artisanal skills and values involved. Wardle's willingness to cooperate with Morris was life-changing, as the historic practice of hand-block printing was a skill that had almost disappeared, as had the allied craft of wood-block cutting. Wardle introduced both into Leek, possibly for the first time, mobilising different teams of skilled workers. His investment in the necessary equipment, labour force and materials to nurture the demanding crafts would have been a considerable financial outlay and demonstrated a great leap of faith. There must also have been a huge process of adjustment, as the livelihood of both men depended on the success of their endeavours, which were vulnerable in new and changing markets.

As colour was a major element of Morris's complex designs, this change of working methods created technical challenges that, unsurprisingly, resulted in occasional tensions. It all proved to be worthwhile, however: the textiles that this alliance produced are now recognised as exceptional.[18] Wardle, who was acknowledged as a strong force operating at the highest level of fine craft production, used the best traditional methods designed to get the finest results from natural materials, but, as they were seeking the maximum results, Morris and Wardle were both willing to experiment with technical and aesthetic factors. This sparked one of the great dialogues about textiles during an era marked by diverse creativity. These two exceptional men had many other interests in common. They visited Paris searching for historic herbals, took long walks, fished together and made each other laugh. Wardle was an early and active member of the Society for the Protection of Ancient Buildings (SPAB), of which Morris was a co-founder, and George Young Wardle its proactive secretary.

The production of hand-block-printed textiles expanded and became a fixture that the Wardle companies maintained until at least the 1950s. Industrialised methods of textile production nationwide, however, seriously threatened to replace hand skills for economies of scale. Compared with mechanised cloth production, hand-block printing and traditional dyeing, as invigorated by Wardle & Co., were comparatively small scale and costly. Nevertheless, a clear understanding of these expensive and tricky processes was nurtured, confirming Thomas Wardle's belief in the craft skills of his local community. Although there was certainly an element of unease associated with industrialised, dehumanising cloth production, Wardle's work was not an ethical or nostalgic gesture. He was far-sighted and realistic, and his ideals did not conflict with the practicalities of running a company. Respect for tradition became a way of giving attention to detail, which offered the ability to tailor production to specific markets. He combined the spirit of the Arts and Crafts movement with the reality of commerce, which provided the means by which this could be achieved. The introduction of hand-block printing proved to be a pragmatic direction for the company to take. As different Wardle companies grew stronger, the town of Leek became renowned as a place where historic skills thrived.

In the right hands block printing was a flexible process that, when imaginatively used, produced vibrant contemporary fabrics for an expanding market. Wardle & Co. hand-block printed fourteen of Morris's complex designs on different fabrics using natural dyes. Even though his subsequent patterns were produced at Morris's own Merton Abbey site, the original series remained in production with Wardle companies well into the twentieth century.[19] Thomas Wardle gained a reputation as a printer who was committed to the social role of the designer as a producer of beautiful, desirable, useful things that required the input of a skilled workforce. As he gained in reputation many of Morris's followers, also troubled by the increasing pace of industrialisation and the attendant loss of individual talent, sought him out. They, too, had their ideas turned into glorious original patterns, printed onto fine fabrics in Leek.

Morris and his followers must all have realised that successful designs did not end with the concept on paper. A great deal more needed to happen before a working drawing emerged as a fully formed textile, and much of this was often in the form of the unacknowledged but important 'hidden' or 'intangible' designing, which frequently happened in a workshop[20] and was usually due to the symbiotic relationships that existed between prominent designers, architects, local craftspeople and members of the Wardle family.

Both location and a skilled workforce were important to the development of different Wardle companies and that remained the case as the small family dye works evolved to become an international market leader by the 1880s. Its goods were the result of a measured evolution and the ability to adapt to changing conditions, along with the blending of history and nature. The colours used were rooted in plants, shellfish and insects, and fixed in the river water.[21] They were also the result of an expanding body of knowledge. The full variety of dyed and printed cottons, wools, velvets and silks produced were in great demand internationally. A number of the printed patterns were used as bases for embroidery and became an essential component of the Leek Embroidery Society's success. Thomas Wardle's skills were then merged with those of his wife Elizabeth, an experienced embroiderer, and a whole new set of opportunities was opened up. Consequently, the Wardles contributed to the noticeably increased global recognition of India's improved raw materials. An immediate outcome was a growth in exports of raw silks and dyestuffs from the subcontinent to Europe.[22]

The launch of the Leek Embroidery Society, managed by Elizabeth Wardle, took these developments further. As a vertical structure was already in place, the

Figure 3   Portrait of Sir Thomas Wardle. Photographer: W.H. Horne.
Staffordshire Libraries and Arts Service

various family companies could cover all the processes, from the initial transformation of raw materials right through to the finished lengths of printed fabrics and elaborate needlework. All aspects of this expansion are fully detailed in the following chapter. Through the Society the Wardle family taught skills to others, creating jobs in their community for women as well as for men. This put a new vigour into the town, as the growing variety of goods produced there attracted a great deal of attention. The Society reinforced an already growing role for Leek as a centre of diverse and exceptional arts and crafts activity, and the Wardles' maintenance of their strongly rooted lives in this community continued to contribute to its success.

Thomas Wardle developed his own ranges of printed fabrics, including a series of velvets inspired by complex Byzantine, French and Renaissance silks and other historic examples that had stood the test of time. His choice of designs confirms that he understood that the present could learn from the past. A further series of patterns based on traditional Indian textiles gave rise to many simple repeat patterns and border designs. Both printed and embroidered goods were selected for the prestigious Arts and Crafts Exhibition Society events in London, where embroidery was a prominent feature,[23] and were displayed at international trade fairs in Amsterdam, Berlin, Boston, Dublin, London, Manchester, Melbourne and Paris, where they won awards, admiration and gold medals. Exhibits included designs by Tom Wardle Jnr that were regularly promoted by art and craft journals as models of excellence. As Wardle & Co.'s profile rose, the much larger Churnet Works also owned by the Wardles, on the opposite bank of the river, rose to become the largest family-owned dyeing and printing firm in the country.[24] Sir Thomas and Arthur Wardle Ltd was still hand-block printing in the 1950s.[25] Ultimately, Thomas Wardle was acknowledged globally as the greatest British textile dyer and printer of his time. Awards, honours and acclaim followed, including a knighthood, the Freedom of the City of London and France's highest honour, the *Chevalier de la Légion d'Honneur* (Figure 3).

Networks of Influence

When Morris was working at the Hencroft Dye Works he stayed with Thomas and Elizabeth Wardle at their family home. Number 62 St Edward Street, Leek, is a stone-built Georgian townhouse in which Thomas and Elizabeth lived from 1866 to the mid-1880s. By then Morris knew Elizabeth's brother, George Young Wardle, very well. All four demonstrably had many things in common with other major figures and those connections were to deepen. Morris would have noticed that the Wardles' work was closely integrated with family life.

One appeared to blend with the other in a manner similar to that of his own household, as, for both families, the domestic sphere was a place of flexible boundaries that was also firmly connected to the production of useful and beautiful things. Under the Wardle family's guidance standards and confidence had risen and craft production expanded. As these matters were of great concern to him, Morris must have realised that the family's pioneering attitudes and the constant creation of new skilled work made it possible for other people of the town to enjoy creative freedom. They, too, could follow their principles and aspirations while contributing to the town's prosperity and cultural life. He would almost certainly have discussed embroidery with Elizabeth, as it was a passion they shared. Jane, Morris's wife, who was a noted embroiderer, was known to order embroidery silks and patterns from Thomas Wardle. When she visited Staffordshire in 1907 she also stayed at the Wardle home.[26]

As the Wardles' front door gave direct access onto a busy central thoroughfare the household was closely connected to the sights and sounds of the town. When Morris left the house he would have stepped straight into the hustle and bustle of silk workers, horse-drawn carriages, hand carts, cyclists, vendors and herds of animals on market days. To his left he would have seen the parish church, a short walk away, where the Wardles were married. Ten years previously it had been restored by Morris's former mentor, the vastly influential architect George Edmund Street.[27] Later it acquired stained-glass windows by Morris & Co., including one commissioned by Thomas Wardle in memory of his wife. George Frederick Bodley was involved with a later restoration.[28] John Dando Sedding, also a former associate of Street, had finished his restoration of St Luke's church in the town just two years earlier. Thomas Wardle counted Sedding as a friend, as did Richard Norman Shaw.

On the right, just a few doors from the Wardles' home, Shaw had built the splendid townhouse 'Spout Hall' in about 1871. Shaw had by then renovated a church at nearby Meerbrook, although his magnificent All Saints, Leek, had yet to be built.[29] When completed it was almost in sight of the Wardles' home. From 1865 Elizabeth collaborated with many of these outstanding figures, embroidering their designs for their churches. Morris knew these men, and their intense interests in Gothic Revivalism chimed with his own. He would have seen their buildings in Leek, built of local stone, by local artisans, and would have known that they contained exquisite silk embroideries made by members of the local community for the community, supervised by Elizabeth Wardle. He would have realised that the decorative arts were an important aspect of daily life and played more than a minor role in many people's lives; they were a considerable cultural force in the town. Creativity was a serious matter and not simply a case of supplying random soft furnishings to soften the contours of a large stone public building. Embroidery was planned from the outset to take centre stage in a church interior.

Elizabeth Wardle was one of a number of highly successful women whose work has only recently come under scrutiny. Like her husband, she became prominent in the affairs of Leek and made her mark on the town. She never simply fitted her activities around her husband's increasingly busy life, but in her own right accepted many commissions from major architects who worked in her home town. She must have had absolute self-belief and the determination to succeed early in her life, along with an awareness of the importance of her work, to achieve what she did. Even as a young mother, with four children under the age of four, she formed an alliance with George Gilbert Scott Jnr to stitch his designs for embroidery. The family grew until there were ten offspring to care for; from 1858 to 1877 Elizabeth was either pregnant or nursing a baby. In total she gave birth to fourteen children, although four babies died in infancy and her youngest son, Francis, died in 1886 aged eleven years. The relentless routines of childcare and managing a busy home did not, however, trap her in domestic drudgery and prevent her from achieving great things: she had the confidence to take on high-profile projects for decades, completing many important embroidery commissions. Taking on the challenges her varied life presented, she developed interests and contacts far beyond the household, as did numerous other talented women of the time. Her embroidery evolved in parallel with her husband's research, although she independently formed alliances with Watts & Co., the famed church furnishers, and the Royal School of Art Needlework (RSAN). Like her husband, she was also in contact with members of the royal family. In addition, she was renowned as a teacher who passed on her skills to others. From her first commission in 1865 Elizabeth enjoyed public approval ten years before Morris came to work in Leek, and constant recognition and awards led to an international profile. Clearly she was not held back by living in a small provincial town or by any low expectations that being a wife and mother engendered. Hers is a story of steady progress, as one success built on another, leading in time to the launch of the Leek Embroidery Society, the role of which is fully explored for the first time in Chapter 2.

Elizabeth Wardle's story upends simplistic views of exploited needlewomen of the late nineteenth century – a theme explored more in the Conclusion. Unlike those who were forced to stitch shirt seams for a pittance, or who churned out dreary patterns to fill their time, she had a creative freedom that matched her ambition. She was not just dabbling with stitching as a hobby for her idle hands: she was a highly regarded craftswoman who frequently exhibited her work in prestigious international exhibitions alongside the work of other women. As the co-founder and superintendent of the Leek Embroidery Society she rapidly gained a wide renown as an exceptional director of a dynamic organisation. She was, furthermore, an astute businesswoman who combined the conventional, demanding role of wife and mother of a large number of children with that of a creative embroiderer. She remained highly visible and active in the town where she lived for her entire life, even though, as her status grew, she developed a noteworthy enterprise and a distinguished career with an international profile and strong links to influential institutions.[30]

Elizabeth Wardle's embroideries were on permanent display at the South Kensington Museum (now the Victoria and Albert Museum) in her lifetime and were regularly exhibited at other prestigious venues. The Leek Embroidery Society won significant awards and was consistently praised in prominent journals. The facsimile of the Bayeux Tapestry, produced in Leek in 1886, achieved serious acclaim when it travelled across Europe, America and South Africa. It is discussed in detail in Chapter 3.

Her achievements, and those of numerous other women in Staffordshire alone, suggest that we must revise our views about the range of activities available to many, if not all, women in the nineteenth century. They demonstrate a life of multiple interests, and one in which domesticity was balanced with motivation and achievement. A particular combination of economic, aesthetic and ecclesiastical factors (such as trade with India, gothic revivalism, the arts and crafts movement, the growth of art needlework and the expansion of middle-class homes) allowed Elizabeth Wardle to make astute career choices that in turn meant that the Leek Embroidery Society quickly became renowned. An impressive array of evidence shows that, despite her demanding home life, she continued to create fine needlework that brought her international recognition. Fine needlework required discipline, aesthetic awareness and attention to detail. As a superintendent she needed to multitask, organise groups of other needlewomen and meet deadlines. Many women in Leek, though, not just Elizabeth, found that the family home could be a place of liberation. Trade directories reveal that a number set up businesses related to embroidery in the town, which indicates that there is still a lot to learn about the scope and diversity of other successful women's lives in a number of spheres. Accounts of Elizabeth Wardle's dynamic alliances with major designers and architects who worked in north Staffordshire provide further insight into shared values and strong links to the best ornamental textiles of that time, confirming just why this history matters.

Elizabeth Wardle published two books. Her *Guide to the Bayeux Tapestry* (1886) is given detailed coverage in Chapter 3. Her other publication was a cookery book – *366 Easy Dinners Arranged for Young Housekeepers* (1891) – with a different recipe for every day of the year. Anyone who could produce such a variety of recipes had extensive domestic skills and a wide knowledge of seasonal food. As they were intended for households they must have taken into account the limitations of a family kitchen. The whole initiative suggests a highly practical person who felt that domestic skills and understanding should be passed on in order that others could benefit. This subject must have been important to her, as for a number of years she was honorary secretary of the Leek School of Cookery, one of several of her charitable concerns that encouraged working-class women to learn healthy culinary skills (Figure 4). There are also several recorded instances of her supporting other needlewomen. She helped run bazaars, which sold embroidery to raise money for charities, as well as assisting at art emporia. These latter organisations allowed women to sell their work

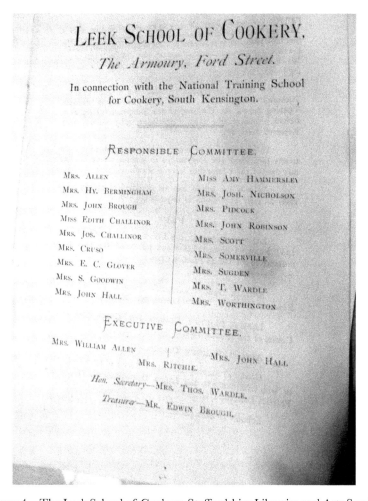

Figure 4   The Leek School of Cookery. Staffordshire Libraries and Arts Service

through cooperative ventures, which took less commission than a commercial enterprise would have done. Her numerous achievements are discussed in Chapters 2, 3 and 4.

Part of this story is about our understanding of the alliances of local makers with major architects, as epitomised by Elizabeth Wardle's collaborations with significant architects of her day. Regionalism was often a significant factor in their practice as Gothic Revivalists, yet, although their buildings are famous, the embroideries within them, made in the locality to their designs, are hardly known. The Leek Embroidery Society was a magnificent example of high-level partnerships, and knowing more about this increases our appreciation of eminent men such as Gerald Callcott Horsley, George Gilbert Scott Jnr, John Dando Sedding and Richard Norman Shaw. Understanding the context of their needlework designs highlights different aspects of their ingenuity. The architects who feature in this history went beyond designing buildings to create designs for embroidery, which involved working on quite dissimilar scales, textures and materials that behaved quite differently. The same men frequently understood embroidery techniques and when working with local craftspeople their combined skills produced exquisite needlework for the focal points of their churches. As a consequence, the residents of Leek experienced buildings by the most distinguished of architects as part of their daily lives. They were at the heart of the community, as places where the important stages of life were celebrated, and they contained the best examples of craft practice by leading figures of the Arts and Crafts movement. The Wardles' skills contributed a great deal to these histories, which are more than simply regional in scope.

The correspondence between Thomas Wardle and Morris, which continued over a number of years, provides a great deal of detailed information about their preoccupations, mainly related to their businesses. Concurrently, George Young Wardle was also persuaded to learn new skills by Morris in order to develop Morris's firm. It was George Young Wardle who supervised the strategic move of Morris & Co. from Queen Square to Merton Abbey. He was a perceptive man and his writing has proved to be invaluable to anyone wanting to understand more about Morris the man and the development of his company.[31] May Morris, the younger daughter of William Morris, described George Young Wardle as a 'chemist and artist' and although Ray Watkinson thought that this was a 'terse description' he felt it was 'exactly right'.[32] Watkinson considered George Young Wardle to be a 'delicate draughtsman and close observer' who guarded his privacy. His keen powers of observation and subtle remarks reveal him as an intelligent eyewitness. George Young Wardle's *Memorials of William Morris* (1897) and *The Morris Exhibit at the Foreign Fair, Boston* (1883) are both lucid and revealing publications for which many Morris scholars have been grateful.

George Young Wardle wrote *Memorials* just after Morris's death in 1896 at the request of Morris's biographer J.W. Mackail, who had taken on the task of writing the biography at the special wish of Edward Burne-Jones. In *Memorials* George Young Wardle gave shrewd insights into Morris's character, offering reasons for many of Morris's actions. He must have been content working for Morris, as he wrote: 'of the work at Merton there seems nothing to say except that it was altogether delightful'.[33] He ended with a heartfelt tribute: 'no-one having worked for Mr Morris could willingly have joined any other workshop or, having passed through any other, would have given up Mr Morris's for that'. He revealed how he acquired numerous skills when working for the firm, having learnt the craft of wood cutting in 1866 in order to transfer Burne-Jones's drawings into woodcuts. This prestigious project, *The Earthly Paradise*, was profusely illustrated by the artist and required the cutting of about thirty-five wood blocks. Some were done by Morris and the rest by George Young Wardle, who also provided his own subtle illustrations for Morris's poetry. He took on a great deal of responsibility, performing in addition other highly skilled tasks, such as overseeing production in the stained-glass and carpet workshops at the Merton Abbey site. This released Morris to concentrate on other growing interests. George Young Wardle clearly understood the importance of colour to a design, whether that was for stained glass, a tapestry, chintz or embroidery. Mackail was convinced that Morris was fortunate in finding a man like George Young Wardle, 'who caught this energy from him [Morris] and yet retained with it a full measure of shrewdness and caution', adding that 'the choice of a good manager is in effect good management'.[34] This is supported by Charles Harvey and Jon Press, who note that George Young Wardle's contribution to the success of the firm 'has rarely received the recognition that it deserves'.[35]

George Young Wardle produced a detailed catalogue for Morris &Co. when the firm exhibited its goods at the Boston Foreign Fair of 1883. It was described by Charles Faulkner as 'a fascinating document, organised in such a way as to take one around the exhibition and lead one to appreciate the qualities of design and material in each of the six rooms devoted to the company's work'.[36] The catalogue is thought to be 'possibly the most important document on Morris (and Morris & Co.) never to appear in print'.[37] Not only did it itemise the complete range of goods available from the firm, but it also advised purchasers how to use them. George Young Wardle discussed different types of fabric, often with detailed instructions on hanging them to best advantage in different interiors. He acted as an interior designer, advising on colour schemes and the patterns in wallpapers and fabrics that might look best with the variety of wooden floors and furniture then preferred in America. He was clearly aware of numerous aspects of niche markets.[38]

George Young Wardle's drawings were as impressive as his writing. While working as a freelance draughtsman in medieval churches across East Anglia on a project spread over two years, he recorded a range of decorative features, even those on high ceiling beams. A series of his drawings taken from the region's rood screens became the foundation for distinctive figurative embroideries produced by his sister in Leek. Other drawings by him were purchased by Morris, Marshall, Faulkner & Co., and some were used by Philip Webb during the restoration of the chapel ceiling at Jesus College, Cambridge, which began in 1866. Another series of drawings was made during a tour of major Gothic buildings across Europe. From 1862 George Young Wardle travelled through Belgium, France, Germany, Holland and Italy recording ceiling decoration, stained glass, stone carvings and other architectural details.

His surviving measured drawings show that George Young Wardle would linger over the smallest detail of ornamentation. The exact colouring of a panel or the precise profile of a moulding was noted. His drawings were kept and later donated to the V&A by May Morris and Aymer Vallance, an early biographer of Morris, in the 1930s, where they remain. His associated letters divulge that although his frame of reference was wide he could keep to the job at hand as he concentrated on the physical details of sacred places. He revealed that he was not copying features in the many churches he visited simply for commercial use; he was trying to establish a framework for understanding a national phenomenon. As he recorded decoration he sought to comprehend the relationship of one material to another as well as the transformation of one material by another. He examined paint samples, suggesting that he was conducting a technical survey, and also formed opinions on the workers who painted the rood screens of Norfolk and Suffolk. His analysis suggested that a particular school of artists worked there, as he identified certain common schematic characteristics in the decorations of a number of churches in that region.

Michael Hall reports that when George Young Wardle was working in Cambridge on the painted chapel ceiling of Jesus College he wrote revealingly to the college bursar, E.H. Morgan, in 1869 about a fellow workman, named Leach, as follows: 'he certainly had not quite hit the colour of the red. ... I have now shown him how to improve the colour of the red – make it a little fresher – & I also left a specimen of another way of painting the cornice.'[39] Frederick Leach, described as an art worker, had a leading decorating company in Cambridge before opening a branch in London. He was employed by Bodley and worked on a number of prestigious projects across the country, including the decoration of St James's Palace in London. His standards were, however, not up to those set by George Young Wardle.

George Young Wardle's study of the Charterhouse building in London, originally a Carthusian monastery, is a detailed extended essay that, similarly, reveals the author's great powers of observation.[40] Throughout he notes the smallest detail of the building's construction and decoration, indicating his insight into the efforts invested by craftsmen and their understanding of the materials they controlled. Implicit in his writing is an awareness of the nature of human ingenuity, which is both shaped by, and shapes, the physical aspect of the buildings and their contents. It is a work of subtle, intelligent scrutiny grounded in a reverence for the work of the artisans and their sense of scale, colour and beauty.

George Young Wardle's interest in historic buildings continued through his work for the Society for the Protection of Ancient Buildings (SPAB), which celebrated its 140th anniversary on 22 March 2017. Writing in 1897, Valance argued that Morris saw SPAB as his finest achievement. He was present at the inaugural meeting, and with Morris and Philip Webb he drafted its manifesto in 1877, which outlined its aims.[41] George Young Wardle was a major figure on the vital Restoration Committee, which inspected sites and wrote letters of protest. Thomas Wardle also joined SPAB in its early days and was an active member in Cheshire and Staffordshire.[42] In addition to his work with SPAB George Young Wardle was also politically active in the Socialist League, along with his wife Madeleine. He was asked by Morris to draw up a scheme that would give workers a share of his firm's profits and Morris accepted his proposals. It would seem that, at least in politics, Tom Wardle Jnr took after his uncle. In a letter to his daughter Jenny in 1886 about his own political public speaking, Morris noted that 'Young Tom Wardle was summoned for speaking at Harrow Road Station some weeks ago and appeared at the police-court yesterday: he was committed for trial; he says he will not pay a fine – item his father says he won't.'[43] Although young Tom was then only fifteen years old he was clearly passionate about politics. We do not know why he was in London, but clearly Morris was aware of his activities and expected Jenny to know who he was talking about.

After he retired from Morris & Co. in 1889 owing to illness, George Young Wardle maintained contact with the architect Philip Webb, a co-founder of SPAB. Webb's letters show that George Young Wardle retained a great interest in historic buildings and their condition and he continued to prepare detailed papers for SPAB. Webb clearly knew him better than most and refers to him in letters to others, including May Morris and Dante Gabriel Rossetti.[44] Webb's correspondence with Sydney Cockerill acknowledged that George Young Wardle was much more than a business manager; he was a man of artistic discernment and taste. Webb's letters also reveal that, as George Young Wardle suffered from poor health, he regularly changed locations in order to find healthier places to live. He tried Kent, Richmond, Surrey and Bognor before moving to Italy, after which time little is known of him. We do know that when he lived in Charlotte Street, in Bloomsbury, London, with his wife Madeleine, they were near to George Bernard Shaw and other members of the socialist movement. Madeleine was an embroiderer who produced at least one small item for Sedding's church in Leek and other work for the Leek Embroidery Society, and reputedly stitched items with Jane Morris and others in London.[45]

Like his brother-in-law George Young Wardle, Thomas Wardle was usually engaged with multiple projects simultaneously. He was not only a craftsman but also a strategic thinker who understood the international market place and the need to promote the silk industry in various countries. His actions convey his unbounded curiosity about, and his ability to investigate, the world around him. As the first president of the Silk Association of Great Britain and Ireland, in 1887, he developed an over-arching view of the silk sector and used that knowledge to help the global silk industry evolve and survive multiple changes. This energetic polymath invented a new fabric, 'Sealcloth', and revived challenging chiné printing in Leek – a complex warp-printed technique that transformed block-printed designs. His influence was widespread partly because he was a prolific, articulate writer who published on multiple topics. His range of expertise also developed outside the textile sector at the highest level and in a number of spheres, covering topics as varied as geology, palae-ontology, statistics, art and technical education, history of art, architecture and stained glass. He was passionate about music and composed, played the organ and led local choirs. He published more than fifty scientific papers and learned documents as outcomes from his research, some in French, and presumably spoke other languages, as he constantly conducted business across Europe, where he had many contacts and friends. Wardle remained true, however, to the essential craftsman within, and remained embedded in Staffordshire, playing an active part in town life. He was therefore acutely aware of Leek's outstanding buildings, congregations, societies and charities, and somehow he found time to be a Justice of the Peace, as well as encouraging numerous inter-esting people to visit the town, where he and Elizabeth gave them hospitality.

Like Morris, Walter Crane and Lewis Foreman Day, Thomas Wardle was closely involved with art school education as a lecturer and an examiner. He talked regularly to elite metropolitan societies, Cambridge University and schools of art across the country. He felt strongly that access to the finest examples of art, craft and design should be a prerequisite for anyone entering the textile and other creative industries. In an address he gave at Burslem School of Art he agreed with John Ruskin when he said that 'beautiful art can only be produced by people who have beautiful things about them, and leisure to look at them; and unless you provide some elements of beauty for your workmen to be surrounded by, you will find that no element of beauty can be invented by them'.[46] The links between museums and industry were important. It was, however, difficult for apprentices or students in north Staffordshire to make the journey to London's museums and galleries. One solution to this came in the form of loan exhibitions, which were sent out from the Circulation Department of the South Kensington Museum to provincial textile centres, including Leek. This system allowed the best fine art, ceramics and textiles from other cultures and eras to be viewed by a much wider audience.[47]

The Wardles themselves collected paintings and drawings, including some by George Young Wardle, and they lent their extensive collection of Rossetti's drawings for a memorable display in the town. Although he was often involved in major projects, Thomas Wardle still found time to organise art exhibitions in Leek and was described in the local press as a very zealous worker for the cause. His commitment was clear; he knew just how significant such exhibitions were to manufacturing towns and continued to organise displays of exemplars for decades to come. He was also involved with events of international importance in London and Manchester for the same reason. Other prominent events, including lectures and ambitious exhibitions, were held regularly in Leek. Many noted speakers were attracted to talk there, including Morris in 1882, as well as Oscar Wilde, Robert Stephenson Smyth, Robert Baden-Powell and J.W. Mackail. Walter Crane, then principal of both Leek's Nicholson Institute and Manchester School of Art, gave an address titled 'The Relation of Art to Education and Social Life' at Leek's town hall;[48] along with Wardle, he also made his mark in other ways on the town.

According to reports in the *Staffordshire Sentinel* and other newspapers these events generated a great sense of excitement, as they gave opportunities for everyone to see and hear the finest orators. Many of these occasions were the result of Thomas Wardle's connections, which allowed him to stimulate creativity in the region. He understood, as did Ruskin and Morris, the range of decorative design. Like Ruskin, he agreed that it was the duty

> of manufacturers to form the market, as much as to supply it. … if you resolve from the first that, so far as you can ascertain or discern what is best, you will produce what is best, on an intelligent consideration of the probable tendencies and possible tastes of the people whom you supply.[49]

The wide scope of Thomas Wardle's interests suggests a man with an urge to comprehend the world about him. It was not enough to acquire general knowledge; he needed to understand things in depth, and explored subjects as diverse as geology and Coptic history in forensic detail. The emergence of geology as a science drew the interest of many people, including Wardle, whose engagement with the region's familiar landscape included what lay below its surface. As a geologist he regularly made field trips across Staffordshire and Derbyshire, an area rich in pickings. There he discovered new fossils and had a fossil fern *Adiantites Wardlei* named after him.[50] Wardle's trips resulted in learned papers, which gained him a Fellowship of the Royal Geological Society in January 1863.

Wardle was a prolific essayist, as noted above, and contributed articles to specialist journals as well as to the journal of the Staffordshire Field Sports Club, just one of a number of organisations of which he was president. He produced a regular column for a church magazine and, as a churchwarden, he developed an interest in Gothic architecture, stained glass and ecclesiastical textiles, overlapping with his professional interest in silk, which was an important medium for the transmission of power and wealth through elaborate designs. Wardle wrote scholarly articles on silk for the *Encyclopædia Britannica* and *Chambers Encyclopædia* and produced, among other things, a detailed catalogue on Indian silks for the South Kensington Museum. Silk-making tested the most skilled craft workers and from these crucial documents we can discern his attitudes to aspects of the global silk industry and his own driving forces as a dyer. He was frequently invited to lecture at learned societies, giving lantern-slide talks often with specimens of textiles to show to the audience. We know

Figure 5   Visit of the Duchess of Teck, Old Stockwell House,
Leek. Staffordshire Libraries and Arts Service

he addressed a number of institutions with which he had some connection, including the Art Workers' Guild, the Society of Arts, the Royal Female School of Art, London, the British Association, Cambridge University, the Society of the Chemical Industry and the Royal Society of British Architects. He was also invited to speak at conferences in France and India as well as at a great many art schools. As well as the first president of the Silk Association, he was the first president of the Bradford Society of Dyers and Colourists.

Thomas Wardle corresponded regularly with Morris, occasionally with Shaw and Bodley, and was friends with Sedding. As many of his research papers were published we know that he produced clear, informative and often passionate prose based on experience. The publications project the confidence of a man who had a grip on the data and a good explanation for them. He demonstrated over and over that he had the intellectual agility to move comfortably between the nitty-gritty world of the dyers' workshop and the politics of the Anglo-Indian silk trade and leading art establishments. He was always engaged with the problems of global silk production and its challenges and strategically raised its profile with the general public by involving members of the royal family in the promotion of British silk via their input into numerous exhibitions. He also attended many events with the duchess of Teck in a valiant effort to publicise the English silk industry (Figure 5). She even designed silks. His research resulted in productive cultural cross-fertilisation and he took pains to share this knowledge with others, including craftworkers in India. In 1903, on an ambitious second visit to India to rejuvenate the Kashmir silk industry, he made no concessions to his age when he went on field trips.[51] Thomas Wardle was, moreover, an all-round outdoorsman; he excelled at field sports, particularly fishing, a pleasure he shared with Morris.

Taming the Wild

Thomas Wardle was a strategic thinker, deeply immersed in the demands of the modern English silk industry, while looking to the past and the East for inspiration. When he embarked on his major study of India's wild silks he was not only continuing but also reinforcing a long tradition. His was the first systematic project to use science to unlock the secrets of the structure of wild silks and recalibrate their potential. In parallel, he made investigations into all the known indigenous dyestuffs of India. This was a government-backed initiative and the scope of the study was remarkable; in the process he became the first to discover how to permanently dye the wild silks, transforming them from their familiar golden shades to any desirable colour using India's natural dyes. Through an intensive programme of research and development, which occupied his time, skills and energy over at least eight years, he overcame a number of problems that had always prevented a wider use of this silk. This project grew exponentially and resulted in an entirely fresh understanding of the properties of the raw materials. The results were met with equal enthusiasm by British, European and Indian makers.

Throughout his investigations Wardle followed a key argument about human agency: that people should understand and use what is there in front of them. He challenged the international silk industry, urging it to reconsider India's wild silks as a raw material. The result was a joint English–Indian project that joined the raw materials of India with expertise from Leek. As early as 1873 he was ready to display the first results of his research at the major International Exhibition in South Kensington, London. The hand-painted, photographic copy of the Bayeux Tapestry was also displayed there. It was a prescient event.

Thomas Wardle's early experiments attracted the attention of leading figures linked to the Indian government. They encouraged him to extend his work using more raw materials from the subcontinent. The official documents from that time clearly state that the aim was to encourage an increase in international markets for India's resources. Ultimately, Wardle sent thousands of cloth and yarn samples, which documented the outcomes of his research, to India. The fifteen hard-backed volumes arrived in Calcutta (now Kolkata) in 1886, after which they disappeared for decades. When they resurfaced, in around 2009, they caused utter amazement among contemporary Indian dyers. The volumes and their relevance today are discussed in detail in the Conclusion. When Wardle visited India in 1886 he was greeted by dyers in Bengal's villages with warm enthusiasm as a friend who had helped them extend their craft. He also addressed a large business audience in Calcutta and demonstrated how India could benefit from his findings related to cultivated silk production.

Wardle had rescued the relics of an historic local dyeing tradition and rebuilt it into a living, thriving business that knew no borders. At the same time he tested the natural resources of India in the face of a huge man-made chemical onslaught and succeeded beyond anyone's imagining. In his traditional dye works there was a constant interplay between local and global, art and science, historical and contemporary, and craft and industry. There was no inconsistency in this, as opposite forces can and do come from within craft practice as well as from external stimuli. Traditional skills have always evolved as makers respond to market forces and to their materials, and many have the desire to explore their craft to its limits. There is no doubt that Wardle was inspired by India's rich textile heritage and admired what ancient dyeing methods had already achieved. His successes chimed with what was happening elsewhere, as leading figures in the Arts and Crafts Movement, Gothic Revivalism, Art Needlework and Aestheticism were seeking well-made goods produced by traditional methods, which were rapidly disappearing. As Wardle extended his knowledge these leading figures found what they were looking for in Leek.

Once Thomas Wardle had dyed wild silks with rich shades of colour from India's dyestuffs he set out to broaden their use, encouraging Elizabeth Wardle to devise a method of stitching that would bring out the beauty of the wild silk thread that he had transformed, and her stitching experiments revealed the potential of the thread's possibilities. Their joint understanding of colour, newly made available in silk embroidery yarns, was to play a decisive role in the formation and evolution of the Leek Embroidery Society. Theirs was a collaboration of some magnitude, as they employed their individual and combined skills to launch what proved to be an extensive new project. Their authority rested on an understanding of how designs work and of the use of colour, on their knowledge of technology and on the creative combination of all these factors. Both had a highly developed visual intelligence, a strong work ethic and a sense of discipline and workmanship, and both were always conscious of the true purpose of their work. Together they showed that India's improved materials offered great opportunities for creative expression, including artistic embroidery.

The market for a wider range of embroidery silks was huge. An increasing international interest in innovative Art Needlework saw the demand for decorative arts and good-quality traditional materials expand and massively raised the consumption of goods produced by the Wardle companies. Thomas and Elizabeth Wardle opened up the possibilities for India's materials in striking ways, often adopting the traditional colours and patterns of India in the process. The activities of the Wardles were typical of other practitioners following an Arts and Crafts philosophy, in that they drew motivation from pre-industrial methods without simply imitating historic examples. Both continued to absorb new ideas and adapt their technical skills to meet changing demands and satisfy new markets. Their surviving textiles demonstrate that integrity. They are a powerful reminder of the different forces at play in that creative era. Thomas and Elizabeth Wardle passed on the same attitudes to the following generation, as some of their children adhered to the same standards. Despite the increasing pressures of industrialisation, the family companies, run by Gilbert and Bernard Wardle, continued to produce specialised products.

Chapter 2

THE BUSINESS OF STITCH

Does the silkworm expend her yellow labours for thee?
For thee does she undo herself.
    Thomas Middleton, *The Revenger's Tragedy*, 1607

Praised by all who came into contact with it, the Leek Embroidery Society was noted for its ingenious use of design, fine materials, innovative techniques and distinctive colour schemes. It is also an interesting example of how the ethos of the Arts and Crafts movement was interpreted in diverse ways and in a variety of places. Although the Society was the result of many different conditions and connections, the vision and skills of Thomas and Elizabeth Wardle lay at its heart. Through their initiatives a multitude of forces were united in 1879 as members of the Wardle family caught a widespread mood that fitted their interests and talents. Their sensitivity to local issues also informed their decision making. There were benefits in being a comparatively small but flexible company that had the ability to pick up ideas and match them to the talent available locally. The dynamism and diverse talents of the family meant that new projects could be developed swiftly. Risks were certainly taken, but as far as we can tell all were successful.

The Leek Embroidery Society was launched in 1879/80 in the Wardle home in the town centre. The house is there still, halfway down a broad street of handsome buildings. Later the family moved from 62 St Edward Street to more spacious premises at No. 54. As Figure 6 shows, it too is a Georgian townhouse, although larger and of rose-red brick, occupying a commanding position. Today it is a solicitor's practice. In the mid-1880s smaller premises next door at No. 56 were converted into the headquarters of the Society and other family companies.[1] There was then space for a dedicated workroom with a shop. While St Edward Street remained the location for the Society it was moved across the road to No. 21 in the early twentieth century. This was its

Figure 6   The Wardle Family Home, 54 St Edward Street,
Leek. Photograph: the author

last known address. The workroom and shop continued under the direction
of Mrs C. Bill until Miss Annie Sutton bought the business. Helped by Miss
Annie Redfern, she offered a repair service for historic pieces until 1937, when
the shop was bought by Miss Winnie Rawsthorne, who managed it until the
outbreak of the Second World War.

It was an opportune time for creative needlework, and the Leek Embroidery
Society flourished, growing swiftly into an extraordinary venture that lasted for
over fifty years. While the stitching was women's work, it is important to note
that the organisation was a family enterprise. Although some needlewomen
were anonymous, many were identified and their skills publicly acknowledged
in the town and beyond, pointing to a great deal of confidence in women's
work. However, the role of the skilled male workforce has remained relatively
under-appreciated. They, too, were experienced craftworkers with a vast
store of knowledge who understood the materials they worked with and were
essential to the success of the Society. Cloth and yarn dyers, wood-block carvers
and hand-block printers were invariably male, while silk weavers and braid and
fringe makers could be either male or female. They all served long apprenticeships in local artisanal family-run workshops and their skills and understanding

were the result of a crucial and complex blend of design-related and technical knowledge that was crucial to the successful production of fine embroidery.[2] Nevertheless, apart from Thomas Wardle, his sons and a dyer named Kay, who was active when William Morris was working at the Hencroft site and was mentioned in Morris's correspondence to Wardle,[3] it has proved more difficult to name the men who produced the cloth and silk yarn without which the Society would not have flourished in the way that it did. Figure 7 shows a team of male dyers on the banks of the river Churnet beside a wooden plank placed across the river; the dyers would stand on this in order to immerse hanks of silk into the water flowing beneath, a precarious process which no doubt led to many cold-water soakings.

A provincial location and numerous pregnancies did not prevent Elizabeth Wardle achieving widespread acclaim in her own right, as described above. Well before the formation of the Leek Embroidery Society her needlework skills attracted public attention. Due to particular local developments ecclesiastical work of a fine standard was stitched by her and other women in north Staffordshire as early as 1865. This was reported in the local press, where the needlework was praised. It was from at least that time that she set out the themes for her life that would emerge again and again in the coming decades. She was a craftswoman who must have been visionary, determined, focused,

Figure 7   Skilled dyers on the river bank. Staffordshire Libraries and Arts Service

proactive and talented in order to achieve what she did. More details of her life and work are covered in depth in Chapter 4.

A knowledge of colour, materials and techniques lay at the core of Thomas and Elizabeth Wardle's success. The best craft skills require years of continuing practice, involving the understanding of raw materials and the tools needed to manipulate them to bring out their beauty. The capacity to produce even basic stitching is a commonplace yet astonishing human activity, involving complex hand movements. A simple stitch done well can be a deeply satisfying act, when control of the needle and thread allows a person to carry out what appears to be a routine task. The core of this rhythmical action is that well-designed object, the needle. Although it has no function other than to carry a thread it does the job well. It may seem to be employed almost without thinking, yet it requires considerable skill comprising intricate hand and eye coordination to make a needle do what is wanted, even at the most rudimentary level.

From the beginning of her needlework activity Elizabeth Wardle must have set herself the highest standards, and she maintained and perfected her craft skills over a lengthy period, presumably at least in part for the personal satisfaction that it brought. To achieve this she needed to fully understand the qualities of the different yarns and cloths she was using. Skilled needlewomen would adjust their stitching according to the type of textile being embellished, the yarn chosen for stitching it and the nature of the design being worked. Elizabeth Wardle's exploration of the qualities of India's wild silks, at an early stage of their development by her husband, resulted in many commissions and alliances.

Handwoven tussar silk cloth had a loose structure, which provided little resistance to a needle and thread. Like most softly draping fabric it needed to be stretched taut in a frame when being stitched. Loosely twisted tussar silk thread presented challenges, as it was likely to untwist during use, and so a soft cloth of tussar silk was the ideal base for tussar yarn embroidery. Elizabeth Wardle's ability to combine both materials in a finely judged way, which enhanced them for a specific purpose, proved fundamental to the success of the Leek Embroidery Society. The distinct qualities of India's wild silks were undoubtedly worth the extra skills needed. They have a particular structure that dictates how they absorb natural dyestuffs and their characteristically uneven surface results in scintillations of rich, yet subtle shades with a subtle iridescent sheen. Colour Plate 2b, a beautiful panel of distinctive wild silk, demonstrates these qualities clearly. This pattern was hand-block printed onto a base cloth that was available in a variety of colours. As we can see from this example, even the simplest stitches allowed the embroiderer to play with colour and texture in a satisfying way. The creation of a formal workshop was, however, quite different to an individual working from home alone.

An Inspired Partnership

Given their skills and preoccupations, along with wider national developments, founding the Leek Embroidery Society must have seemed an obvious project for Elizabeth and Thomas Wardle. It was a turning point in their lives, as it represented both a consolidation of their core interests and an integrated awareness that they could develop in a number of ways. Ultimately they functioned jointly and independently as practitioners, collaborators, facilitators, researchers, teachers, managers and leaders. They were far from unique in seeking to produce the finest needlework possible, as there were other, larger and long-established workshops responding to increasing requests for fine embroidery across Britain. However, as the demand locally and nationally was evidently for specialised embroidery, which they could provide, it was a logical step to aim to meet that demand and expand as orders grew. They were well placed in Leek to react to the seemingly boundless demands for well-made and beautiful objects for church, home and fashionable dress and to meet deadlines, and their particular brilliance was to harness the skills of different family members to produce unique work. As a result the Society was based on a firm foundation of interlocking family enterprises in which the various branches of the company strengthened one another. This combination of skills meant that control of the supply chain for the Society was in family hands. There were huge advantages in this relating to quality control and it was likely that cloth and threads were processed on demand, which must have been more cost-effective. Colour Plate 1c shows some of the subtle colours available, with their shades clearly numbered; some are labelled as suitable for washing and some have the brand name of a major supplier Pearsalls. Numerous other yarn types are not shown here. This new and exciting episode in the family-run business brought some of England's most creative figures to Leek, their combined talents producing astonishing outcomes that are still visible in the town today. They were, moreover, closely linked to the local silk industry, which manufactured many of the core materials, such as fringes, braids and other trimmings regularly used by embroiderers.

Had the Wardles been unable to satisfy the expectations of notable architects, designers and retailers and complete complex work on schedule, however, the Society would never have developed so swiftly and gained the reputation it did. However, within a very short time it was attracting attention at the highest level. As demand spread rapidly, special pieces for international exhibitions were produced. The panel of angels seen in Colour Plate 5 is likely to have been an exhibition piece. The earliest phase of the Society included the use of designs by renowned architects. Elizabeth Wardle's first ecclesiastical commission quickly led to others, as one major architect after another came to work in the region and designed embroideries for their churches. They recruited the talents of Elizabeth Wardle, who proved she was a versatile needlewoman capable of working with an array of subjects, in a variety of techniques and on different scales. Her output ranged from smaller items such as alms bags to extensive, site-specific altar frontals for large churches as a result of collaborations with Gothic Revival architects, discussed in full in Chapter 4. As a prominent figure in the town her activities were regularly reported on in the local press and prominent art journals such as the *Journal of the Society of Arts*, *The Studio*, *The Queen*, *Ladies Field* and *The Lady*.

Significant Silks

In November 1881 the revelatory Exhibition of Modern Embroidery, organised by Elizabeth Wardle, was held in Leek (Figure 8). A variety of items from that exhibition can be seen in Colour Plates 7a, 7b, 8a, 8b and 8c. They remain in remarkable condition and are a testament to a huge variety of skills. Although only open for two days, the exhibition's significance was lasting. It was far more than a display of embroidery; it was an assured exhibition of the finest talent, which indicated that significant relationships existed between Thomas and Elizabeth Wardle and major figures in fine textile production. The exhibition was held in connection with the Leek Mechanics' Institute Art Classes on the occasion of the annual prize-giving. Sir Philip Cunliffe-Owen, director of the South Kensington Museum, distributed the prizes, which was an extraordinary event in itself. By then Thomas Wardle's links with the Museum, mainly related to the Indian silk trade, were strong. Cunliffe-Owen knew that Wardle had an astute awareness of the international consumption of silk in its varied forms, which was matched by his ability to turn that awareness into desirable goods. The Museum was, moreover, committed to collect and display the best objects from different cultures to inspire British manufacturers. Promoting trade was an important remit, silk was part of a complex international economy and developments in Leek were integral to an interdependent global market. Because of its responsibility to support trade the Museum purchased many items of Leek embroidery, while other examples were borrowed from the Wardles in order to include their joint work in the important Indian section of the Museum. Along with a comprehensive collection of India's wild silks, dyed in Leek and supplied by Wardle, these exhibits demonstrated the improved potential of India's raw materials and so were prominently displayed for commercial reasons.

Wild silks differed significantly from cultivated silks and were valued for a number of reasons, strength being only one. Thomas Wardle had carefully chosen a wide variety of types for the Museum to demonstrate the material's

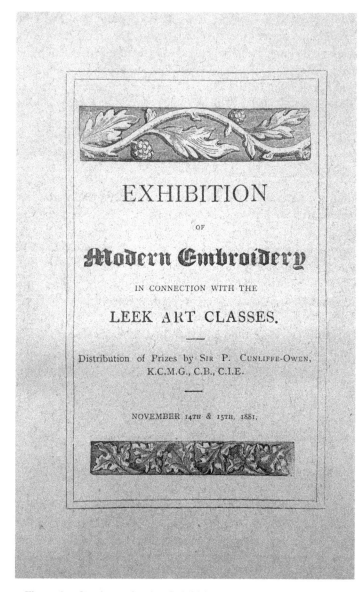

EXHIBITION

OF

Modern Embroidery

IN CONNECTION WITH THE

LEEK ART CLASSES.

———

Distribution of Prizes by SIR P. CUNLIFFE-OWEN,
K.C.M.G., C.B., C.I.E.

———

NOVEMBER 14TH & 15TH, 1881.

Figure 8   Catalogue for the 'Exhibition of Modern Embroidery',
Leek, 1881. Courtesy of the Royal School of Needlework

varied characteristics. Examples of Leek embroidery vividly revealed how the raw materials could then be transformed as never before. Techniques employed in Leek emphasised the distinctive sheen of the wild silk thread, which was more subtle than the vibrant shine of cultivated silks. The Museum's displays were aimed at the international silk industry, as the silks were considered to be 'one of the most wide-spread and important natural productions of the Indian empire, and would thus be a means of increasing the material prosperity of Her Majesty's Indian subjects'.[4] Thomas Wardle was commissioned by the Museum to write an extensive illustrated catalogue to bring attention to these specific collections, which was published in 1881. This was the same year as the embroidery exhibition in Leek, which also reinforced the importance of Anglo-Indian trade. Cunliffe-Owen was, therefore, very aware of the important role that Leek embroidery had in extending trade with the subcontinent.

The South Kensington Museum was a suitably prestigious venue for the joint promotion of India's improved silks and Leek's traditional skills. In the process Elizabeth Wardle was acknowledged as the first person to use India's dyed tussar silk thread for embroidery. Records reveal that a variety of pieces stitched by her were purchased by the Museum in 1880,[5] soon after her initial stitching experiments. As Cunliffe-Owen requested occasional changes to displays, other embroideries were acquired in 1881 and 1884, and a major purchase of twenty-one items of tussar embroidery was made for the Indian section in February 1894. One display case held altar cloths, along with a variety of fringes intended for use with needlework, all made entirely of tussar silk. The Museum's displays were a focused validation of India's silk production and a clear indication of the continuing relevance of craft for the Anglo-Indian silk trade in an increasingly mechanising nation. The displays represented the future, promoted a sense of valuable diversity and demonstrated the quality of work from Leek as well as the town's prolific output.

Meanwhile, in north Staffordshire, the catalogue for Leek's Exhibition of Modern Embroidery highlighted the work of the Society beyond South Kensington Museum by firmly placing it in the context of the Art Needlework movement. It was a defining event, with leaders in the field of embroidery collaborating to show their work. This centre of dyeing excellence was, thereafter, also known as a place for fine needlework. The exhibition was held at the Temperance Hall, originally a chapel, in the town centre. Although the venue was frequently used for staging exhibitions and drama nothing of this magnitude had been done before. Conceptually this was a major event and we may never know why such a significant undertaking lasted for only two days. At that point the Society was still a relatively new organisation, which seemed to have sprung up fully formed in a very short time. To some extent, however, the exhibition was a retrospective, as some exhibits, such as pieces for Cheddleton church, dated from 1865. Along with the other exhibitors the Society made a significant contribution to the elevation of Arts and Crafts and Gothic Revival embroidery that was recorded by the Staffordshire press in some detail.

The range of exhibits tells a story of commitment, vision and collaboration. These were not humble rural pieces, the products of a limited provincial outlook; rather, they were luxurious items showing evidence of a creative influence that had been gathering strength in the region for some time. The exhibition publicised named local needlewomen who were capable of producing subtly different work with great ingenuity. Embroidery for large works by three major architects, along with pieces by eminent designers including William Morris and Walter Crane, were included for the public to admire. It is likely that this was the first example of such a range of embroidery designs by so many nationally renowned people being gathered together in a small market town, albeit a town that was a centre of silk production. Here were examples of the finest designs, materials and traditional skills used to make useful and beautiful objects by local people for the local community and beyond. It was a groundbreaking event that demonstrated that Thomas and Elizabeth Wardle were both vital figures in the English Arts and Crafts movement and contributing to other creative movements. The local had quickly become a national and international force.

The exhibition offered a remarkable opportunity to view some of the finest needlework then known in Britain. It was the result of the rich interchange that happens when collaboration between like-minded people takes place across disciplines. In what was a spectacular explosion of creativity and refined skills it represented traditional and contemporary work at its best. Packed displays illustrated how historical, modern and global influences combined to satisfy varying user-centred demands and stimulate a growing confidence in local needlewomen, and demonstrated excellent design by some of the nation's leading practitioners from a variety of disciplines. The selection of site-specific ecclesiastical embroideries, stitched in the region to designs by influential architects, must have been a high point. These were unique, elaborate and costly pieces planned specifically for the region's buildings by George Gilbert Scott Jnr, John Dando Sedding and Richard Norman Shaw. Their designs were embedded with emblematic features manifest in their colouring, motifs and costly fabrics. The catalogue lists at least six large altar frontals with matching superfrontals, together with a selection of smaller items to complement them. All but one, shown in Colour Plate 7b, which was of linen and wool, were of expensive silks and gold thread. Both materials were historically highly prized and symbols of power across centuries, cultures and continents. They clearly reflected the wealth and aspirations of the community. Pieces such as alms bags and pulpit falls were on view alongside a chancel carpet and sanctuary mats. They were shown together with items designed by George Young Wardle, brother of Elizabeth.

The needlework had been produced by skilled local embroiderers, supervised by Elizabeth Wardle, over a period of thirteen years. It confirmed the strength and range of the women's skills, many of whom were named in the catalogue. Pieces that were never meant to be seen alongside each other were arranged so that work could be compared and contrasted. All of these ecclesiastical exhibition pieces have now been tracked and identified for the first time and we can see from the colour plates shown here that they are all distinct. Remarkably, most are still in the churches for which they were made.

Alongside the ecclesiastical items were at least twenty-two secular pieces stitched in Leek; the catalogue confirmed that the 'colouring (was) by Mrs Wardle'.[6] A learned use of colour was always a vital element that lent distinctiveness to Leek work. Much thought went into the use of iridescent, softly shaded colours, colour contrasts and colour harmonies. As well as describing Elizabeth's specialist skills, this demonstrated that there was a new dimension to silk production that considerably expanded the choice of silk yarns available. The qualities of India's wild silks were consciously highlighted, as it was noted that each item was worked with 'floss of tussar silk on native Indian woven tussar silk in Indian designs'.[7] 'Tanjore Lotus', shown in Colour Plate 2a, is one of many such designs that were considered typical of Leek embroidery. The promotion of this particular silk indicated that a branch of the Wardles' enterprise was gathering momentum. Yet, it was not only about the materials; a distinctive aesthetic had also emerged, which became a characteristic feature of Leek work for decades to come.

Every secular piece had a purpose; they were mainly functional domestic items that demonstrated the potential of raw materials and designs from India to great effect. They were worked by members of the Leek Embroidery Society and others, including Madeleine, the wife of George Young Wardle, who had stitched a chair back. There were curtain borders, a pocket handkerchief bag and a mantelpiece border. Colour Plate 1a shows an embroidered photograph frame with the pattern Allahabad Marigold printed onto a hand-woven Indian wild silk. It is stitched with tussar silk thread using just three stitches: stem stitch, long and short stitch, with couched gold thread highlights.[8] The image within the frame is the only one known to show Elizabeth Wardle stitching. A selection of unfinished pieces and a variety of samples cleverly utilised traditional patterns alongside studies in colouring of Indian designs. By this early stage of its development it was evident that the embroidery demonstrated, through the creation of a variety of goods aimed at specific national and international markets, a carefully considered uniqueness that had much to offer.

This extended marketplace was a decisive factor in the survival of the British and Indian silk industries.

In 1881 it was made clear that the Leek Embroidery Society was firmly allied to a variety of high-level contacts. The importance of India to the British empire was also evident, as the exhibition's displays conveyed the richness of silks and patterns from the subcontinent. This was a vital sign of intercultural concern for economic sustainability in the global silk trade. It must also have been evident that needlework skills, which for years had been mainly confined to domestic use, had been honed to perfection in Leek and employed in the production of the finest embroidery for domestic and ecclesiastical purposes. Local embroiderers had pushed the expressive potential of silks and stitching practice, while retaining traditional symbolic motifs and other cultural references. These developments were closely connected to the work of progressive, London-based architects, all of whom were dedicated to understanding the many deep, emblematic subjects related to their buildings (see Chapter 4).

Besides the embroideries produced in Leek visitors to the exhibition viewed a huge display of work by the Royal School of Art Needlework (RSAN), then based in South Kensington, London. 'A charming collection of embroidery' by this prestigious School contained 'upwards of forty articles',[9] including designs by Morris, Crane, George Aitchison, Lady Fitzhardinge, Frederic, Lord Leighton, Mrs Stuart Wortley and Mrs Madeline Wyndham. This selection of work, by major designers, artists, an architect and prominent members of the School's Managing Committee, indicated that the Leek Embroidery Society was accepted at the highest level. Additionally, Morris & Co. 'sent a small collection of rare merit' to the exhibition.[10] That alone was a conspicuous endorsement of Leek's status. After all, this was the same town that was still hand-printing a number of Morris's early textile designs.

In this small Staffordshire town was the finest needlework by a group of prominent people who explored and advanced craft skills, established design theories, used global supply chains, worked with local industries and critically challenged aspects of mechanised production. Crucially, they understood how to merge these elements with excellent design to produce goods that provided alternatives to those pouring out from the immense, automated textile industries. Implicit in their attitudes was an engagement with deeper issues related to their understanding of people and the forces that combine to shape societies. Although industrial innovations imposed fierce competition on traditionally structured textile workshops, their owners often found various ways of facing those challenges by meeting the demands of different consumers. In the case of the Wardle family each stage of expansion sprang logically from advances in the dye and print works, which supplied commissioned materials to retailers and other clients as well as completing its own assignments. The materials that were processed and transformed by Thomas Wardle and his craftsmen ensured that a local enterprise swiftly became one of world renown. As a result regional forms of hand production became more firmly integrated into global systems and functioned on similar lines to workshops along the ancient Silk Road. The distinctive handcrafted goods in Leek were always linked to the established international silk industry with its extensive networks of makers, suppliers and traders, whose combined forces produced sumptuous silks. Developments by the Wardle family in Staffordshire helped strengthen this transnational network as they created new markets.

The continuation of specialist crafts, including natural dyeing, thread preparation, handloom weaving and block printing, meant that an interconnected cluster of small and large businesses fed directly into the establishment of the Embroidery Society. Expert authors pointed out how its work was distinct from other work in terms of colouring, design, materials, technique and the combination of these in any one example. These unique features of the embroidery remained constant, which meant that, despite the Society's relatively modest size, it stood out, gaining many prizes and accolades, along with an international reputation.

Webs of Influence

There were, moreover, significant and varied connections between the different exhibitors of 1881, which went as far back as the 1860s. It is possible that the strong show of solidarity with the most prominent designers, architects and organisations, as represented by the exhibition, may have been due to the fact that the exhibitors were all clients of Wardle & Co. Yet to some degree they were all, at the same time, commercial rivals. Morris had his complex hand-block-printed textiles produced in Leek. Lord Leighton chose some of those furnishing fabrics for his spectacular Leighton House interiors. Crane's design, the 'Four Seasons', considered to be a tour de force, was hand-block printed by Thomas Wardle in 1892 for Liberty & Co., and in 1892 Crane became principal of the Nicholson Institute in Leek. Wardle's company supplied yarns and cloth to Watts & Co. between 1878 and at least 1884, and also to the RSAN and Morris & Co. Elizabeth Wardle supplied embroideries to Watts & Co. at least as early as 1878. George Young Wardle provided designs for both Watts & Co. and the Leek Embroidery Society. Meanwhile, Morris produced designs for the RSAN. Elizabeth supplied the same School with embroidery, while yarns dyed in Leek were used in its workshops. Such was their widespread influence and interdependence that the Wardles' metropolitan contacts were happy to display their work in Leek and to have it linked to local art classes. Morris distributed the annual Leek Art School prizes on 12 December 1882, when he also delivered his lecture 'Art: A Serious Thing'.

So why did an exhibition of such magnitude happen in this historic silk town? There were a number of reasons, and all the elements of this significant event are explored in the following chapters. In particular, the links between several prominent architects and the textiles produced by the Wardle family are examined in detail for the first time. These important connections go back to at least 1865 and the parish church of St Edward the Confessor, in Cheddleton, Staffordshire: during the restructuring of the church, which is about 6km (four miles) from Leek, the lives of five dynamic young people intersected – the architect George Gilbert Scott Jnr, Thomas Wardle, Elizabeth Wardle, George Young Wardle and Morris. All were remarkable individuals and critical thinkers engaged with different aspects of design and craft. Each one went on to become a leading figure in their chosen field. They shared a keen interest in history as well as overlapping skills, passions and concerns. This was a formative time for them all and their successful lives continued to connect for decades afterwards. Two of them, Morris and Scott, have many publications devoted to their lives. The remaining three, the Wardles, are less well known and it is the intention of this volume to bring them in from the margins.

Once India's wild silk thread was developed in rich jewel colours as well as a range of delicate shades, a different colour palette was available for embroidery. Wild silk threads, furthermore, had a softer bloom than the high sheen and vivid colours of cultivated silk yarns and this creative potential was exploited by Elizabeth Wardle to great effect. It must have been exciting for her to help develop a greatly extended colour palette for embroidery. Initially she stitched a series of samples that Thomas Wardle took to his public talks promoting India's silks. The first record of this was at the Royal Society of Arts, London, in 1879, where tussar silk cloths embroidered by her were shown to a learned audience.[11] He also used his wife's examples to promote Indian silks elsewhere. We know that he showed two curtains of tussar silk embroidered with a design by Morris and an example of the design 'Ajanta' while delivering a lecture in London in 1891. This was to the Ladies Silk Association, an organisation led by Lady Egerton of Tatton with which Wardle worked closely to help promote English silk production. The striking design 'Ajanta' is illustrated in Colour Plate 1b, and it reveals just how varied is the range of India's historic designs.

The fact that Elizabeth Wardle could demonstrate the yarn's effectiveness using just a few stitches proved to be vital. Here was a crucial benefit, which she must have quickly realised when testing the thread's qualities. Simple stitches, worked in a lightly twisted floss thread, produced the best results. When stitches were packed closely together it was possible to create a variety of rich effects, which was particularly important for elaborate ecclesiastical work. Thereafter, embroidery produced in Leek was generally developed through the use of four ancient stitches: stem stitch, long and short stitch (sometimes known as feather stitch), French knots and buttonhole stitch. Some specialised work involved the use of laid and couched work, also an historic technique.

By restricting the number of stitches, Elizabeth Wardle cleverly optimised the potential skills of a community workforce. Anyone setting up a needlework enterprise as she did would recognise that access to many skilled hands was fundamental. It would have been absolutely necessary for local needlewomen to swiftly master some basic stitching techniques thoroughly before attempting anything more demanding. Of course, the placing of stitches also played an important part in the aesthetics of a piece. The direction of each stitch and the precise position of a small knot contributed greatly to the overall texture, determining how colour was perceived and how light was refracted from the yarn. It was realistic to recognise that a small community could never consistently provide the wider range of skills that more complex techniques required. It made sense, therefore, to limit the number of stitches. Such a pragmatic level of understanding must surely have underpinned the enormous critical and commercial success of a society based in a modestly sized town.

The methods selected by Elizabeth Wardle were not simplistic; they still needed practice and expertise to satisfy a high level of expectation and close scrutiny. But the fact that there was a limited range of techniques to perfect would have made both teaching and learning a simpler, faster system. Accepting this from the start must have made it easier to recruit and teach more women this streamlined version of a historic craft than would otherwise have been the case. It would then have been feasible for another group to be taught relatively quickly, followed by another as demand grew. This would pave the way for a skilled workforce to develop and would account for the high number of experienced needlewomen who were operating in a comparatively small area. Clearly Elizabeth Wardle needed to know that there would be sufficient women available in the region to produce work of a quality that was consistently commercially viable. Her earliest work indicates that there was already a body of skills, a previously untapped reservoir of ability, from which to draw. This preliminary stage was presumably an essential prerequisite for the initiative to emerge, survive and expand to become a celebrated enterprise. And in fact it was the case that the Leek Embroidery Society rose rapidly, flourished and never looked back, as commission after commission came in. This may not have been the case if it had followed a model that offered a more ambitious variety of stitches.

Initially the use of India's tussar silk thread and cloth was unique to the Leek Embroidery Society and was one of its identifying features. The Society had positioned itself well in a crowded marketplace by offering something that no other embroidery workshop produced. That position changed slightly as others realised the silk's qualities. Once Thomas Wardle had successfully dyed and then printed India's wild silks he promoted them widely and in the process gave other embroiderers many new shades and types of yarn with which to work. The transformed thread was demonstrated to be outstanding and was advertised in publications as being effective for the production of opulent effects. Before long Wardle & Co. was supplying a discerning clientele that including Liberty & Co., Morris & Co., Watts & Co. and the RSAN, among others. Undoubtedly this was in part due to the rise in status of fine fabrics as a result of the impact of major art movements and the growth of Art Needlework. The impact on trade with America was also significant. However, it involved more than simply developing a greater range of colours: commercial success globally was also due to the fact that, because of its particular qualities, tussar silk produced shimmering effects. Embroiderers were encouraged to use supple tussar silk cloth supplied in its natural golden state, as well as dyed and often hand-block printed with patterns, as a base for their embroideries. The picture frame in Colour Plate 1a is an example of the effective use of an undyed base cloth, although it is printed with a simple repeat pattern. The hand-block printing side of the family business expanded rapidly, which must have helped recoup the essential investment that allowed hand printing to develop.

Elizabeth Wardle was aware of the RSAN, its structure and why it was instigated. The School was founded in 1872 to revive 'a beautiful and practically lost art', and in the process would offer employment to distressed gentlewomen.[12] It had a rigorous selection process for prospective employees, who paid in advance for their training. They followed an extensive curriculum: as Lynn Hulse notes, 'training consisted of nine five-hour lessons in art needlework'.[13] The School was based in London, as were many of the other leading embroidery workshops. It had a deep pool of talent from which to draw and could offer a greater variety of techniques, which were taught in specialised workrooms by a number of tutors. Each workroom had a mistress with an assistant. There was a large room for preparation, a store room and a showroom with specimens. These were not amenities that a smaller, provincial organisation, based in a family home, could offer. Many kinds of stitch were taught at the RSAN, with lessons for each technique lasting an hour. Private lessons could be arranged in a pupil's home. Ecclesiastical work was not undertaken at first, although that did change, and learning the necessary techniques was more expensive. From 1875 the School was run by a Managing Committee, an Artistic Committee and a Finance Committee, and employed twelve administrative staff. It was clearly very different from the domestic environment that prevailed in Leek.

In response to the great demand for Art Needlework the RSAN produced kits or 'prepared work' from 1874 and published a *Handbook of Embroidery* in

1880. The latter carried up-to-date information on developments in thread production, including lengthy coverage of Thomas Wardle's research into India's wild silks. The author, Miss Letitia Higgin, praised the qualities of tussar yarns, which she was convinced 'would create a revolution in embroidery' and were half the price of cultivated silks from Italy, Japan and China.[14] She explained: 'Within the last year successful experiments have been made in dyeing these Indian silks in England. The exact shades which we admire so much in the old Oriental embroideries have been reproduced, with the additional advantage of being perfectly fast in colour.'[15] The School bought a considerable supply of silk threads from Pearsall & Co., which were dyed by Wardle, who used 'Unfading Eastern Dyes' as a well-known trade mark. Examples can be seen in Colour Plate 1c. The silks, which were both utilised and quickly put on sale by the RSAN, were predicted to be 'an important element in decorative needlework'.[16] In July 1875 Morris was invited to submit designs to the School and helped form a committee of artists. This coincided with his remarkable collaboration with Thomas Wardle in Leek.

Embroidery was the first textile technique attempted by Morris. His wife Jane stated as early as 1855 that he was interested in embroidery 'before he knew me'.[17] He designed and stitched his first embroidery in 1857, just two years after viewing the Bayeux Tapestry in France. Although he designed a great many more he left the stitching of those to others, including his wife and her sister. The formation of Morris, Marshall, Faulkner & Co. in 1861 took the embroideries from the domestic sphere and placed them in a more commercial setting. The company provided embroidery of all kinds and displayed items, including an altar frontal, on its stand at the International Exhibition of 1862. The frontal, featuring a repeated pomegranate motif stitched in silks and gold thread, appliquéd onto crimson velvet, is now in the church of St Martin-on-the-Hill, Scarborough, a building designed by George Frederick Bodley. He was one of the first architects, along with George Gilbert Scott Jnr, to commission Morris's firm to provide interior fittings and stained glass for his buildings. When the firm was re-established as Morris & Co. in 1875 orders for ecclesiastical embroidery were a significant part of its business. Linda Parry states that Morris's designs for embroidery become more refined from the mid-1870s, as silk was increasingly used for both cloth and yarn. This is attributed in part to Morris's strengthening interest in colour, which grew during his collaboration with Thomas Wardle.[18] Morris gained considerable knowledge from his time at Leek, as Wardle provided him with facilities to experiment with dyes using different materials. Morris's study of historic textiles also gave him an increased understanding of stitching techniques. He developed a preferred range of stitches, including stem stitch, satin stitch, long and short stitch, running stitch and darning stitch. As his reputation as an embroidery designer grew,

Morris became a sustained and important influence for the Art Needlework movement. His public stand against mind-numbing canvas work, popular from the 1830s, focused on the widespread revival of traditional skills, which allowed for a greater degree of creative expression.

Morris & Co. received important commissions to create series of large embroidered wall hangings for private houses. Morris and Edward Burne-Jones produced the designs, while Morris took charge of cloth preparation and instructions for the work. Stitching was sometimes done by the female members of the household that gave the commission.[19] As demand for Morris's embroideries grew freelance embroiderers were employed; outworkers were supervised by Bessie Burden, Jane Morris's sister. Other family members were involved as Jane and her daughter May Morris became increasingly engaged with workroom management. Recently published letters reveal that Jane ordered silks directly from Thomas Wardle on several occasions.[20] Letters were written by her on 25 and 28 February 1879, shortly after Morris finished his work at Thomas's dye vats. The first states:

> Dear Mr Wardle I am glad you have written straight to me about the tussah, as I find My husband had forgotten to return the pattern. The only one I like is the one wrapped in blue paper, which is exactly what I wanted. What will the cost be? Thanks for your congratulations on the address, it was plain speaking without doubt, the people liked it though. I am yours truly, Jane Morris.

The second reads: 'The tussah patterns were sent by me to Queen Square for you to be forwarded, but I now learn that as you are coming up to town next week, the goods were not sent on.' It would seem that Jane received printed tussar cloth samples from Leek, probably with a view to purchasing examples and then stitching over the pattern. We do not know which pattern she preferred, but it is highly likely, given the date, that it was Indian in origin. In a letter to Sydney Cockerel dated 10 September 1907 Jane wrote: 'I had a good time in Staffordshire, but unfortunately got a chill soon after I came home which I can't throw off.'[21] A footnote explains that she visited Staffordshire in mid-August, when she stayed with Thomas Wardle. It is not clear whether she stayed at his Leek home or at Swainsley Hall, in the Manifold valley, where he kept his important collection of drawings by Dante Gabriel Rossetti. By then Wardle was Sir Thomas Wardle, having received a knighthood for his extensive research into India's wild silks and dyes.

Embroidery remained central to the success of Morris & Co. long after Morris's death. May Morris became manager of the embroidery department in 1885, when she was twenty-three years old. Apart from her knowledge of embroidery gained in the family home she had taken a rigorous three-year course at the South Kensington School of Design. From 1890 a number of needlewomen recruited from local schools worked under her supervision at her home, 8 Hammersmith Terrace. Her authoritative book *Decorative Needlework* was published in 1893. While outworkers were employed, work was also completed in the rooms above and behind the firm's shop in Oxford Street, London. Small items for domestic use proved to be popular, particularly when sold as kits to be stitched by the purchaser.[22]

The domestic setting and family involvement that produced Morris's early embroideries were presumably not dissimilar to the conditions in place during the early stages of the Leek Embroidery Society, although without the presence of so many lively children. The domestic sphere was certainly no hindrance to Elizabeth Wardle's creativity; indeed, it must have had advantages. There were, however, great differences to the systems in place at the RSAN and in the many convent workshops. In contrast to the spacious, dedicated workrooms run by the RSAN and the relative peace of a convent workroom, the Leek Embroidery Society was organised around the demands of a boisterous and growing family. But Elizabeth must have known in advance exactly what this involved. Her mother had taught in her family home in Leek, so she was aware that women could negotiate the boundaries that often divided domesticity off from a career. She arranged her life to accommodate a large family, a successful vocation and a talent that deserved to be nurtured. In one of his many letters to Thomas Wardle Morris makes a warm-hearted mention of the then nine Wardle children when he suggested delaying his next visit until '"the ruffians" (to whom I offer my congratulations on their youth, their holidays and their capacity for noise)' had returned to school after their Christmas holidays and the house was presumably considerably quieter.[23] Elizabeth gave birth to two more children in that time; Gilbert, the oldest, was then thirteen. It could not have been easy. There were presumably few separate rooms kept specifically for the peaceful practice of embroidery or for administration and the storage of materials. Although this in itself must have limited Elizabeth's activities, there were probably some advantages, as she did develop a successful career that was entirely home-based.

Joined-up Thinking

The Wardles' response to increasing demands for embroidery was a triumph. They discovered a number of opportunities as their output evolved and ultimately they supplied finished work that was for both ecclesiastical and secular use. Surviving pieces demonstrate a fusion of various craft skills and a superior understanding of the nature of materials, design and colouring in domestic and church work. Importantly, the family had control over the whole enterprise, as their companies produced most of the materials needed for embroidery. Although cloth and thread production generally had separate markets, when combined, using Elizabeth's needlework skills, the overall production of both must have expanded substantially as soon as the Leek Embroidery Society was established. The Wardles' son Tom and Elizabeth's brother George Young Wardle, moreover, provided designs. Other companies in Leek supplied additional materials and many local people benefited. The Society strengthened links between technical innovation, commerce and entrepreneurship while sustaining a strong contribution to the growth of Art Needlework.

It must, nevertheless, have taken considerable confidence for Elizabeth Wardle to presume she could take on more commissions by eminent architects, run a business and train other needlewomen. Generally embroidery workshops employed sub-divided processes, particularly where ecclesiastical work was concerned. Some tasks were quite basic, while others were exceptionally demanding. Different needlewomen had different capabilities and some were more proficient than others in various techniques. Small segments of a large composition could be worked as 'slips' by women in their homes. Their finished pieces would then be brought together and assembled on a big frame. In some ways the needlewomen of Leek epitomised the role of modern women in that they were engaged as independent individuals and some were paid for practising a skill that previously was mainly for their own use in the domestic sphere. They were also preserving knowledge while producing beautiful objects for their community and gaining a degree of financial freedom.

As its superintendent, Elizabeth Wardle performed a number of crucial roles for the Leek Embroidery Society. There was considerable scope for her organisational, creative and teaching skills, which she had in abundance. In journal articles she was often admired for complex skills such as 'arranging' work, which included the aesthetics involved with colour and texture in a design. The more intricate aspects of some pieces, such as gold or flesh work, needed specialised technical skills that she had, although not everyone was capable of such dexterity. We do not know where she acquired this expertise. It is likely that it was when she was away at school in Stone, Oulton or Codsall in north Staffordshire, although this cannot be confirmed. Her work for the Society must have been carefully balanced with her many charitable concerns and the considerable demands of a large family. From the earliest known surviving examples of her needlework at Cheddleton to pieces produced in the late 1920s, we can see how the embroidery evolved under her direction and then her daughter's. Other Leek women of equal social status were occasionally involved with specific commissions, presumably according to their particular ability and interest. The Wardle daughters and nieces, and the wives, daughters and sisters of yeoman, accountants, doctors, solicitors, vicars and tradesmen worked alongside others from humbler backgrounds. As most lived in the small town or its vicinity, many of them were connected in some way to one or other of the prominent families.

Patterns of Consumption

One crucial aspect of the Leek Embroidery Society's success stemmed from Thomas Wardle's collaboration with Morris. Wardle started a new venture when, prompted by Morris, he revived the declining craft of hand-block printing. This was entirely dependent on the fine skills of a number of artisan communities who had undertaken long apprenticeships; wood-block carvers served on average seven years before they were fully trained. Despite his inexperience in this field, Wardle soon had teams of capable men covering cloth with patterns at his Hencroft Dye Works. This was by no means a nostalgic regression: although block printing was expensive, it was a flexible technique. A carved wood block in experienced hands could be skilfully manipulated to achieve multiple effects. One block could provide an all-over pattern of motifs, which repeated horizontally, vertically and diagonally. The same block could be used to print a border design, or a solitary motif could be isolated from a pattern and printed in a number of different ways. Block printing was particularly useful for patterning expensive cloth such as silk, especially when only small quantities were required, or where a pile was present, as with velveteen. What began as a localised craft developed for one challenging client swiftly became a speciality of Wardle & Co., and in due course a distinguishing feature of the Leek Embroidery Society.

Many distinctive printed patterns were suitable for stitching over and were regularly used by the Society and by others, who could purchase the printed cloth and stitch the pattern themselves at home at their leisure. Colour Plates 1a, 1b, 2a 2b and 3b are good examples of this. Apart from the outstanding range of complex patterns he produced for Morris, there were three main design traditions that Thomas Wardle selected for block printing that provided a suitably patterned base for embroidery. Notably, he introduced what he described as a 'more decorative phase' for hand-woven wild silks. After many fruitless attempts and considerable investment, as described above, he succeeded in hand-block printing tussar silk cloth with permanent, natural dyes. He considered that designs from the East were naturally the most suitable for cloths of wild silk, and Dr Forbes Watson, of the former India Museum, lent Wardle a series of expertly cut printing blocks from India, which he used to illustrate the potential of the silk. Dr George Birdwood of the India Office especially admired those patterns, as did the director of the South Kensington Museum, Sir Philip Cunliffe-Owen. Several of these had small-scale designs often utilising just one simple, solidly outlined motif in a repeat pattern. Using Indian wood blocks, Wardle created a number of such repeat patterns for Arthur Lasenby Liberty, which were soon in great demand.[24] Allahabad Marigold, used for the picture frame shown in Colour Plate 1a, is one of these designs. Wardle's alliance with Liberty was to prove vital to them both at a critical early phase of their businesses. The prints for Liberty were exhibited by Wardle in Paris in 1878, at the Universal Exhibition, and the display was awarded a gold medal.[25] The printed tussar exhibits were later acquired by the South Kensington Museum, where they formed a permanent display.[26] All of those patterns were used extensively as a base for Leek embroidery by Elizabeth Wardle, which extended their market potential considerably. When needle-women took the dyed and printed cloth and embellished it with tussar threads both materials were transformed. Importantly, the printing technique simulta-neously removed the necessity of laboriously transferring a design from paper to cloth.

Many of the patterns printed onto tussar silk were given names suggestive of India, including 'Allahabad Marigold', 'Bengal', 'Champa Chrysanthemum', 'Indian Ceiling', 'Poonah Thistle' and 'Tanjore Lotus'. The artistic colours that Thomas Wardle printed for Liberty using natural, non-fugitive dyes were described exuberantly in the press thus: 'the faintest amber to the deepest sunset gold, the palest cerulean blue to the darkest sapphire, the daintiest rose blush to the richest maple red' and 'Persian Pink, Venetian Red, Terracotta, Ochre-Yellow, Sapphire and Peacock Blue, Sage, Olive, Willow Green, Soft Brown and Drab'.[27] Articles in leading journals also praised the printed tussar silks. *The Mayfair*, using aesthetic terminology, wrote, 'These soft silks are all "sincere"', while *The Medical Examiner* could imagine nothing more delightful, and even *La Mode Illustrée* recognised competition for France in describing them as 'The best finished silks we have seen'.[28]

The striking 'Ajanta' was a larger-scale, more complex design inspired by cave paintings near Aurangabad, in Maharashtra in western India. These twenty-nine heavily decorated man-made caves, rediscovered by chance in 1819, contain some of the most expressive examples of early Buddhist art, thought to date from the second century BC; indeed, they were considered to be the finest wall paintings from any known ancient civilisation. They were probably the oldest source used by Thomas Wardle, who visited the remote site when touring India in 1886. The beautiful repeat pattern that resulted from his visit was based on a painted ceiling design from one of the caves.[29] Wardle described the pattern of pomegranates, water lilies and elaborate birds as an example of graceful and artistic decorative treatment, which he thought few designs surpassed. Facsimiles of the paintings were made available in the South Kensington Museum soon afterwards. 'Ajanta' was printed as a repeat pattern and a border onto velveteen and silk. When it was used for embroidery Leek needlewomen embellished the cloth with Indian silk yarn and gold thread. The results were outstanding. Colour Plate 1b depicts an embroidered version.

Other bold compositions printed in Leek had their roots in historic European examples such as Sicilian silks. These designs had proved their worth over time as balanced, two-dimensional, sinuous arrangements that lent themselves to the rhythm of stitching. Thomas Wardle also produced an acclaimed series of printed velveteens – substantial designs often based on complex, cut-silk velvets mainly from centres of excellence in Renaissance Italy. They were the pinnacle of the dyers' and block printers' craft and eminently suitable for ecclesiastical purposes. Although velveteen was notoriously difficult to stitch, some designs were selected to become a base for embroidery. 'Indian Poppy', depicted in Colour Plate 3b, was based on an historic French damask.

Subsequently a number of renowned designers who followed an Arts and Crafts ethos had their designs printed in Leek. Leading contemporary designers tended to produce designs that were complex and on a large scale. They required bigger printing blocks, which presented a significant challenge to the carvers and printers. A number of these were transformed by embroiderers. When enriched with lustrous silk thread, with its rich tones and semi-tones of colour and the textures from different stitches, the same basic materials and patterns could be used to create a variety of beautiful items. In Colour Plate 1a Elizabeth Wardle is seen stitching 'Crown Imperial', a design by Lyndsay Butterfield. All these patterns were equally well received and the Leek Embroidery Society became increasingly acknowledged as a source of good design.

As so many of the designs used by the Society were block printed, multiple copies continued to be available as a base for embroidery. Block printing continued for special orders at the Churnet works into the 1960s, which may explain why the cross designed by Shaw was still being used until at least 1927. It was stitched then for a small rural church in Cheshire, where it remains today. Unsurprisingly, however, orders for new ecclesiastical work eventually slowed down, as most churches in the region had been supplied with all the costly embroidered items they would need for some considerable time.

Leek embroiderers clearly understood the natural materials they used. They explored them, changed them and transformed them into marvellous things that were enjoyed on a daily basis. They displayed a great deal of self-expression, in strong contrast to the ever-growing mechanisation of textile production elsewhere. The wide range of designs, their flexibility and the quality of fine stitching observed in surviving domestic pieces reflect a clear opportunity for individual interpretation. Although multiple variants of some printed designs were produced, no single surviving example is the same, as individual stitchers could create a personalised version of any pattern, revealing that, even with a limited repertoire of uncomplicated stitches, a variety of effects was achievable. The clever blending of colours, the imaginative placing of textural effects as a result of an array of techniques and the qualities of the thread itself and the finishing touches of gold thread, spangles, decorative cords, fringing and borders of velvet meant that one simple repeat pattern of just a few motifs offered many possibilities. A design could appear dramatically different when the base fabric was changed, so that, for example, in the case of 'Ajanta', satin was changed to velveteen and cream to crimson. Whether the same pattern was printed as a border or as an all-over pattern expanded the potential yet again. Clients who purchased completed embroideries could choose from various patterns and permutations of patterns, which could be combined in one piece. Most designs were given names and were numbered accordingly so that orders could be customised. Many items for domestic use had a rectangular central field surrounded by a series of narrow borders in the manner of traditional Indian textiles. The piece shown in Colour Plate 2a demonstrates this: narrow block-printed borders frame the lotus motif. Each element relates to the other as well as to the cloth to form a balanced composition. This border treatment was particularly suitable for use in table runners or chair backs.

Imaginative Homework

Different products were ingeniously developed by the Wardles to allow for consumers' varying skills. Embroidery was sold as a completed piece or as a kit that was partly worked, with stitches and colouring shown, so that the purchaser could finish the stitching using the yarns provided. Tussar silk cloth was used extensively as a base and, along with cotton, velveteen and, occasionally, finely woven wool, was supplied block printed in one colour with an outline repeat motif. One range of patterns, labelled as 'Outline Design for Embroidering', was specifically intended to be stitched at home; these consisted of bold motifs block printed in outline in blue or terracotta, usually onto cotton. Thomas Wardle described one such design, 'The Nubian', as an ancient pattern that originated from the Sudan.[30] A select few were printed onto wool challis. Consumers could also, if they wished, acquire any Wardle & Co. cloth by the yard to stitch at home according to their preference. As there are a number of surviving examples we can see just how enterprising the stitchers were.

Fabrics originally produced for furnishings were sold by the yard through Liberty and other prestigious London retailers. Liberty also stocked a variety of patterns designed by leading figures, which Thomas Wardle had been commissioned to print in the early 1880s; they displayed the Liberty stamp block printed on the selvedge. Some of these are known to have been transformed with stitching. They generally had strong curving lines as major elements of the composition, often with continuous trailing vines and tendrils linking pattern motifs together. They provided ideal forms for stitching, as curving shapes lent themselves to the rhythmic use of the needle. Surviving examples demonstrate how an enormous change had evidently taken place, showing how the standard of needlework made in and for the domestic sphere was far removed from the mindless deluge of Berlin wool work. This had dominated domestic production in the first half of the nineteenth century and had drawn outraged condemnation from Morris and others. While hand embroidery was steeped in history and culture, we can see that it was nevertheless always open to adaptation and change.

Leek's domestic pieces were invariably designed to be functional. Produced for sitting rooms, bedrooms, parlours and foyers, they took the form of portières, cushion covers, chair backs, table covers, curtain borders, fans, nightdress cases, picture frames, blotters, letter racks, reticules and fire screens. Colour Plate 3a shows the cover of an ink blotter, with its tussar silk base cloth, silk embroidery and silk velvet border with cord trim, which clearly demonstrate the creative potential of simple useful items for the home. The range of fire screens surviving in Leek homes alone is an interesting example of how creative embroidery was used in a variety of ways throughout the domestic interior (Figure 9). They are mainly in private hands, kept carefully by families whose relatives had often belonged to the Leek Embroidery Society. The rectangular format of panels intended for fire screens gave opportunities for bold design, generally involving a central motif radiating outwards. 'Tree of Life' compositions based on Jacobean crewelwork, which was popular in the seventeenth century, lent themselves to this format. Elaborate floral motifs, with their patterns within patterns, frequently including exotic birds, encouraged rich colour schemes. Invariably the surface of tussar silk was covered with densely packed silk stitching, creating an opulent and strikingly beautiful piece. Colour Plate 2b is typical of such a composition. While the standard of the work is generally excellent, unless we know that it was supervised by Elizabeth Wardle it cannot be described as the work of the Leek Embroidery Society. It may have been completed simply for the pleasure of the embroiderer, to be used in her home.

Further possibilities arose when a pattern was adapted from domestic to ecclesiastical applications. Continual changes were made to the production

Figure 9   Embroidered fire screen, Staffordshire interior. Courtesy of Nigel Brearley

and use as much as to the meanings and values of historic textiles. There are numerous surviving examples of a particular pattern's adaptability, as historic symbols were reinterpreted for ritualistic purposes, the motifs and colouring then assuming associations freighted with Christian symbolism. Embroideries gained a communicative role when they were situated in a wider sociocultural position in a church, signposting the congregation's gaze to the altar through their significant motifs and rich colours. The Wardles were not limited to reproducing traditional Christian designs from the past, although contemporary forms often took their lead from older versions. Block printing was an invaluable asset, as it allowed sections of a pattern to be employed in a variety of ways, as noted above. Elements from the secular design 'Cortessa' were regularly and ingeniously reconfigured to become component parts of a number of superfrontals or pulpit falls. One version of this, printed onto velvet, was utilised for an altar frontal destined for a church in Khartoum. The design, 'Ancient Gothic', originally appeared as an all-over pattern; block printed onto velveteen, it was employed to cover royal palace furniture in Stockholm.[31] Surviving examples demonstrate how one motif has been isolated from that design and applied repeatedly to an ecclesiastical piece produced for the church of St Luke, Leek.

Although a subtle regional character was manifest in Leek embroidery the broad range of products available was probably just as often destined for urban markets as for local consumption. Accordingly, the economic base of the Society changed to nationally and internationally recognised Arts and Crafts-focused production. As this became an increasingly sophisticated, intellectually driven, London-centred movement, it gave added value to Leek needlework. While Leek was central to their life, the Wardle family increasingly operated in wider circles, in London and beyond, and were closely associated with a number of major figures in a variety of sectors. Thomas Wardle, moreover, contributed to prestigious, learned societies at the heart of the art establishment. These contacts were to prove beneficial to Leek in many ways, as a network of metropolitan connections undoubtedly contributed to the transformation of locally significant products into globally sought-after goods.

The skills of Thomas and Elizabeth Wardle were instrumental in the success of a number of other companies. From the mid-nineteenth century London church furnishers such as Watts & Co. and Morris & Co. were in the business of supplying a rapidly increasing demand as the rate of church building escalated. Records show that Elizabeth provided Watts with embroideries at least as early as 1878, while Thomas also had regular business contacts with that company between 1878 and at least 1884. Elizabeth was, in addition, renowned as a teacher who passed on her skills to others. Her picture in Colour Plate 1a – in profile, wearing a costly figured silk dress and intently concentrating on her needlework – suggests a scene of domestic intimacy, but is a posed studio portrait. The image can be dated to at least 1892, as the cloth she holds is printed with the design 'Crown Imperial' by Lindsay P. Butterfield, which was registered in that year, although no stitched version has yet been found. Retailers such as Liberty, thread producers, importers of textiles, raw silks and dyestuffs all played a part in this success. James Pearsall & Co. used the high status of the Leek Embroidery Society for its product placement, noting that it had 'arranged with the Leek Embroidery Society to commence all our Tussah Needlework of this character, and for the future it will bear its name'; five types of embroidery silks were dyed with traditional natural dyestuffs in Leek for Pearsalls and the company's detailed advertising stated that 'tussah silk threads had been used with great success by the Society'. It likened the range of colours to those found 'in ancient oriental, Italian and Spanish needlework, often three or four centuries old', and promoted the special arrangement it had with the Society, 'which allowed them to stock plain and patterned tussah silk cloth, for embroidering upon', declaring that 'the designs are mostly from Indian suggestions and types and are the registered property of the Society'. Despite the detail, the advertisements omitted to say that the silks had been dyed by Wardle & Co. in Leek.

As a response to this advertising and to commercial success, and as producers grew ever-more sophisticated, the choice of thread types for embroidery developed, and colour ranges expanded as new shades were added as a result of a greater understanding of natural dyes. Much of this was down to Thomas Wardle's research into the properties of India's wild silks and indigenous dyestuffs. The diversity of the Wardles' output was astonishing and much of this came together and was reinforced with the launch of the Leek Embroidery Society.

Exhibiting Leek

Once the Society was launched it developed rapidly. Exhibitions were important to its progress. They established selection criteria, suggested hierarchies and standards, allowed comparisons to be made and created much publicity when medals were awarded. When the Society held the first exhibition of its work in 1881, described above, it publicly demonstrated to new audiences just how far and how fast it had risen. The event confirmed that the Wardles understood the national marketplace and, by setting out such a wide range of high-status exhibits in a very assured way, it indicated that a sophisticated creative society clearly had a strong organising capability at its core. Everything that was to earn the Society great acclaim in the years ahead was already in place.

Exhibitions were important to the general public as well, and the exhibition of 1881 had a particularly strong connection with the local community. They could experience the range of colours, see the size of pieces and, importantly, view many items side by side and understand at a glance what they had in common, unmediated by journalists. The public saw the reality of the silks, designs and stitching, and could reach their own judgement about the producers of this magnificent output. It must have been revealing for many local residents to see work done by their fellow citizens exhibited alongside work from some of the greatest names. It must also have been thrilling to see the products of their own skills as dedicated artisans incorporated into the designs by some of the most renowned architects of the day. What was regularly displayed in their local churches was seen alongside and no doubt compared with other fine work away from the chancel for the first and probably the last time.

Thomas Wardle recognised the values of embroidery on a national scale. The reaction the organisers of the exhibition were looking for was undoubtedly complex and went beyond aesthetics. The Leek exhibition provided a platform where the nature of embroidery and its diverse roles were visible to all, allowing a number of themes to develop. While the talents of the embroiderers, dyers and printers were crucial, it was important to demonstrate what the actual materials could do. Some items were intended to perform serious, ritualistic roles, and were juxtaposed with secular items that had a domestic purpose. They were all there in the same venue for viewers to enjoy, and many were designed by the greatest names in the field.

This significant event revealed that the Wardles were able to mobilise a large number of highly regarded designers and producers. They were plainly already well connected to powerful people, including other renowned embroidery producers, and just about every high-profile individual and organisation associated with Art Needlework was included; it is unlikely there has been another occasion like it outside an international exhibition space. Such a public alignment with so many prestigious names at an event in north Staffordshire was a strategic move that showed where the Wardles stood in the national textile hierarchy. The impression was that they were undeniably running a confident, dynamic enterprise.

Thereafter the Wardles made a systematic effort to keep a high profile in national exhibitions, which entailed the production of a series of pieces that would act as beacons for the Leek Embroidery Society. Once needlework from Leek was increasingly displayed more widely it gained in status; shortly after being shown in its home town, Leek embroidery appeared in the Fine Art and Industries Exhibition in Manchester, where the exhibits included Indian tussar silk needlework that the *Manchester Guardian* thought was 'noticeable for much delicate originality of colour and design'.[32] The newspaper highlighted the 'extraordinary progress made in this branch of decorative art in the last few years'.[33] Leek needlework featured in all the prestigious Arts and Crafts Exhibition Society events in London. At The Workmen's Exhibition in July 1893 Leek's facsimile of the Bayeux Tapestry, shown in the Women's Industry section, was singled out for special notice. At the Manchester Arts and Crafts Exhibition, the Colonial and Indian Exhibition, Manchester Royal Jubilee Exhibition and the Grand County Bazaar in Manchester Leek work was repeatedly praised. In addition, Leek embroidery regularly took prizes in the 'Professional category' at the Cheltenham Fine Arts Society. It was shown in Derby, Dundee, north Wales, Matlock Bath, North Yorkshire, Liverpool, Lincolnshire and Birmingham, and, abroad, in Amsterdam, Berlin and Australia. It gained gold medals in Amsterdam in 1883[34] and at the *Women's Exhibition* at Earls Court, London, in 1900. Unfortunately there are no surviving documents that indicate who organised the Leek Embroidery Society's exhibition programme, not to mention the logistics of supplying labelled items for display, the transportation of delicate work or meeting associated costs. The facsimile of the Bayeux Tapestry was, likewise, displayed across the UK and beyond, providing further global exposure for the Society from 1886 onwards. Its reception in America was remarkable and is discussed in detail in Chapter 3.

Marketing Stitch

There was clearly a growing desire for the Wardle family to expand the market for Leek Embroidery Society products while remaining firmly rooted in Leek, where generations of the Wardle family lived and worked. Their skills and enthusiasm were tailor-made to a sustainable marketplace and so eventually outlets for embroidery were established in London and elsewhere. Between 1882 and 1888 the company's customer base widened considerably, with an important development in the form of a showroom at 71 New Bond Street. It must have seemed the perfect, central, prestigious location: on its façade were, and are, peculiarly fitting sculptures depicting Art, Science and Commerce. The shop, then known as Wardle & Co., was advertised as an 'Indian Art Drapers, Embroideries and Decorative Furnishers' (Figure 10). Eight departments stocked different luxurious textiles, wallpapers and ceramics, with one assigned entirely to Leek embroidery.[35] Prospective clients received letters from Thomas Wardle in which he set out the company's aims 'to put before the public the results of a lengthy experience in true and artistic fabrics for dress and household purposes, avoiding all that is bad and spurious in colour form and material.'[36] He went on to state, 'We shall have associated with us the Leek Embroidery Society, which is now so widely known. The embroidery branch, under the superintendence of a lady of experience will, we are sure, be a great convenience to our lady customers.' Advertisements to promote the new store were printed in *The Queen* and other respected journals. Thomas Wardle came to an agreement with Morris & Co. and Liberty, as both clients stocked his goods, not to undersell them in his own shop. At some point there were discussions with the RSAN, which considered taking rooms in the building. Records show that Elizabeth Wardle had formed links with the RSAN prior to this. As early as 1880, at the start of the Leek enterprise, she was contracted to produce needlework in the form of tussar silk samples in various designs and colours for the School under strictly monitored conditions.[37] This was just before the Leek exhibition was staged, so it was an exceptionally busy time for her.

However, after serious organisational difficulties with its manager the London store was forced to close. Thereafter Debenham and Freebody and other London stores took on the sale of Leek embroideries with great success, and the Wardle family remained in command of its own retail outlets as they

Figure 10   Advertisement for the London store, 1884. Courtesy of Bud Abbott

increased in number. They employed different systems to disseminate products and accommodate various needs, ranging from huge pieces for cathedrals to homely tea cosies. All items could, of course, also be purchased in person in Leek or obtained through a mail-order system, which provided samples of stitching, threads and cloth on request. Increasingly, items could also be acquired from agencies in selected stores in major cities in England and Scotland. Large commissioned pieces were usually for church interiors, and were generally designed by leading architects, some of whom would indicate colouring and stitches. These are discussed in depth in Chapter 4.

Cloth and yarn were combined by needlewomen at home who could, by following Elizabeth Wardle's example, bring out the best in the materials. They controlled unruly silk floss thread, taming it so that it lay flat and formed firm outlines; they stitched yarn so that it was of an even height and created dense, shaded patches of colour. Printed patterns were completely transformed when covered with closely packed silk threads. A clever needlewoman could produce the same flower head in a variety of tones and textures using a few simple stitches. Even uncomplicated patterns contained endless permutations, which was something completely understood in India. Different surviving examples of 'Allahabad Marigold', seen in Colour Plate 1a, reveal how, with just a change of a stitch or yarn colour, a great many effects could be achieved. Colours were selected according to an embroiderer's preference, while stitches could be placed to emphasise elements of a pattern differently, giving unique results. Extant versions of 'Tanjore Lotus' are varied in texture and colouring. This design was usually stitched onto an undyed tussar silk ground, although one example has apple-green tussar silk as its base. The centre of the main lotus flower motif, which is different in each case, was occasionally executed in couched gold thread and French knots. A selection of single flower heads was extracted from a number of such patterns to provide a set of embroidered dessert mats trimmed with lace. Endless variations were therefore possible, allowing individual creativity to play an important role in the production of these pieces. Generally, whatever its nature, there is an overall harmony in the colour schemes of surviving pieces, many of which are more than a century old. When over a hundred examples were recently collected together for an exhibition none clashed, as every colour seemed to blend perfectly. The tussar thread reflects light softly and lustrously, undoubtedly as a result of the nature of the natural dyes and the specific qualities of wild silk thread, which seem incapable of creating dissonance.

A great many of the printed textile designs that were registered by Wardle & Co. in the early 1880s expanded the repertoire of the Leek Embroidery Society. They were generally bold, detailed, repeat patterns with recurring motifs. 'Strility', for example, was originally a multicoloured cotton print of Indian derivation, which was printed in Leek in strong shades of blue, green and yellow. Surviving examples reveal that the pattern changed dramatically when it was printed onto undyed tussar silk and stitched as a decorative panel in delicate pinks, blues and gold highlights, every one of the many repeated flower heads being stitched differently. In another version single flower heads were applied to purple velvet and edged with gold for ecclesiastical use. Versions were still being produced in the early twentieth century. Adaptations of 'Indian Poppy', also known as 'Papaver', demonstrate clearly the flexibility of the patterns. The design was transformed over and over again through the use of various ground cloths and colourways. One striking example was block printed in shades of blue onto white velveteen; it was then stitched over in a subtle blue and gold colour scheme and mounted into a Morris & Co. wooden fire screen surround. We do not know who chose to work this example, which has survived in remarkable condition in a private collection. A further version in the collection of Staffordshire Moorlands District Council, seen in Colour Plate 3b, was block printed onto an undyed, naturally golden tussar silk, stitched with shades of yellow and green and framed with green silk plush. Yet others in a private collection and in the Rijksmuseum, Amsterdam, were worked in an alternative colour palette. All vary dramatically in stitch and colouring.

As numerous examples have survived, we are able to see that the embroidery was challenging work that demanded great skill.[38] The often subtle handling of colour and stitch reveals a high level of sophistication; although limited to just a few stitches, the standard of needlework is excellent, while the costly fabrics and yarns still glow with colours extracted from natural dyes and the gold thread still glimmers in the light. Embroiderers in Leek knew just where to place the couched gold thread from Japan[39] – whether to use it with an intentionally light touch for delicate highlights or densely packed for a more dramatic, calculated opulence. The background cloth generally reflected the needlework's different roles. Velveteens, silk damasks, complex brocades and slubbed tussar were the fabrics most often used for ecclesiastical work. They are testament to a number of things – as this history reminds us, there was a serious element to embroidery in terms of its enormous creative potential for women of all social ranks. For many, needlework was not simply a form of gentle therapy or a way of filling time for those whose lives were otherwise confined to the limiting domestic sphere. Far from being passive victims of male authority, women often had the ability to act more independently than has been acknowledged.

Individuals who produced needlework under the aegis of the Leek Embroidery Society were capable of stitching pieces for more than their own amusement. Indeed, a number of prominent designers and architects depended on their needlework skills to complete the focal points of their interior schemes. Demand for embroidery grew as it was recognised as an important expressive technique. Consequently, for those talented women who could produce fine needlework there were increasing opportunities to create pieces for important public spaces that reflected their Christian faith. Although many ecclesiastical embroideries were made in convents, where women were supervised by nuns and employed to stitch items for church use, many were not. For some the time involved in this work was voluntarily given; for others it was paid employment.

Unlike much domestic embroidery of the eighteenth and early nineteenth centuries Leek embroidery was generally made to be sold as useful domestic items or created for a major church project. This provided makers with the opportunity to perfect a craft that allowed for the practise of a refined, challenging skill and it was also a form of income for some that had significant implications for their independence. The important place of embroidery in many outstanding churches frequently involved members of the congregation, who contributed to the considerable cost of lavish work either by donating their skilled time or through the funding of these costly pieces. Makers and benefactors were from the same close community, often worshipping together in the same church where the embroidery was a central feature.

One major advantage of embroidery for many women was the ability to practise a creative activity at home without the need for specialised, expensive equipment. Embroidery could combine with childcare or other family duties; it took up little space and could even be a social activity. Unquestionably, collaborative embroidery projects in Leek created possibilities for a female community to grow. There were advantages in joining other women with similar interests, which were about more than stitching and could include a set of mutual expectations that went beyond public duty. The benefits of working collectively in groups in each other's homes would have been huge, with the transfer of craft skills an important interdependent aspect for some. Any member of a group that was collectively responsible for making fine work presumably gained from a supportive network. Teacher and pupil could both reap the rewards from such interaction in incalculable ways. Women's community activities were no doubt pleasurable as, together, they were producing things of great beauty. Art Needlework gave the more talented few many additional benefits that were not always about earning power. What was once a routine domestic task was elevated into an outlet for artistic expression. Through shared enterprise there was the potential for self-development and social advancement, which may not have been possible for those many women working in nearby silk mills. Embroiderers were able to define their identity and express their creativity with like-minded others. The Leek Embroidery Society presented opportunities, no matter how small, for women to improve their lives while contributing to a distinctive heritage. While women's skills were valuable in their own right to the women concerned, they were also acknowledged in the local and national press as a matter of civic pride and honour.

Staffordshire newspapers regularly reported on embroidery activity and individuals were named for their contributions. Newly finished ecclesiastical pieces were often on public display in the town before they were installed in a church. This suggests that embroidery played a prestigious role in the community and was the subject of regional admiration. A number of Leek women took part in fundraising by selling embroidery at mission bazaars in Leek and Manchester. Art emporia were formed on a cooperative basis, which allowed needlework to be sold at events, raising a small income for the makers, who did not have to pay a commission; many had no other means of selling the work they produced at home. Elizabeth Wardle supported these developments and was willing for her name to be used as a referee should Leek women wish to sell their work in this way.[40]

Reactions

Women wrote about other women's work in the increasing number of journals and manuals devoted to arts and crafts. In one of her many articles on needlework for the *Art Journal* Miss Letitia Higgin declared 'that no art has a nobler history or finer ancestry than decorative needlework. Its beginnings are pre-historic.'[41] She recognised how important it was that the great designers of the day had turned their talents to needlework design, just as they had in the past. In a lengthy article she uses an image of Allahabad Marigold, captioned 'Indian Design for Tussar Embroidery. Mrs Wardle, Leek', to illustrate her points on good design.[42]

Although occasionally some of her facts were wrong, Higgin was an experienced needlewoman with strong links to the RSAN. She knew what she and others wanted and was clearly impressed by the properties of tussar silk and the work of the Leek Society. She made a major feature of this in a subsequent article for the *Art Journal*: 'nor must we forget to mention the wholly distinctive and very beautiful "Leek embroidery" produced by Mrs Wardle's society in Staffordshire'.[43] Higgin was in favour of Thomas Wardle's new products and her well-informed comments typify much of what was written about his research. She states:

> He made an embroidery yarn from the wild silk, which has a character of its own, possessing precisely that appearance of a broken lustre, by which the woven silks of the same class are known. The embroidery of tussar upon tussar is wonderfully effective, partly from the peculiar broken lustre of the materials, and partly from the fact that the yarn made from this wild silk takes colour with great softness. To Mr Wardle also is due the reproduction of the beautiful Eastern dyes, and the rendering of them to a great extent fast.[44]

She acknowledged that, owing to Wardle's efforts,

we are already a very long way from the fatally fugitive and harsh aniline dyes and the old process of topping up the colour, for the work executed with these unreliable dyes was frequently spoiled before it was out of the embroiderer's hands, the colour entirely changed and, the harmony upset.[45]

In the same piece Higgin praised the Leek Embroidery Society further for its honest work. While admiring everything that went on at Leek, Higgin expressed regret that institutions then producing fine needlework were all private ventures for the production of orders and that lessons were given only to amateurs. No school for the training of needlework teachers had by then been introduced as in other countries to ensure that work to a high standard continued. This was a subject alluded to by Cunliffe-Owen, shortly after he opened the Exhibition of Modern Embroidery in Leek in 1881. He indicated that Elizabeth Wardle was ideally placed to train others to run schools of needlework, which were much needed in Britain. As he put it, 'Mrs Wardle's active and organising mind would become a model throughout the country. From Leek would go out teachers for the numerous schools of art needlework and embroidery which would spring up throughout the United Kingdom.'[46]

The Lady also had unstinting praise for Wardle & Co.'s products and the work of the Leek Society, which were acknowledged as increasingly demanded by more aesthetically aware needlewomen and the general public. In a lengthy piece titled 'Art Needlework',[47] the anonymous author devotes the bulk of the article to her discovery of Leek embroidery. In the context of the time the title was not intended to convey that Art Needlework was a form of fine art. It suggested that a degree of skill and aesthetic understanding existed that was in contrast to the stultifying form of cross stitch, also known as Berlin wool work, that for so long had suppressed creativity. The author was delighted with the patterns, the materials, the methods of working and the many options available, stating that 'The designs are traced on a kind of tussore silk, which can be had in several good background colours, and worked with a soft sort of silk on the most exquisite art shades.' The author understood that Leek work was useful for all manner of domestic items, particularly when combined with plush, as well as an adornment for clothing. 'I saw the other day a waistcoat, collar and cuffs of this work which were to give the finishing touches to a very stylish costume; but I think this embroidery more suitable for evening wear, as it lights up so remarkably well.'[48] Messrs Debenham and Freebody of Wigmore Street were recommended as agents, as specimens of Leek work could be seen at their showroom and all the materials, including gold thread, purchased there. Tellingly, she went on to implore readers of the magazine to consider giving needlework orders 'to one of the many poorer ladies who ask so constantly through the medium of these pages for employment'.[49]

A long article in *The Ladies Field* described how a daughter of the Wardles used what must have been a form of pantograph to transfer designs onto cloth in a 'cosy little studio, … overlooking the tennis court at the back of the house' (Figure 6).[50] *The Studio*, a sophisticated journal that reported extensively on the fine and decorative arts, was founded in 1893 by Charles Holme, a great supporter of the Aesthetic Movement. It became a focal point for articles on and by prominent members of the Arts and Crafts and Aesthetic movements. The very first volume carried a lengthy, detailed and well-illustrated article on the Leek Embroidery Society,[51] clearly indicating the Society's wider significance. The article's author, William Kineton Parkes, principal of Leek's College of Art, was yet another creative, charismatic resident of the town. The piece featured images of altar frontals by Gerald Horsley, Norman Shaw and Tom Wardle Jnr, with two litany desk hangings by the younger Wardle. All but the desk hangings have been traced to Leek churches, where they remain.

Numerous other publications confirmed that the Leek Society was a national rather than a local institution. In *The Gentlewoman's Book of Art Needlework* (1892) Ellen Masters singles out Elizabeth and Thomas Wardle for extensive praise regarding their choice of designs 'by artists of high position and well-known excellence'.[52] The term 'artist' is used loosely, as throughout she refers only to designers and architects. She highlights a striking repeat pattern by the architect Sedding, originally produced as printed cretonne by Thomas Wardle for furnishings. Although Sedding designed many ecclesiastical embroideries (see Chapter 4), this was possibly his only design for secular use. It was transformed when printed in outline onto fine green wool challis and retailed as an embroidery kit. Masters considered it suitable for curtains and hangings of medium size as it would 'lend itself admirably to the decoration of a small curtain, such as is often used across an open bookcase or corner cupboard'. It was important that 'the curtain should not be so full as to prevent the beauty of the embroidery from being appreciated in spite of the folds in which it hangs'.[53] A further transformation of Sedding's design took place when the pattern was block printed onto undyed tussar silk. This was finely stitched with silk threads dyed with natural dyes; the principal colours used were dull red, white, a little blue and soft shades of green. This panel was then turned into a lavish table centrepiece with an elaborate border for an exhibition. The border design has now been identified as the same one used for a superfrontal for a Leek altar cloth.

Another favourite highlighted in Master's article was a handsome border 'Indian in character worked on printed silk at the Leek workshop, the silk itself being manufactured by Mr Thomas Wardle of the same town'.[54] The design was the ever-popular 'Tanjore Lotus'. Evidently she knew Leek work well. She asserted that, it is owing entirely to the exertions of Mr and Mrs Wardle that a great deal of beautiful embroidery is executed at the Leek Embroidery School upon printed silks and velveteens. Many of the Leek velveteens are splendid in design and often display flowing scrolls, admirably suited for enrichment with needlework. The silks are generally printed in 'all-over' designs and find few rivals as portières where the portion of the pattern that is the middle field of the curtain is left plain.[55]

Discussing materials, she added:

Leek embroidery silk may be depended on as being pure and therefore likely to wear better than mixed threads, though there is a slight roughness about it to which some workers object. Much of the old embroidery was executed with floss silk, which is nowadays to be had in perfect colouring.

Through articles such as these we have a good idea of how the variety of needlework produced by the Society was widely received. There are, however, still many questions about the nature of the Society itself for which we do not have answers. As so few documents have survived, we do not know even the simplest things, such as precisely what 'The Society' was. We can surmise its role in general terms because of what it achieved and the context within which it operated. But there are no workroom accounts, order books, patterns, lists of purchases or client details to indicate just how the workplace operated or whether the system changed over time. We can only refer to conditions that prevailed elsewhere, which suggest that similar workrooms were run with a supervisor and teams of workers with varying degrees of skill.

There is a famous photograph, taken around 1888, which shows Elizabeth Wardle surrounded by a group of young local needlewomen (Figure 11). Owing to recent research we now know who most of them were and in some cases exactly which items they helped create, particularly some ecclesiastical pieces or parts of the facsimile of the Bayeux Tapestry.[56] But there must have been many others working over the decades who are not yet identified. They could be, for example, the women who finished off the pieces, completing tasks that were less demanding. Many hands were needed to line and back large frontals, and to weight them with cords, fringes, borders and other trimmings to make them ready for use. Even smaller domestic items required a considerable number of finishing-off processes.

While we can read about 'members' of the Leek Embroidery Society, it is not clear exactly what that entailed. If there was an organised, documented membership with specific skill requirements and a set of rules, no evidence is forthcoming. Nor do we know how needlewomen were recruited – whether places were advertised locally or filled through personal contact. Was someone

Figure 11   Elizabeth Wardle and Leek needlewomen.
Staffordshire Libraries and Arts Service

acknowledged as a 'member' if only one item was stitched, or was it a matter of producing work supervised by Elizabeth Wardle and then, later, by her daughters? Legal documents from 1896 and 1897 set out conditions of employment, indicating that some women were hired as employees, with an option of homeworking.[57] This suggests that some work was produced on the Wardles' premises and other work in employees' homes. Although not all needlewomen who worked for the Society worked *exclusively* for the Society, they were not free to work in competition with it. But whether the same conditions were applied to all or just to some, or whether they developed over time, is simply not known. What, then, of others who were not directly employed, but possibly supplied work intermittently for particular projects, such as a large altar frontal? How was their status defined? Did a fluid arrangement allow 'members' to come and go as they pleased? It is possible that some brought needlework skills to the town and others came to the town to learn them. Presumably those involved in whatever capacity needed to reach a high standard of proficiency; we must suppose that there was a system of testing and monitoring quality and that formal meetings were held. We do not know whether anyone was refused the status of membership of the Leek Society, as so much information is lost to us. Nor do we have much information about whether instruction was paid for, although documents do refer to this in a few cases. Some teaching was available but it is not known who taught what to whom or whether 'members' were taught all they needed to know to reach a desired standard. What we do know is that the many surviving pieces clearly illustrate that Leek women were undoubtedly skilful.

From the beginning Elizabeth Wardle was the superintendent of the Society, initially responsible for making technical and aesthetic choices, managing the teams of needlewomen and dealing with clients. But she could not possibly have done all of those things throughout the Society's long existence. Someone else must have taken over from her at some point, but who was it and when? Clearly some pieces were created by particular women in the early years, some of whom may have gone on to produce more work over decades while others may not have done so. As the workforce was probably constantly evolving we do not know whether there was an archetypal Leek needlewoman. If there was such a category, did this change over time? A surviving letter indicates that a Leek needlewoman was turned down by the RSAN. She was known to be somewhat idiosyncratic, so perhaps not typical. Many Leek women were certainly business-minded and numerous small enterprises based on needlework, such as millinery and dressmaking, sprang up in the town. Figure 12, showing a women's trade procession, reveals a great many elegantly dressed women representing a variety

Figure 12   Women's trades procession, Leek, 1907. Courtesy of Neil Collingwood

of trades that they practised in the town in 1907. This was characteristic of activity elsewhere, as trade directories throughout the country show page after page of embroidery workshops, needlework emporia, depots, warehouses and other retail outlets. Most entries were advertising skills in domestic and ecclesiastical work. Needlework warehouses supplied patterns and materials for both. There is another interesting aspect to this, which contributes to a nationwide debate. Can a division really be made here between the amateur and the professional, with all the implications that such a distinction entails? A number of the younger embroiderers attended art classes in Leek, which were conducted under the authority of the Science and Art Department attached to South Kensington Museum. Did this alone make them professionals, or was it the standard of an individual's work that decided this? Or did it depend on whether or not they received payment for work that placed them into one category or another? It is not always easy to know what is meant by these terms as they were used then and subsequently more recently by some historians.

Thomas Wardle maintained that an understanding of colour was the most important aspect of a successful design and that this could and should be taught. We do not know whether Leek embroiderers were taught colour theory or principles regarding the placement of stitches to create textural contrasts, or whether any of this was learnt elsewhere or even intuitive. While an array of simple stitches gave enough variety to produce a wide range of work, sometimes more demanding techniques called for superior skills. Gold work, flesh work, the assembling of frontals and arranging of complex designs, preparatory work and the transfer of designs from paper to cloth required diverse expertise. Certain challenging cloths, such as velvet, needed greater proficiency to work without puckering. Yet it is not clear how these variations were managed. For example, Mrs Clara Bill was the person who assembled all the sections of the Bayeux Tapestry facsimile; presumably she had prior experience to equip her for that crucial task?

By the 1890s the effects of art school and technical education were beginning to have effects. An awareness of aesthetic principles and technical expertise were increasingly considered vital for those entering the textile industries. This more formalised education, which often included craft-based courses, replaced the traditional, more informal system of teaching hand skills. The role of college education as a route into creative employment was a increasingly important factor for inventive needlework in the last decade of the nineteenth century.[58] May Morris was a student at the National Art Training school from 1881, where she studied embroidery.[59] Embroidery became recognised as an expressive craft that allowed for individuality to be explored. The increasing numbers of women who gained access to colleges across the country may have helped to swell the ranks of those engaged in Art Needlework, but it was not a prerequisite. Women still could and did gain experience of fine needlecraft from accomplished local teachers such as Elizabeth Wardle.

Leek was also used to seeing the best examples of art and design. Students in this small town had access to the work of major artists and designers through the series of exhibitions organised by Thomas Wardle. He was acutely aware of the links between industry and museums and the need to study the finest objects in order to produce better goods that would be more internationally competitive. Through his persuasive powers and personal contacts he organised loans of priceless paintings and ancient textiles from South Kensington Museum and elsewhere for those local citizens who could not easily make the journey to London, such as the exhibition of drawings and paintings from Albrecht Dürer to Francesco Bartolozzi in 1878. Textiles displayed included Turkish and Persian carpets, Japanese hangings and antique needlework from Greece, Albania, Rhodes, Crete and Turkey. Exhibitions such as these were doubtless intended to exert a positive influence and counteract what many considered to be the monstrous results of cross stitch.

Oscar Wilde's famous lecture 'The House Beautiful', a version of which he gave in Leek in February 1884, was well reported in the Staffordshire press. Detailed flyers naming the patrons and others were produced to advertise what was a prestigious event. Figure 13 shows the poster advertising this, which includes a long list of local dignitaries who supported this event. One subsequent newspaper article, 'Oscar Wilde at Leek', gives a good indication of the high standard of other events that were arranged for inhabitants of the town. We also know from this that Thomas Wardle provided a lavish stage set in keeping with the theme, which gave Wilde a suitable setting.[60] As the *Leek Post* reported, the textiles used for this were 'the products of the artistic enterprise of Messrs Wardle & Company'. An elaborately draped room was designed for Wilde, with much use of sumptuous, orange-red velvet arranged above an olive-green dado. This was to disguise 'the total abstinence from all loveliness which marks the interior of the Temperance Hall', where the event took place. William De Morgan's ceramics and Persian pots were placed on ledges and a fireplace, which were painted a deep ivory. The floor covering of rich terracotta red formed a good ground for 'the sombre splendour of the Eastern rugs and carpets which were laid about'. There was also a long-case clock, a canopied settle and other pieces of old carved oak furniture donated by local residents. 'A chastened light was diffused through the apartment from one of Morris & Companies hanging lamps of burnished copper and Venetian glass, reinforced by a detachment of vermilion wax candles.' On either side of the platform were stalls covered 'with antique Turkish and Persian rugs, embroidery and other needlework, pottery, jewellery and metalwork lent by people who had visited far off lands'.[61]

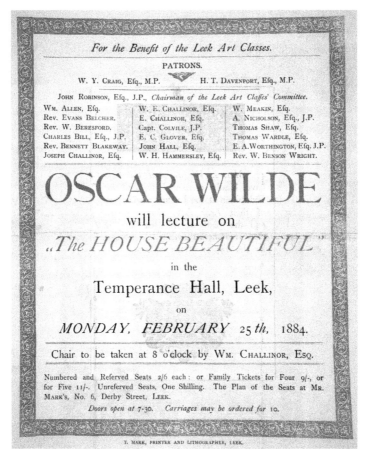

For the Benefit of the Leek Art Classes.

PATRONS.

W. Y. Craig, Esq., M.P.　　H. T. Davenport, Esq., M.P.

John Robinson, Esq., J.P., *Chairman of the Leek Art Classes' Committee.*

Wm. Allen, Esq.	W. E. Challinor, Esq.	W. Meakin, Esq.
Rev. Evans Belcher.	E. Challinor, Esq.	A. Nicholson, Esq., J.P.
Rev. W. Beresford.	Capt. Colvile, J.P.	Thomas Shaw, Esq.
Charles Bill, Esq., J.P.	E. C. Glover, Esq.	Thomas Wardle, Esq.
Rev. Bennett Blakeway.	John Hall, Esq.	E. A. Worthington, Esq. J.P.
Joseph Challinor, Esq.	W. H. Hammersley, Esq.	Rev. W. Benson Wright.

OSCAR WILDE

will lecture on

„The HOUSE BEAUTIFUL"

in the

Temperance Hall, Leek,

on

MONDAY, FEBRUARY 25th, 1884.

Chair to be taken at 8 o'clock by Wm. Challinor, Esq.

Numbered and Reserved Seats 2/6 each: or Family Tickets for Four 9/-, or for Five 11/-. Unreserved Seats, One Shilling. The Plan of the Seats at Mr. Mark's, No. 6, Derby Street, Leek.

Doors open at 7·30.   Carriages may be ordered for 10.

T. Mark, Printer and Lithographer, Leek.

Figure 13　Poster advertising Oscar Wilde's talk 'The House Beautiful'.
Staffordshire Libraries and Arts Service

Leek certainly knew the sort of setting that Wilde's talk commanded as residents were well aware of national developments and preoccupations, the town being concerned with international commerce and the global silk industry. According to the press, Wilde was 'humorous, poetical, critical and satirical',[62] but 'did not aim to direct the audience on particular purchases for their home, or to tie them down to a specific style; his desire was to "develop the spirit of beauty using his engaging wit"'. He spoke for over two hours and the 'large and fashionably dressed audience' were told by him that 'they could have no better guide, than Mr William Morris'. Wilde acknowledged that both Thomas and Elizabeth Wardle had helped raise the standards of good textile design for the home. Referring to the beautiful material behind him, he stated that, thanks to Mr Wardle, England was beginning to see the beauty of Indian dyes when applied to tussar silks, in which their great bloom and beauty were admirably retained; and he (Mr Wilde) figured that when the history of decorative art in Europe came to be written, Leek would occupy a very high position.

He then praised Elizabeth Wardle and the 'Leek School of Embroidery, for the highly artistic work that had been produced by them'.

The aim of the event was to benefit art classes in Leek for workers in the textile industries. The proceeds amounted to £218 7s, a substantial sum. Wilde had given the same talk during his American tour in 1882, in which he discussed how to relate to the aesthete's mantra of 'Art for Art's Sake' in one's daily life. He advised consumers to avoid rudimentary, vulgar mass-produced objects in favour of a more sympathetic, aesthetic approach to all household goods. We do not know whether he dressed outlandishly in Leek, wearing plush knickerbockers, silk stockings and clutching a sunflower, as he was reported to have done in America. His famous wit, however, was in evidence, as journalists reported that the audience was entertained and laughed a great deal. The stage set remained on public view for a few days afterwards, so that others could experience the sensuous Aesthetic interior scheme.

The Aesthetic movement, with its links to the Pre-Raphaelite Brotherhood, helped energise demand for good decorative designs. Aestheticism brought about an increased interest in Japan, sumptuous interiors generally and elaborately decorated clothing throughout the 1870s and 1880s. As the market for embroidered objects grew massively, designs with a distinctive Japanese influence by Lewis Foreman Day were printed in Leek for Liberty. One small cherry blossom pattern became a ground for Leek embroidery; an example can be found in an ecclesiastical piece stitched for Chester cathedral. Other examples were produced as domestic items. Retailers in Europe and America were, moreover, clamouring for embroidered pieces for domestic interiors and costume accessories. The growth of publications devoted to the subject was extraordinary. Magazines engaged in debates promoting 'rational' dress, with its less structured form of women's clothing. The softer silhouette lent itself to velvets and softly draping, richly coloured silks, all of which brought British art and design international acclaim. There were clear links to the Arts and Crafts movement; fashionable Arts and Crafts interiors often featured the same fabrics and decorative details as those described as Aesthetic.

The majority of women who participated in the first Arts and Crafts Society Exhibition (1888) were embroiderers. Thereafter, however, there was a dramatic increase in the number of women designers exhibiting their work in a variety of media. Embroidery subsequently became one of a wide range of techniques that women practised. It also became increasingly common for them to design their own pieces and to stitch designs produced by other women.[63]

The Wardle family legacy was maintained after Elizabeth Wardle's death in 1902 by her daughter Lydia, and major works continued to be produced. Lydia, a talented needlewoman, followed the ethos of the Leek Embroidery Society, while three of her brothers managed the various dye and print works after their father's death in 1909. A number of prestigious embroidery commissions were supervised by Lydia, including the stitching of a superb festal frontal and chancel carpet designed by Gerald Horsley. They were created by the Society for his All Saints church, which was built in Hanley, Staffordshire, between 1910 and 1913. These, along with a Passiontide frontal designed by Horsley and which is still in that church, demonstrate that exceptional standards were continued in collaboration with Horsley up to the start of the First World War. Members of the congregation still talk of how the frontals were carried bodily from Leek on a train then brought on foot through the streets of Hanley to the church.[64]

The creation of an important church congress banner was entrusted to the Leek Embroidery Society in September 1911. The complex design was for a large work over 2m (seven feet) in height. It was prepared under the supervision of Lydia Wardle, Mrs C. Bill and Miss Redfern, long-term members of the Society. The processional banner was described in the local press as the most important piece of work yet undertaken by the Society and it was stated that it 'will undoubtedly add to the reputation Lady Wardle's institution has secured'. It was produced for the church of St Peter ad Vincula, in Stoke-on-Trent, where it is permanently on display today. Lydia Wardle completed the faces for the large figures in this dramatic pictorial piece, which is an outstanding indication of her skills. The central oval composition consists of a prison scene: two dominant forms with swirling drapery are set into a detailed architectural framework. They are surrounded by local coats of arms and various regional symbols, including a tiny figure of a potter at his wheel. He is placed just above a shield containing a minute motif of the Portland Vase, which had been reproduced by Josiah Wedgwood, who is buried in the churchyard. There is a long quotation stitched in couched gold thread on red velvet; the stitching is very fine throughout, evidence that the Society was still capable of producing exceptional work. The designer is unknown. Meanwhile, in conjunction with all of these major developments Elizabeth Wardle embarked on a distinctly different project in 1885 – a copy of the famous Bayeux Tapestry, the production of which is examined for the first time in Chapter 3.

Chapter 3

STITCHING NARRATIVE: LEEK'S FACSIMILE OF THE BAYEUX TAPESTRY

… it has been thought that it would be a matter of some interest for the reader to learn the conditions under which this piece of embroidery has been commenced and completed.

Elizabeth Wardle, 1886[1]

Creating a facsimile of the Bayeux Tapestry was a bold endeavour on the part of Elizabeth Wardle. Although there are no documents that tell us why she took on this monumental task, she did leave clues as to her intention. It was a project that on the surface appeared to be very different to those usually undertaken by the Leek Embroidery Society, as discussed in Chapters 2 and 4. It is only when we consider several different factors, however, that we can appreciate that the task was not too far removed from what she was already doing. Contextual evidence presented here for the first time helps us understand the relevance of the facsimile to other demanding projects that she completed during her life.

By the time that she had tied herself publicly to such a famous work Elizabeth Wardle was an established embroiderer who had completed a number of high-profile commissions, and was widely acknowledged as a significant woman across a range of artistic movements. The facsimile was certainly much more than a vanity project or a publicity stunt, as the huge costs, the massive investment in time for many people and the immense organisation involved suggest a more serious intent.

The Bayeux Tapestry, now exhibited in a purpose-built display in Normandy,

France, is a work of embroidery that illustrates the significant events that took place between 1064 and 1066. Through the use of stitched images it depicts the events of 29 September 1066 when William, duke of Normandy, landed in England and won the Battle of Hastings. Still considered to be one of the most famous dates in British history, 1066 was the year that William the Conqueror, at the height of his power, brought England under his control. After he had seized the English throne he started to restructure the country, forming a French-speaking court to rule over the Anglo-Saxon population. This reshaped the political map of England. Under his rule England became firmly Norman, with consequent seismic changes. 'The Norman Yoke', as this became known, was something that concerned William Morris and a great many others. The Bayeux Tapestry is one of the main sources of information for these most significant events, the narrative power of which has riveted observers for centuries.

The Tapestry has stimulated countless publications and discussions attempting to unpick its ambiguities, indicating the compelling nature of the original Tapestry and of its facsimile – that made in Leek. Despite all the print and debate devoted to the original, no one really knows who designed it or where it was stitched. Interpretational inconsistencies and contradictions remain unopposed and questions unanswered, and so the Tapestry continues to challenge and tantalise in equal measure more than 950 years later. While acknowledging that there are speculations over its origins, academics currently agree on one aspect: that although it was probably designed by a Norman artist it was stitched by English embroiderers. Certain historical facts and features suggest potential locations: Winchester, for example, had an important embroidery workshop at that time and Canterbury was then a centre of needlework excellence. There are other possibilities.

The material nature of the work is more readily comprehensible. Although known conventionally as a tapestry, the original is an immense length of embroidered linen. Eight sections of linen, one of the few English-made cloths then available, were stitched together to form a base 70m (227 feet) long and 50cm (twenty inches) wide. It was almost certainly longer at first, as parts of the historic chronicle are absent. The scenes were stitched with wool, a readily accessible staple English yarn, dyed in eight colours.[2] Over centuries the Tapestry was subjected to different environments, uses and treatment in northern France. There is evidence that it was documented in 1476, and in 1842 it was repaired and displayed at eye-level, behind glass, in a purpose-built gallery in Bayeux, Normandy.

Regardless of its enigmatic background, the many scenes throughout the length of the work still delight viewers. Even though today it may seem principally a decorative work on an impressive scale the scenes were designed to describe events of enormous importance to English people at the time of its creation, thought to be the 1070s. Using a horizontal format, the embroidery narrates the story of the invasion of England by the French and the subsequent dramatic battle. It is astonishingly ambitious, featuring over 600 people and almost as many horses, birds and other creatures in a series of action-packed sections. In addition, there are thirty-seven ships, thirty-three buildings, many trees and plants and fifty-seven Latin inscriptions. Playing along the narrow upper and lower borders are fantastical images and motifs, including scenes of everyday life.

Despite its fame, we do not, as mentioned, have the most basic facts about the people who planned the composition or drew out the animated scenes along the length of cloth. Unquestionably the designer, or designers, understood how narrative worked in a two-dimensional format and developed various strategies to structure and develop the story so that it captures different aspects of war. Viewers of the Tapestry needed to travel its full length from left to right in order to follow the individuals in the drama through various stages of their epic journey. As the colour plates reveal, every section was composed by someone who was skilled in depicting both action and closely observed detail. They organised dynamic crowd scenes and carefully considered the aesthetic integrity of each section, some of which portray numerous animated figures within carefully balanced groups. A number of scenes have an embedded subtext.

The historic account begins with events in 1064, leading up to the death of Edward the Confessor and the Norman Conquest of England in 1066. The opening scene is one of the few comparatively static compositions, which acts as a form of introduction to the three main characters: it shows King Edward the Confessor seated, along with Prince Harold and William, duke of Normandy. A Latin inscription tells us briefly what the scene represents. The sections are organised to illustrate the exploits of William the Conqueror and his opponent Harold, another pretender to the throne of England. They depict journeys and a battle, and all are vividly and realistically expressed with recognisable details. This is despite the fact that there is no perspective, no distinct vertical borders to contain each portion of the story and little use of three-dimensional forms. This was something that John Ruskin understood, as he considered it as 'one of those bold pieces of picture history' that was, 'in our pride of perspective', something that we would not attempt.[3] As David Hockney explains, medieval artists often used isometric perspective, which means that 'lines don't meet at a vanishing point; everything remains parallel'.[4] This was not because they did not know how to get it right; it was an approach that Hockney considers to be more realistic. 'Because we have two eyes, which are constantly moving, perspectives are constantly shifting.'[5] If vanishing points were used in the Bayeux Tapestry they would interrupt the linear flow of left to right action, which is a strong feature throughout the design. It is this that gives the viewer the sense that they are moving through time and space just as the figures in the scenes do.

The sense of progress across a scene, as characters frequently move location, and the clever use of space and proportion, reveal that skilled hands and eyes were involved. Sections merge into one another as figures in the drama travel through the landscape and through time along a horizontal plane, crossing from one side of a linen panel to the other and on to the next panel in the sequence, keeping the momentum flowing. Each scene is carefully considered in its own right and all explore the theme of people at war. They are generally bursting with energy – a riotous mix of humans and animals shown constantly on the move and eager for violent conflict. Colour Plate 4b shows a section from the facsimile in which a group of horsemen are setting off to battle. Although not realistically coloured, the mounts are distinctive and well-drawn, with a sense of pent-up energy as they are reined in by their riders. The signature below is that of Ellinor Wardle, who stitched that section. The designers' skill produced an extraordinary balance of pronounced simplicity and extreme subtlety. Similarly, illuminated manuscripts from the time of the original Tapestry were works of great sophistication, which indicate that tools such as compasses and rulers were available to apply the geometrical principles that help to balance a composition. It is feasible that such tools were used to maintain the equilibrium of such an extensive stitched account.

Alongside the action-packed scenes there is occasionally an isolated individual or two, set apart from the crowds. They are usually employed in some task and, even in outline, reveal distinctive aspects of human nature through gestures, facial expressions and clothing. Small details in the scene shown in Colour Plate 4a provide a good example: soldiers, who are carrying hounds, have removed their stockings to avoid soaking them as they wade through the sea to board their ship. This is just one of many examples drawn by an acute observer of everyday life. The signature below this scene is that of Phoebe Wardle, Thomas Wardle's sister, who was an experienced embroiderer.

Someone also took into account how each individual form would be stitched and how that contributed to the overall, lengthy configuration. Several figures, for example, appear to be smiling, so that at times events seem almost carnivalesque rather than martial in nature. The Anglo-Saxons can be recognised by their shoulder-length hair and moustaches, although they have no beards, while the Normans' hair is cut high at the back. Clothing, too, is used to emphasise an individual's origins. It would seem that the use of colour was meticulously planned throughout, often acting as a harmonising medium as well as an aesthetically pleasing element. Despite the limited colour palette there were many choices to be made regarding the juxtaposition of each tint. Bold colours and strong shapes complement each other beautifully and work together as well-planned devices. They are systematically combined and repeated to distinguish forms that otherwise would be very alike in size and shape. Colour is cleverly used to differentiate figures and objects in groups while at the same time uniting them. Colour Plate 4c, for example, shows a group of soldiers stitched by Anne Clowes. Although the visible clothing is all quite similar each item is part of a finely controlled arrangement employing the constant balancing of a limited number of colours – green, blue, yellow and red – to gain the greatest effect. A green tunic is worn with yellow shoes, red hose, red cap and red belt. The red tunic-wearer also has red shoes, but is given yellow hose and a yellow belt. Each part of the outfit has stitched outlines in contrasting colours. This distinguishing device continues throughout the composition, suggesting that it was not an arbitrary choice. On the contrary, it demonstrates a clear understanding of how colour contrasts and harmony work and how a sense of variety can be achieved with a restricted palette. The depiction of clothing is seemingly part of a carefully conceived scheme perhaps developed to identify specific figures, which helps the viewer navigate their way through a complex story. The colouring of the horses also seems to have a broader purpose: while the many mounts of the Normans – noted archers and horsemen – are accurately drawn and clearly recognisable, they are not always naturally coloured, as already noted. Despite what at first glance can seem to be a naïve and random use of colour in Colour Plate 4b, a second look reveals it to be more than that. Variations including blue bodies, red legs and yellow hooves make each animal more noticeable as an individual. Without this lively use of colour the composition would have been just a dull, if realistic, blur of natural shades of brown and grey.

Kay Staniland notes how dense areas of stitching 'give solid form to the main elements of the narrative – the men, their horses, weapons and ships – so that they stand out boldly from the linen ground'. This 'indicates a high level of competence and interpretive skill'.[6] Ships are vibrantly coloured with patterns on hulls and sails; in addition, they are depicted elegantly, as shown in Colour Plates 4d and 4e. The designer was clearly knowledgeable about shipbuilding and had the ability to capture vital features in the few lines allowed for embroidery stitches. They were also clearly aware of the power inherent in a curving line and how that can be enhanced with colour. Boats at sea are shown with gracefully arched sails puffed out with wind. The shape of the sail is repeated in the oval shapes of shields held by soldiers on board; it is repeated again in the prow of the boat, which in turn is echoed in the curl of a wave. This strong rhythmic treatment is emphasised by the use of colour, which is handled with sophistication. Each boat's sail is differently coloured and patterned. Although stripes on hulls are common, they vary in width, which adds an element of liveliness. In one scene containing eighteen boats only two of the hulls have identical configurations of stripe, width and colour. We do not know if this painstaking attention to detail represents reality, but it certainly provides an apparently deliberate playfulness. As the same sensibility is applied to animals it creates a distinctive type of graphic wit throughout. This suggests that it was the designer who thought carefully about the flowing lines, although it may have been the embroiderer who decided on the colour scheme, which contributes so much to each scene. Whoever was responsible understood the potential of the wool yarn dyed with natural dyes then available, and cleverly exploited it. It is probably the case, however, that it does not fully capture the pugilistic reality of the Norman fleet heading rapidly to England's undefended coast. The Norman ships numbered over a thousand and they carried over 1,400 soldiers and a great many horses.

Once the Normans landed the two great armies confronted each other. The detailed scenes of the resulting battle are astonishing. The frantic gestures of wounded soldiers in violent combat, with tangled groups of frenzied horses falling during the conflict, are graphic and animated. Curiously, trees are not portrayed realistically but are stylised throughout, often providing a boundary to a scene. The narrow borders that run the length of the composition along the top and bottom edges lend a different rhythm and scale. They illustrate fables and mythical, hybrid beasts, together with scenes of agricultural labour. Depictions of farmers sowing seed and hunters killing birds with slings give some insight into rural life and serve to add comment on the main sections. Because some of the original images were sexually explicit it is thought unlikely that the Tapestry was ever intended to hang in a church. Although the intended destination is not known, Staniland argues convincingly that it was probably envisaged as a hanging for a large hall or chamber.[7]

Even though the Tapestry constitutes a determined effort to describe the cruel reality of battle this does not, of course, constitute anything like evidence. The visual simplicity with which ancient complexities are represented can be read in many different ways. The scenes are very suggestive, however, and demonstrate the power of images, even 1,000-year-old images, in a narrative form. Undoubtedly this would have been something Elizabeth Wardle understood.

As well as giving a graphic history lesson, the stitching reveals what medieval designers and embroiderers were capable of in their workshops. The direction of stitches, individual threads and the texture of both the original and facsimile are all still clearly visible, as are the colours for the most part, despite some inevitable fading.[8] Although nothing that could tell us anything about the makers has survived we can surmise that there were a number of them and that they could have been men, women or both. The stitches emphasise the form drawn beneath, suggesting a symbiotic relationship between the designer and embroiderer. Occasionally facial features and hands are given heavy, dark outlines; generally, facial features were stitched in outline only, leaving the naturally coloured linen ground cloth to provide skin tones. For the most part, only two relatively straightforward stitches, commonly used in the Middle Ages, were deployed in the original to produce these colourful, dramatic scenes. Laid and couched work filled the main sections, while stem stitch created distinct outlines. As Staniland explains, stem stitch 'predominated as an outline stitch … [and] was one of the most important stitches used on the Bayeux Tapestry'.[9] Split and chain stitches occasionally created outlines of sections. Together this small group of stitches was capable of constructing a rich medley of textures, materials and all manner of creatures and things: garments, armour, plants, animals, weaponry, royal regalia, boats, buildings, furniture and leather, along with the Latin inscriptions. It is not surprising that this absorbing work ultimately became one of the most famous embroideries in the world.

The Facsimile of the Bayeux Tapestry

It is easy to appreciate why a work such as the Bayeux Tapestry would have had a powerful impact on anyone interested in stitch, history, narrative and bold public projects. A number of copies of the original embroidery have been made in different media. The earliest full reproduction recorded was in the form of engravings by Bernard Monfoucault, executed between 1729 and 1730. In 1816, the 750th anniversary of the Battle of Hastings, Charles Stothard was commissioned by the Society of Antiquaries, London, to produce a series of drawings of the Tapestry, which were then engraved by James Basire. Stothard, the historical draughtsman for the Society of Antiquaries, returned to France on several occasions with the engravings, which were hand coloured to match the original. They were smaller than the Tapestry, each measuring approximately 35 × 76cm (13¾ × 30 inches), and although they captured a great deal they were not a suitable medium for the recording of the texture of needlework. Wax impressions of sections of the surface were subsequently taken by Stothard, who painted the plaster casts (13.5 × 11cm, 5⅜ × 4⅜ inches) to replicate the colours of the original stitching. Impressions reproduced texture and technique, as they were taken directly from the surface of the threads and ground cloth. Although taking a cast was a controversial act it is an interesting indicator that the stitching was considered important.[10] Between Monfoucault's engravings, Stothard's engravings and Joseph Cundall's photographs several changes in some details took place, although the overall composition remained constant in all reproductions.

Stothard's hand-coloured engravings were published in *Vetusta Monumenta* between 1821 and 1823. It was 'the first time that a complete colour reproduction of the tapestry had been made available to the public'.[11] They were completed after the Tapestry was damaged during the French Revolution, but prior to repairs undertaken in the nineteenth century. They are, therefore, an interesting record of a particular stage in its long life. Stothard used fragments of original threads to recreate 'sections of missing embroidery and reveals [*sic*] scenes lost through damage'.[12] A further set of engravings produced by the Society of Antiquaries between 1819 and 1822 did reproduce the 'fine detail of the individual stitches'.[13] Measuring approximately 53 × 72cm (20¾ x 28⅜ inches), they were the source for subsequent copies.

Cundall considered the original to be a work of national importance. He photographed the tapestry in 1873 using the autotype (Woodburytype) process, preparing 180 glass plates, each 50.8 × 38.1cm (20 × 15 inches), by this method. The resulting photographic prints were the size of the original and hand coloured to match the tints of the Tapestry as perceived at that time. It is still possible to observe skilled repairs and individual stitches on the prints, although some sections are clearer than others. Unquestionably the original dyes had by then faded to a certain degree over the centuries, as they continued to do subsequently. The artist Walter Wilson was engaged to hand colour the prints when they were reproduced on paper. The whole exercise was carried out for the Department of Science and Art, and photographic prints were issued through the Arundel Society, the government publishing house. The Lords of the Committee of Council on Education approved the scheme, acknowledging the educational aspect of the project.

It may have been at the hand-colouring stage that some images were censored, as the blatant nakedness visible in the original was removed. Hand-coloured photographs, now in the archives of the V&A Museum, London, reveal that images of genitalia had been scraped off the photographic paper on roll numbers 6 and 12. As the photographs were to be made available to the public it is possible that the images were amended because they may have been seen by children. This act of modesty was a source of disquiet and amusement for a number of commentators over time. It has been said that the needlewomen of Leek were responsible for this, when in fact they were faithfully following the photographic version they had borrowed. The naked figures, both male and female, acted as a subtext to the main drama unfolding in the central battle scenes, and appear to be a comment on the spoils of war.

An agreed number of copies of the photographic portfolio version were then purchased by the Arundel Society, with plain images available at £50 and hand-coloured versions at £75.[14] Both types were produced for the South Kensington Museum: one took the form of twenty-five separate rolls of prints, while the other was backed with linen to form a continuous strip of images.

The latter could be hung in a similar manner to the original Tapestry and went on public display at the opening of the International Exhibition of 1873 in London. Thomas Wardle exhibited at that major event, which attracted a huge number of visitors, and it is highly likely that he saw the images then. The photographs were displayed for some time at the Museum on a drum-like, rolling mechanism until this was broken, never to be repaired.

We know Thomas and Elizabeth Wardle viewed the images at South Kensington Museum and were also inspired to visit Bayeux to see the original for themselves. In France the Wardles were following in the footprints of many eminent people, some of whom recorded their reactions. Thomas Carlyle, Charles Dickens and Alfred, Lord Tennyson made the journey. Ruskin visited with his new wife Effie in 1848.[15] He later compared the Tapestry to a mosaic in St Mark's cathedral in his influential *The Stones of Venice* (1851–3), and referred to it in other publications. Ruskin discusses the ornamental value of waves, among other things, in Chapter XX, 'The Material of Ornament', as for some cultures and eras they were a sacred symbol. Open water has been given different conventionalised or naturalistic treatments over time, often through the use of simple, undulating lines representing currents and rippling surfaces. He notes that the Bayeux Tapestry has identical wave patterns to those depicted on many significant monuments, including the Ducal Palace in Venice.[16] Colour Plates 4a and 4e both depict wave patterns, as do many other scenes in the storyline. In the same chapter Ruskin discusses 'Quadrupeds and Men', stating that 'the horse has received an elevation into the primal rank of subjects owing to its association with men'. He felt they were the noblest subjects of ornament next to the human form,[17] and concentrates on the treatment of the subject: how to express the subject and how to arrange it according to its purpose, whether that be with reference to sight or to the mind: to reality or imagination.

William Morris and Edward Burne-Jones, with their friend William Fulford, viewed the Tapestry in 1855 when they made a tour of the cathedrals of northern France. Morris, who had a portfolio of Stothard's engravings in his library, wrote to his mother saying that the Tapestry was 'very quaint and rude & very interesting'.[18] Fiona MacCarthy interprets 'rude' as meaning 'unstudied', rather than vulgar.[19] Morris was interested in the political aspects of the Battle of Hastings and the perceived impact of the 'Norman Yoke', the contentious view that the battle instigated years of oppression of the Anglo-Saxons by the Norman ruling class.

While versions on paper effectively told the story of the battle they did not capture the full richness of the original stitching, which adds a great deal to the scenes throughout. Although Cundall's photography was excellent the smooth surface of the paper visually flattened out the contours of the stitched surface. Perhaps Elizabeth Wardle felt the lack of impact and definition that came from the contrast of the raised textures with the smooth linen ground, the ripples of colour that stitches give and the carefully placed defining outlines. The Leek facsimile was the first of the replicas to include these elements.

We know that at some point Elizabeth Wardle decided to make a duplicate so that England would have its own copy. Although there has been much speculation regarding the origin of the facsimile, there is little in the way of documentary evidence to answer the obvious question: why did she do this? Although she wrote a preface to a printed guide to the facsimile it does not reveal what motivated her to take on this epic challenge.[20] By 1881, however, Thomas Wardle was well connected with the South Kensington Museum and over decades had many dealings with its director Sir Philip Cunliffe-Owen, who became a friend. Wardle borrowed a number of items from the Museum for different projects and lent Leek textiles in return, including a number of embroideries by Elizabeth Wardle. So there was a precedent in place, and she clearly states in her preface to the *Guide to the Bayeux Tapestry* that in the spring of 1885 'Fac-simile [*sic*] water-colour drawings of the original tapestry were kindly lent by the authorities of the South Kensington Museum' for her use. They could well have been the original set of photographs, referred to as drawings, or another set of prints made especially for her from the full-size negatives. The V&A still has two of the original versions with their hand-coloured photographs. It is immediately obvious that sections vary in terms of the density of colour, which may have changed over time. The watercolour paints are evenly applied, with scarcely a brush-mark visible. The effect is that of a glaze, although some outlines are not as subtle and appear to be done in heavy black ink. The clarity of the images is excellent, as it is possible to see repaired sections and individual stitches. The overall impression is that the draftsman had a wonderful sense of balance.

Although borrowing the full-scale 'drawings' did not seem to present the Wardles with any difficulty, transporting them to Leek and finding a suitable place to store the many long rolls of photographs must have a been a logistical headache. That said, their business required the constant movement of bulky textile goods and raw materials across the country as a matter of course, so presumably they would have been familiar with the necessary organisation involved. Evidently the challenges were thought to be worthwhile.

It is likely that Elizabeth Wardle had several reasons for wanting to produce a copy. She may have been inspired by the fact it was a significant political history in pictorial form, created very shortly after the event and seemingly done with a passion. It was probably the fullest and most important pictorial document of a turning point in English medieval life. Although made more than 800 years before, the images were still gripping and provided a vivid account of a pivotal battle. It was certainly the largest and one of the most famous stitched objects from Norman times. A lot of what we think we know about that era comes from the Tapestry, as it was also a source of cultural history, giving insights into the way ordinary people were represented in the eleventh century. It was, furthermore, executed in stitch, a technique over which Elizabeth had great command.

It must surely have been the case that from the start she carefully considered what was going to happen to the facsimile on its completion. Owing to its great length she must have taken into account where it was going to be displayed and stored. The Wardle home could not take it and there was then no suitable venue in Leek for it to hang permanently. It is likely, then, that touring the facsimile must have been factored in from the beginning. There were precedents for such a project in north Staffordshire: Josiah Wedgwood's recreation of the ancient Portland Vase, a superb example of Roman cameo glass, was made in Etruria, Staffordshire, after which it went on tour. This may have provided Elizabeth Wardle with a model for the important multi-venue aspect of the project. And at least one venue, Derby, displayed a Portland Vase replica owned by a member of the Wardle family alongside the facsimile of the Tapestry.

Elizabeth Wardle was certainly a woman who took on challenges. Viewing the original Tapestry may have stirred some deep impulse in her to complete an ambitious project for the public sphere, or perhaps she simply thought that it was something she was capable of doing. It was a high-profile venture that, if done well, would bring great acclaim to her, her husband and the family businesses. By the time she embarked on this project in the spring of 1885 she had already experienced a number of important personal triumphs and had a wealth of experience that gave her the skills that such an undertaking demanded. With more than twenty years' experience of working with major architects and designers to complete prestigious commissions for large altar frontals, she had already received a great deal of public praise. Many ecclesiastical pieces produced by the Leek Embroidery Society under Elizabeth Wardle's direction had elements that were comparable to different aspects of the Tapestry. Throughout previous projects she had proved that she was good at managing people and meeting deadlines. This combination of skills must have generated the necessary confidence to convince her that she could meet the challenge.

At that time Thomas Wardle could not have been busier. He was involved with the organisation of two major international exhibitions for 1886 and 1887, which entailed his first trip to India at the end of 1885.[21] Although the cutting of the Suez Canal had shortened the voyage from Europe to India to about three weeks, he was away from home for over two months. He was also conducting an intensive research project into Indian dyestuffs and wild silks while still running a busy company. He still had a major input, however, into the facsimile project, a fact that has generally been ignored, even though it was a joint venture – something that Elizabeth was keen to acknowledge in the final panel of the work. By then Thomas was recognised as the leading dyer and printer of his day, with an unsurpassed mastery of natural dyeing. His extensive knowledge was crucial for the correct preparation of eight dye vats to transform wool yarn with colours equal to those in the Tapestry as it was then. In all dye houses matching colours from one batch of yarn with another was a perpetual problem. Blacks and blues were difficult to get right at any time. Indigo was notoriously temperamental and the same dye recipe could result in variations due to changing temperature, the state of the vat water or human error. Thomas Wardle's reputation as a master dyer was therefore critical to the success of the Leek facsimile. Accurate estimates for the production of each of the eight colours would have been necessary to avoid expensive wastage. Once the correct dye recipes were obtained and the wool yarn coloured satisfactorily the amount of thread needed for each panel would have been matched shade by shade. Black silk thread was also needed, mainly to stitch the lettering of Leek's copy.[22]

By the spring of 1885 Leek embroiderers had already tackled numerous and sizeable pieces of work using a variety of techniques and materials. The rectangular format of a Bayeux Tapestry section was not unlike that of an altar frontal and the Leek Embroidery Society had produced a great many of those. Altar frontal designs stitched in Leek did not usually have a vanishing point, with its illusion of perspective. Those designs often featured wide, flat compositions, some with a linear organisation, as in the Tapestry. They were invariable carefully organised arrangements, commonly composed of horizontal textile panels, that required the balancing of elements and colour within well-calculated space. Shaw, Sedding, Horsley, Pearson and other architects provide us with good examples of such beautifully composed panels. The production of such large-scale pieces required a well-coordinated team effort, involving detailed organisation and the assembly of the finished sections by someone with the requisite skills. Frontals frequently had a matching superfrontal, which acted as a complementary strip running above the main composition, adding emphasis to the design beneath, in much the same manner as the narrow borders in the Tapestry added commentary and supported the main composition. The work would then hang in a prestigious public space where it would be regularly viewed by a crowded congregation. There were other similarities, in that frontals were usually immensely detailed, and some even had narrative content including people, architectural features, objects, animals, birds and plants. Altar frontal designs often contained figures of saints and angels, so that garments and facial features were regularly stitched. Indeed, figures for ecclesiastical use were usually more detailed than those depicted in the Bayeux Tapestry, and were frequently placed within an architectural framework, although generally in static postures. Colour Plate 8a, which depicts a pelican with her young and was designed by John Dando Sedding, has a variety of features that were similar to a number in the facsimile, while Colour Plate 5, a panel of six angels, illustrates a range of other motifs, including various distinctive metal objects such as crowns, vessels, staffs, chains, censors and helmets. Lettering, which featured in the facsimile, was a common element of ecclesiastical designs stitched by Leek needlewomen. Letters and emblematic motifs were part of a visual lexicon employed by the architects who designed them, who were aiming to make visible many intangible aspects of faith. The stitching of fine details was a regular practice from the early Middle Ages and was especially fine in the era of *Opus Anglicanum* (English work). All subjects were usually described in silk and metal thread. Apart from chancel carpets stitched with wool yarn, work done previously by Leek needlewomen was generally finer and used greater subtlety of colouring. One early exception was an altar frontal stitched entirely with wool yarn onto linen cloth by Elizabeth and Phoebe Wardle in 1875 for St Leonard's church, Ipstones, Staffordshire; Colour Plate 7b illustrates a section of wool stitching on a linen ground. Thus the repertoire of motifs stitched in Leek included many items that were remarkably similar to motifs in the Tapestry, and a variety of elements involved were already familiar to the Leek needlewomen stitching the facsimile. However, action was not a common feature of ecclesiastical work, as even doves in flight were not usually shown in energetic mode; generally static compositions provided a calm centre to a chancel. This suggests that the major differences from a Leek embroiderer's usual experience were the vivid displays of violent action evident throughout the Tapestry and the limited range of stitches.

Each embroiderer may also have had a degree of creative freedom when it came to producing texture and the shading of colours for ecclesiastical work. As Elizabeth Wardle explained in the case of the facsimile, however, 'the method of applying the wool has, wherever possible, been reproduced; and those who have visited Bayeux will doubtless recognise the minutely accurate resemblance which this copy bears to the original'.[23] This precluded any degree of choice for the stitchers of the facsimile.

We can tell a great deal about the methods and standard of stitching of the Leek facsimile as it survives in remarkably good condition in Reading Museum. Although the practicalities of production are mostly lost to us we can surmise a certain amount from educated guesswork. The two main stitching techniques of stem stitch and laid and couched work were comparatively easy to learn. They were regularly employed in ecclesiastical work and would have been familiar to members of the Leek Embroidery Society. Elizabeth Wardle used a simple version of laid and couched metal thread work in her earliest surviving pieces of 1864. It was a useful technique for covering large areas of a ground cloth quickly.

Elizabeth Wardle's *Guide to the Bayeux Tapestry*, written in May 1886, was concise and accessible and included some basic information for the general public. It was a small publication, 20 × 15cm (7¾ × 6 inches), and therefore practical for viewers of the Tapestry to use, with enough information to make sense of the scenes without the more detailed information in the original, much longer guide. Some copies were hardbound in a dark olive-green cover with gold lettering, although the majority were paper-backed. Figure 14 shows the interior of the hardbound 'Guide'. As the main body of the text was extracted by her from the much larger publication by the Reverend John Collingwood Bruce, with his permission,[24] he must have approved the finished text. The short preface to the *Guide* outlined its purpose, which was 'for the reader to learn the conditions under which this piece of embroidery has been commenced and completed'. Only six paragraphs long, it is the sole record we have of Elizabeth's direct thoughts on the project. Although we can gather a certain amount from it, many questions remain unanswered. We do learn that the reproduction of the tapestry was commenced a year previously, which in itself was a remarkable achievement and an important piece of information. If

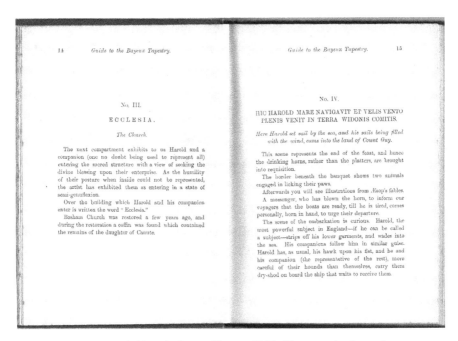

Figure 14   *Guide to the Bayeux Tapestry*, 1886. Photograph: the author

she included the tracing of the South Kensington 'drawings' in that short time span then this monumental task was a very efficiently planned project from start to finish.

Elizabeth Wardle freely chose to take on the organisational challenges of this very public venture. While we do not know what motivated her we do know that she was used to running a busy society efficiently. She was acknowledged as a logical thinker with an active and organising mind, and must have set about this project in characteristic fashion. Organisation was a crucial factor, as was the knowledge that she, along with the others she needed to involve, was capable of sustained output to a high standard. Importantly, Elizabeth Wardle was used to organising group projects, although this was a larger group than usual. As she reveals in her preface, 'Thirty-five ladies, the majority of who are resident in the neighbourhood of Leek, have been engaged on this extensive piece of needlework.' Careful calculations must have ensured that there were the essential materials and skills readily available locally and enough time to meet deadlines. Although Leek was a small town it had a collective momentum and the necessary resources for such a project. Significantly, Elizabeth had vast experience of organising groups of needlewomen for collective projects and working to targets. She would have been conscious of the various stages in the production schedule that needed to be followed and the many tasks that required coordination. No doubt she was also acutely aware of the financial aspects of such an undertaking. Someone had to fund the materials and pay carriage fees to transport the drawings from London before production could even start.

In her preface, in a masterpiece of understatement, Elizabeth Wardle notes that the authorities at the South Kensington Museum kindly lent watercolour drawings 'from which tracings were obtained, which were subsequently trans-ferred to cloth'.[25] The project could never have progressed beyond her original idea without the complete cooperation of this major institution. The very fact that such a prestigious establishment allowed hand-coloured photographs to be whisked away to Leek says, moreover, a great deal about the high status of the Wardles. This Museum was used to working closely with Thomas Wardle for mutually beneficial purposes and had by then purchased a number of items of Leek embroidery for display. A complete collection of India's wild silks, curated by Wardle, had been previously given to the Museum for permanent display. Perhaps the Leek project was seen as educationally worthy by the Museum authorities?

Once the photographs arrived in Leek the preliminary stage of the project could begin. There were opportunities for things to go badly wrong at any one of the many stages, which involved the tracing of the images and then the transfer of the design from tracing paper to cloth. One essential undertaking was the division of the 69m (approximately 226 feet) length of the unfolding drama into twenty-five discrete scenes, which would then be transferred to separate linen panels for stitching. The person with the monumental task of obtaining detailed, precise tracings of the entire length of each panel was Miss Eliza (Lizzie) Allen. Elizabeth Wardle clearly placed great faith in her to accurately complete this pivotal phase.

Lizzie Allen would have required a lot of time, unbroken concentration and a steady hand. Like other needlewomen, she was probably experienced in tracing far more complex designs, as surviving Leek embroideries are revealed to be intricate. Tracings taken twenty years later by another Leek embroiderer show us that processes and materials were still the same. Allen needed to remain alert to the overall balance of the composition for each of the twenty-five panels she traced, as well as recording the minute details. She must have included fine points of stitching along with the texture of the threads as they appeared in clothing, flesh or objects. Copies of facial expressions were crucial if it was to be a faithful reproduction, as the appearance of certain major characters needed to be recognisable throughout. We can presume, then, that Allen was a sufficiently skilled draughtswoman to capture these particulars. She was also based in Leek – an important consideration, as no doubt a degree of supervision was involved because the tracings were such a major aspect of the project's success. Elizabeth Wardle would hardly let anything careless pass her by, as her and her husband's reputations were at stake in such a high-profile venture. Allen, a former student of Leek's Technical School, had some degree of experience, although a number of questions about her role still remain unanswered: did she have help and how long did this stage take?

The time-consuming and large-scale tracing for the facsimile took place in Leek, but exactly where is not known. The busy Wardle family home would hardly have been suitable, as there were still many Wardle children to care for.[26] The coloured photographs of each panel lent by the South Kensington Museum were the size of the original, yet once fixed to a linen backing cloth they were larger. Certainly the roll of twenty-five life-sized mounted photographs would have taken up a great amount of storage space. The unrolled length would have needed a substantial flat surface to allow tracings, as well as colour matching, to take place. When Clara Bill attached the embroidered panels to one another during the final stage she would have required a considerable area in which to work.

Colour matching the traced panels to the original would have been a vital concern, although we do not know how the matches were achieved. In her *Guide* Elizabeth Wardle states 'The wools have all been specially dyed to match each shade the Tapestry presents at the present time.' The eight shades identified by John Collingwood Bruce were: dark and light blue, red, pink, yellow, buff, blue-green and sage-green.[27] Both Wardles certainly had an experienced eye for colour; by that date Thomas Wardle's dye works had achieved thousands of different shades from historic natural dyes, some of which dated back to the time of the original Tapestry. He was internationally renowned for his dyeing expertise – indeed, his business depended on it. He was also experienced in dyeing worsted for carpets and tapestry, some of which was for Morris's use and some for ecclesiastical work. He organised the dyeing of 45kg (100lb) of worsted for the facsimile. The production of such a huge amount of dyed wool yarn, using historical methods, would have been a time-consuming and therefore an expensive business. The wool dyes of the original had faded over the centuries, probably unevenly, and yet it would seem that the Wardles aimed to match the shades as they were observed in the nineteenth century. There was certainly a need for a colour record of sorts so that yarns could correspond. Was it presumed that the hand-coloured photographs from the Museum were accurate? How otherwise could the colours of the original be assessed? If the Wardles had their own methods of colour-matching that knowledge is lost to us, although Elizabeth Wardle's preface indicates that they were successful. Certainly both Elizabeth and Thomas were, furthermore, very aware of the issues surrounding authenticity, which was a hotly debated topic at that time. They worked closely with a number of architects who were Gothic Revival experts, all of whom were deeply concerned about accurate reproduction of medieval ornamentation and materials. As early as 1864 Thomas was particularly anxious, for example, that the correct materials and methods had been used for the restoration of Cheddleton church (see Chapter 4).

After the tracing phase for the facsimile was complete the design on paper would have been 'pricked and pounced' onto linen cloth ready for stitching. This was a standard procedure used to transfer an image from one medium to another. As Elizabeth Wardle stated in the preface, 'the material on which it was worked was chosen so as to resemble the original in texture and colour as nearly as possible'. Although she aimed to produce a faithful copy, the cloth and yarns available to her in the late nineteenth century are likely to have been different to those produced in the eleventh century. The caveat 'as nearly as possible' was, therefore, needed. Owing to improvements in animal husbandry nineteenth-century wool was from a much better-quality staple yarn. Linen production had also changed considerably and various grades of linen, from extremely fine to very coarse, were available to her. But how was she able to check her choices against the original without returning with different samples? We simply do not know what the practicalities of this would involve or even if it was a credible option. John Collingwood Bruce, who viewed the Tapestry in Bayeux a number of times, described the original linen cloth as having 'assumed the tinge of brown holland over time'.[28]

Once the design was in place, the panels prepared for stitching and the quantities for each colour of the wool yarn estimated, the materials were distributed to the thirty-five women who had agreed to work on a section. How the stitching was organised would have depended on the work space available and the number of people occupied at any one time. We can presume that different sections were stitched at the same time, possibly in different locations. Some panels certainly had more than one pair of hands working on them. While most of the women lived in Leek some were in Derbyshire, two in Macclesfield and others in Birmingham and London.[29] As we do not have even the most basic facts we can only presume that each embroiderer came to Leek to complete her work if they were resident elsewhere; any alternative would have been logistically difficult. Whether they worked together on a section or in sequence is not recorded, although each needlewoman signed her name beneath the section she stitched. Nor do we know how long each portion took to complete. Although they were all experienced this was a different approach from their usual working methods. We do not know whether they initially gathered together for lessons in technique or if they produced small trial sections to see if they were fit for the task. We must assume that Elizabeth Wardle set the usual high standards. As she stated, 'the method of applying the wool has, wherever possible, been reproduced'. The needlewomen were expected to match the original as far as possible, but how was this indicated to them? Despite the cautious 'wherever possible', Elizabeth seemed confident that they had succeeded in their aims.

Elizabeth Wardle affirms that 'those who have visited Bayeux will doubtless recognise the minutely accurate resemblance which this copy bears to the original'. The main parts of each motif would have been infilled with laid and couched threads first. This was a comparatively easy technique to learn. Once proficient it was possible to cover a lot of ground cloth quickly with a degree of competence. The bold use of blank space in the composition would have speeded up the task. It is highly likely that outlines of each section were then completed using stem stitch of a contrasting tone. As Leek's facsimile was stitched by many pairs of hands and some panels worked by more than one person, this inevitably must have led to slight differences in stitching across the sections. A small, unpromising envelope in the local history section of Leek Library has recently yielded up important information about working methods. At first glance the envelope, marked 'Notes for Working', seemed to contain insignificant scraps of paper with handwritten lists or scores (Figure 15). They are now identified as records kept by a number of the women who worked on the facsimile. They systematically list body parts, such as noses, arms and faces, as well as garments, including helmets, and references to animals, such as horse's legs. There are comments about wobbly lines and which colour of

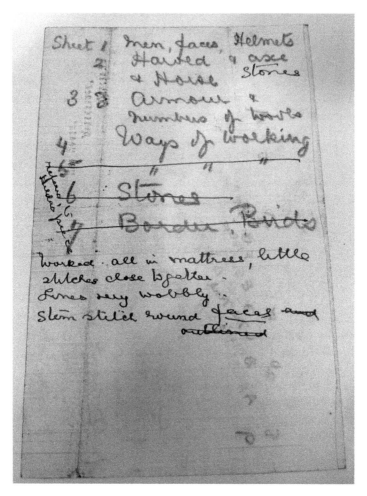

Figure 15   Methods of working, 1885. Photograph: the author

worsted to use. We can also see how each item is ticked off, presumably on completion. Invaluable information about colour matching – 'Left man', 'legs buff' and 'mouth red' – tells us how a needlewomen knew she was correctly reproducing the original colouring by listing even the smallest part. Tiny sketches indicate some of the motifs referred to, while other comments reveal details about different aspects of the task. 'Wobbly lines' might refer to the drawing of the original, perhaps waves, or the copy made by the person who traced the scenes. The lists in the envelope were probably collated by Lydia Wardle, daughter of Thomas and Elizabeth Wardle, who apparently saved as many related items as possible, although little else has been discovered.

As far as the original Tapestry is concerned, the linen strips could easily have been worked by teams of stitchers in rotation, and there is clear evidence that many repairs were carried out over time. But how much does this matter? The main point of the Leek exercise was surely to record the historic subject and not to produce an exact copy of every single stitch. What would have been the point of such a mind-numbing exercise? The Wardles were acutely aware of the deadening uniformity of Berlin wool work and mechanically produced designs and consciously fought against them. Like Morris, with whom they worked closely, and Ruskin, they valued the evidence of the maker and the less than consistent results that the human hand produced.

We know who the needlewomen involved were and which section they worked on because 'the result of each one's industry is shown by her embroidered signature on a strip of blue cloth beneath her work'. This band of signatures is an obvious and deliberate difference between the facsimile and the original. The acknowledgement of each contributor's work with a stitched signature had a precedent in Leek. As early as 1873, years before the formation of the Leek Embroidery Society, the town's needlewomen completed a major commission for St Luke's church. It was based on a striking design for an altar frontal by the architect Sedding. The main section was a narrative scene consisting of a pelican feeding her lively young in their nest. It was placed within a detailed architectural canopy composed of towers, roofs, arches and other structural features based on medieval textiles. The stitching employed the laid and couched technique in part. It is still possible to see the line of embroidered signatures made by the needlewomen above their work today (see Chapter 4). The production of altar frontals routinely needed the input of a number of individuals, as each would contribute various elements for a large piece according to her expertise; flesh and gold work, for example, required highly skilled practitioners who specialised in these techniques. This was not necessary for the facsimile, however, as the stitching techniques were limited and simple throughout. When finished, the separate elements of a frontal were carefully joined by someone very experienced. This stage involved specific technical challenges and practical considerations that would have also been addressed by those working on the panels of the facsimile. The stitching of any long piece of cloth invariably required a wooden frame to support it. This allowed the cloth to be stretched taut, which enabled well-controlled stitching. Various types of frame were available and there were different ways of using a frame as a support.

A textile conservator's report produced for Reading Museum in 1992 revealed that a 'hessian-like' backing fabric was attached and stitched to each of the twenty-five panels of the facsimile and that there were signs that the panels had been washed previously. They were washed again in 1992. The backing may not necessarily have been the original, as at least one previous cleaning and rehanging of the facsimile had taken place in Reading.[30]

Once the stitching of the facsimile was completed each section had its narrow band of signed blue linen attached to the lower edge of the embroidery along its length. Each stitched signature is clear and embellished with a decorative scrolling motif. One motif stands out as different from the others: a solitary needlewoman chose to distinguish her work with what seems to be a South American pattern. The reason for this idiosyncrasy is not known. The assembly of the finished panels was the responsibility of Clara Bill, an important member of the Leek Embroidery Society, who must have had experience for this crucial role. As each panel was firmly attached to another they needed to hang straight along the entire length. In some places stitching over seams had taken place. Elizabeth Wardle added a final statement, in stitch, to the end panel:

> This reproduction of the Bayeux tapestry was worked at Leek in Staffordshire. The drawings were lent by the authorities of the South Kensington Museum. 35 ladies have been engaged on this piece of tapestry and the name of each will be found underneath her work. E. Wardle, Leek, Staffordshire, Whitsuntide 1886. The worsteds were dyed in permanent colours by Thomas Wardle, F.C.S., F.G.S.

The task was complete.[31]

Profit and Loss

In June 1886 the completed facsimile was put on display at the Nicholson Institute in Leek. Thomas Wardle took time away from his official duties at the Colonial and Empire Exhibition in London to attend the opening ceremony.[32] Over 1,200 visitors viewed the work, paying one shilling each to do so. It was possible to purchase a season ticket for two shillings or a family season ticket for four shillings. Due to popular demand the exhibition was extended, although the price was lowered for the final weeks. All profits went to Leek's Art and Exhibition Fund. This was the first venue of a major tour across Britain that was to last for over a year. The facsimile then went on to venues in America and Europe.

The American tour, which began in New York in December 1886, involved major planning, administrative and organisational skills. We do not know who was responsible but we do know that someone must have alerted the major American newspapers to the visit, as it received broad press exposure in advance. The facsimile was awaited with much anticipation and long articles reveal that journalists were well briefed on the 'famous piece of needlework'.

The news coverage started with a well-informed piece in the *Boston Daily Journal* announcing that the facsimile was on its way from England to America.[33] It included details of the original Bayeux Tapestry and the Leek facsimile and predicted great audiences for its tour. 'So marvellous a copy of so marvellous a document written in worsted' was typical of the welcoming articles. Throughout the tour newspaper reports indicated a widespread interest in the facsimile, which was displayed in major venues in principal cities until its return to England in April 1887. The *New York Tribune* provided a long article on 'an important exhibition', which included a detailed context. It also revealed that a poem on the subject would be read to celebrate its arrival in the country.[34]

In New York the facsimile was exhibited alongside the work of Mrs Candace Wheeler, whose influence had apparently initiated the American tour. This must have secured its success. Along with Louis Comfort Tiffany, she was a founder of the New York Society of Decorative Arts and an eminent needlewoman, writer and designer. She was also an 'important activist for American design reform'.[35] Wheeler ran the Associated Artists Rooms on East Twenty-Third Street from 1883 with her son and daughter. It was at these prominent premises that she displayed the Leek facsimile alongside her own work, which was for sale. There were also items in the display of Irish flax-on-flax embroidery, with designs taken from the *Book of Kells*. This work had been awarded a gold medal at the International Inventions Exhibition of 1885. These items, also for sale, had travelled to America in order to raise funds for poor Irish needlewomen in the employ of the Donegal Industrial Fund. It was described as an opportunity for philanthropy and an exhibition of some importance. The *Boston Daily Advertiser* described the New York displays as 'one of the most attractive centres of interest next month'. Another journalist added that they were the 'finest specimens of modern needlework that has ever been exhibited in this country', and included 'an exact reproduction of the famous Bayeux Tapestry'. He referred to Thomas Wardle as 'a man of high intelligence and with a scientific reputation', while Elizabeth Wardle was a woman of 'influence and knowledge'. Clearly this was a prestigious event.

After New York the facsimile travelled to Boston by way of Syracuse, where it was displayed, fittingly, at the armoury. Further details were provided by the *Boston Daily Advertiser*, which carried advertisements for the tour even on Christmas Day. The *Springfield Republican* (Massachusetts) included regular reportage throughout January and February 1887, and Syracuse papers reviewed the exhibition. Coverage extended to the *Daily Picayune*, based in New Orleans, Louisiana. Not to be outdone, in March the *Worcester Daily Spy* (Massachusetts) produced a detailed background to the Leek facsimile and reported on the learned lecture given by Reverend A.S. Garver on the history of the original Bayeux Tapestry at the Art Students' Club, Boston, where the facsimile was displayed. Great numbers of people expressed regret that the work could not stay in the city for longer.

In Philadelphia the facsimile was shown at Gill's Art Gallery, where it 'drew a large attendance of the lovers of antiquity' (Figure 16). One newspaper report included a detailed description of the display, which is revealing as no other account to date has provided such information:

> The long linen strip begins at the head of the stair-way in the south gallery and is stretched around both galleries, while along the sides posts are set out into the room around which the tapestry is brought, forming little alcoves. There is something particularly pleasing about this arrangement, as if it were specially suited to the archaic attractions of the work.[36]

Figure 16   Gill's Art Galleries review, Philadelphia, USA.
Linda Eaton, Philadelphia, USA. Staffordshire Libraries and Arts Service

Over a further touring period of nine years, the facsimile aroused great interest wherever it went. Although we do not know who organised the highly complex tours, we can assume that they would have had many things to consider. A length of embroidery of 68–70m (223–229 feet) required a huge display area. The fact that it was a textile, which needed considerable care when it was in transit and support when it was hung, must have presented enormous logistical difficulties. The practicalities of adapting the embroidery to a variety of very different venues would have been exacting and would certainly require detailed knowledge of each location beforehand. Some exhibition venues must have had enormous problems to overcome when it came to displaying the work in a good light. Then there was also the publicity to consider, which was specific to each venue, along with the packing and transporting of an enormous length of stitched linen and its supports, which would have needed considerable time and skills and suitable transport.

Some locations took the facsimile for only a short period. It was displayed for just two days in Cambridge, England, to coincide with a lecture that Thomas Wardle gave at the University. Chester exhibited it for a month. The busy schedule suggests that there was a team of people who moved the facsimile, installing and de-installing it properly. It would have been vulnerable to damage if badly handled by inexperienced helpers. The details of this are, however, lost to us. Surviving invitations from different venues reveal that visitors could purchase items of Leek embroidery when they came to view the facsimile. This ingenious offer considerably extended the potential market for Leek needlework across Britain. Newcastle-upon-Tyne used the proceeds from its venue to support the local eye infirmary, so it would seem that the possibilities were endless.

Records indicate that a company was formed to deal with the expenses and profits of the venture. The small revenue was divided into shares and each embroiderer was paid according to her input. As some had worked on small sections of a panel while others did a great deal more this was a fair system. Accounts show that shareholders received a dividend in December 1887. The secretary for the accounts was Miss Beatrice Ellen Lowe, whose mother was one of the needlewomen. Despite an enthusiastic reception wherever the facsimile was shown, ongoing costs were considerable and it would appear that the venture made little profit. Nine years after completion the facsimile was described as 'being on loan with the possibility of purchase'. This coincided with its display at Reading Town Hall in June 1895. Alderman Arthur Hill, a previous mayor of Reading, offered to buy the facsimile. He considered 'that this work[,] absolutely unique in its character and historic interest, would be an acquisition of permanent value to our new art college, and the privilege of possessing it should belong to Reading'. Hill purchased the work for £300 and made a gift of it to the town, along with its supports and a large number of printed guides by Elizabeth Wardle. Subsequently Lady Margaret Gaunt, daughter of Thomas and Elizabeth Wardle, stated that her mother 'never thought we should allow such a treasured possession to be sold and leave Leek'.[37] As Leek embroidery was on sale in Reading at an Art Needlework establishment, there was at least some commercial benefit gained from its move to that town.

After its transfer to Reading the facsimile continued its peripatetic life, including a much publicised visit to Windsor Castle in May 1896 at the request of Queen Victoria. When Margaret Gaunt viewed the tapestry in Reading Town Hall in 1927 she was, however, appalled by its condition. It was dirty, nailed to the wall and slit in various places to fit around roof beams, was placed at too high a level to be seen properly and was poorly lit. She offered to buy back the work, as it was clearly not appreciated. Her response motivated the council, which leapt into action. The facsimile was then cleaned and each panel separately mounted into dust-proof frames. At the reopening ceremony at Reading Museum in February 1928 Fred Wardle, then a solicitor, spoke warmly of his childhood home, his parents and the many prestigious visitors they attracted to Leek. With him at the ceremony were his wife and two of the Wardle daughters, Mrs Horace Wardle and Lady Gaunt, as well as Mrs and Reverend Cronshaw, Bursar of Queen's College, Oxford. At the opening ceremony Mr F.D. Kendrick, a former keeper of textiles at the Victoria and Albert Museum, spoke about the textile value of the exhibit. He considered the work to be unique and thought it to be a most excellent and faithful copy. 'He could only think that the South Kensington Museum must have been asleep in some unaccountable manner' when the remarkable object was seeking a permanent home.[38] The tapestry then started another touring phase, which included South Africa.

Copies of Copies

In 1984 the facsimile returned to Leek to celebrate the centenary of the Nicholson Institute, where yet again it was received with great interest. Today it is permanently displayed in Reading Museum in purpose-built, eye-level display cabinets, where it is much admired and still has the power to astonish. The colours of the wool yarns are generally good, with just a few signs of fading, particularly where blue and green was used, and the stitching is sound throughout. Both the Leek facsimile and the original Tapestry in Bayeux are now over 130 years older and it is inevitable that they have changed in that time, so that colours and even the texture of yarns will have degraded to some extent. Given its hectic life on tour and the various rehangings it has endured the facsimile is a remarkable testimony to the skills of Elizabeth and Thomas

Wardle and the embroiderers. Comparing the original with the facsimile today would be a futile activity, given that the latter has been cleaned at least three times and rebacked and repaired in the 1920s and again in the 1990s.

Meanwhile, the Bayeux Tapestry continued to inspire different generations of historians and practitioners. In 1931 the enterprising and well-known needlework manufacturers and warehousemen Vicars and Poirson Ltd (London) offered reproductions of the Tapestry in the form of printed kits 'in the original colourings', prepared for stitching at home. Even though the story was very familiar this proved popular and it was possible for enthusiasts to stitch at least one panel, or more. Over time other women have taken on the challenge of making their copy of the original. Mrs Maud Geare devoted seventeen years to single-handedly stitching her version, although it is not known just how faithful a replica this was. Similarly, Madame Tugis, based in Portsmouth, attempted a version in 1938, although she did not complete the task and severe bomb damage during the Second World War caused substantial harm to her work. Leek retains only one panel, which is a copy of the copy and the work of Alice Allen, completed in 1934. It has much brighter colouring than the facsimile and some figures are absent from the composition. Although Macclesfield Museums Trust has an elaborately framed panel of one battle scene nothing is known of its provenance. Given the expensive, gold-lettered frame it would seem that it was someone's treasured possession. The Whitworth Art Gallery in Manchester also holds a panel in fragile condition, thought to have been made in Leek, although there is no evidence to confirm this. Unless both panels were supervised by Elizabeth Wardle, with her exacting standards, they cannot be considered to be the work of the Leek Embroidery Society. There is a suggestion that the Whitworth's panel was stored in Plymouth, where it was damaged during the Second World War. The remarkably similar fate of the work of Mrs Tugis indicates there might be a connection with the Whitworth's panel. It is hardly surprising that a number of other panels existed, as the hand-coloured photographs issued by the Arundel Society were freely available.

Furnishing fabric based on the Tapestry was also produced. Printed onto textured cream cotton, the brightly coloured scenes made lively curtains and covers in the 1970s. More recently, Alice Kettle, a British textile artist of international renown, has spoken fondly of its influence on her work, which is largely concerned with narrative. She was inspired by Leek's reproduction of the Tapestry, which she viewed as a student at Reading.

Scholars continue to debate the circumstances surrounding the creation of the original and yet a certain amount of mystery remains.

Chapter 4

STITCH MEETS STONE

We should have had no Morris, no Street, no Burges, no Webb, no Bodley, no Rossetti, no Burne-Jones, no Crane, but for Pugin.

John Dando Sedding
Arts and Crafts Congress, Liverpool, 1888

This chapter examines through the medium of embroidery the legacy of a number of talented architects who operated in and around north Staffordshire. It celebrates the collaboration between the architects who created designs, the needlewomen who interpreted their schemes in silk and gold thread and the skilled workers who produced the materials. Viewing the work of major architects from this interdependent perspective offers an opportunity to approach their designs through an entirely different medium and context, expanding our understanding of them. They played a pivotal role in that they combined faith, trade, local community and artistic expression at a time when rituals and communal ceremonies were a part of many people's lives. From what follows we can see that collective talents made numerous beautiful pieces and that many still survive in the churches for which they were made, testifying to the interplay of extraordinary skills.

As a result of complex ecclesiastical and social changes the second half of the nineteenth century witnessed a massive church-building programme across Britain. One outcome of this was a remarkably intricate web of activity in the region of north Staffordshire involving eminent architects and the Wardle family of Leek. The Wardles were closely linked to the architects and the architects were connected to each other through networks of contacts and influences. They all worked closely with the Leek Embroidery Society to produce emblematic needlework for their buildings, which contributed significantly to the overall result. What follows documents their creative alliances.

The county of Staffordshire has a history of attracting the most distinguished men to build there. Augustus Welby Northmore Pugin, Sir George Gilbert Scott, George Edmund Street and George Frederick Bodley produced some of their best work in Staffordshire. This was during a significant stage in Gothic Revival building led by Pugin and inspired by the writings of John Ruskin. Not only did they create magnificent buildings but they also made a conscious effort to revive declining craft traditions and in the process designed many articles, including embroideries, for their interiors. They were firmly rooted in their own time and set a powerful precedent for their pupils and admirers to follow. George Gilbert Scott Jnr, Richard Norman Shaw, John Dando Sedding and Gerald Callcott Horsley, motivated by these masters, were also attracted to work in the county and create designs for embroidery. As a consequence the region's embroiderers had the opportunity to contribute to some of the most splendid Gothic Revival buildings in Britain. In a number of cases we still have the opportunity to see these works as they were first seen: as examples of extraordinary skills that produced beautiful and emblematic pieces.

The histories that follow demonstrate just how important fine needlework was to the completion of a Gothic Revival church interior. Exquisite embroideries were not simply a matter of accessorising with a few well-chosen soft furnishings. They were, and are still, symbolic, intended for ritualistic purposes and not to be admired solely as a beautiful textile. Through their iconography they were an important liturgical device that contributed to a vast and elaborate emblematic scheme. They carried significant status in the church as a result of their vital functional roles as complex ceremonial items: their use of evocative motifs was considered by many to represent the divine in visible form, through which the Christian message was reinforced.

Altar frontals were known to exist as early as the fifth century and were invariably richly decorated with representative themes as an expression of their spiritual importance. They were crucial pieces in that they were situated in a critical position in the church interior as an intentional focus of attention throughout a service. Embroidered textiles were flexible, could be constantly changed and were even mobile, when worn. In contrast, other ornate features of stone, glass or wood were permanent and static. Elaborate textiles were calculated to enhance the ritualistic aspects of a service through their opulence and symbolism, which drew the attention of the congregation to the altar. Each architect who worked with the Leek Embroidery Society recognised the significance of the chancel as the focus of their interior and strengthened the central role of fine needlework accordingly. These noteworthy textiles are an important aspect of Gothic Revival history.

Devotion and Display

Nineteenth-century Gothic Revivalists looked to medieval buildings as models of collaboration, which resulted in complex structures embedded with the strong, communicative power of ornament. The craftsmen who built great Gothic edifices across medieval Europe were master builders who understood materials and the symbolism of the intricate forms they created in a variety of media. Along with their aesthetic values, the results they achieved represented thoughts using foliage, flowers, fruit, human forms, birds and beasts to convey meaning. Medieval churches were filled with costly decorative items, and public demonstrations of faith such as elaborate festivals and pageants needed banners, hangings and robes. Furthermore, and of necessity, medieval builders operated an interdisciplinary, collaborative approach, linking different craft guilds to create these monumental buildings, which stood as role models for nineteenth-century architects.

As one of the oldest and most luxurious textiles, silk was much more than an expensive, beautiful fabric. It was always a prominent symbol of status and power across the globe and through the ages. Silk played a significant role in medieval church interiors, as Eamon Duffy's valuable research into church inventories reveals. Increasingly, trade with the Near East gave easier access to elaborate woven silks from Syria and the Byzantine Empire. The subsequent growth in Italian silk production from the late thirteenth century supplied an even greater variety of luxurious fabrics. Church records list silk in many forms that indicate its central role, utilised on and around the altar. Even small parish churches had altars placed at various points, while huge cathedrals and abbeys possessed a plethora of them. Consequently, a good selection of costly embroidered altar frontals, vestments and other items were provided to churches in large numbers. Unlike stone or wood they were not employed uniformly throughout the building but made their impact mainly on or near the Communion table. As embroidered silk textiles were designed to differentiate those fundamental parts of a church where ritual took place they needed to be noticeable. The eye-catching, sumptuous materials directed attention to the altar through their strong colours and rippling surfaces of silk and gold threads, which acted as a contrast to the muted mass of hard stone. As Duffy states:

> In 1552 even a small and relatively poor city parish such as St Andrew Hubbard (London) retained fifteen highly ornate corporas cases, ten copes including some of sumptuous cloth of tissue, or embroidered velvet, and one retaining the patronal image, and fourteen chasubles and sets of vestments for priest, deacon and subdeacon.[1]

Churchwardens of another parish itemised thirty-nine sets of mass vestments, which were sold in the mid-sixteenth century to defray expenses; others specify 'dozens of copes and vestments'.[2] Fortunately some inventories describe embroidered items in detail and sixteenth-century accounts often record how many items were embellished with images of saints and angels. The church of St Margaret in the City of London owned a number of such pieces between 1486 and 1511 and included the cost of each item in its inventory: 'Item A white Cope of Damaske powered with Archangelles and the Offeraries of the same nedyll were of a parte of the lyffe of Seynt Margarett to the whiche payment of the same Cope … £8 and we paid the overplus'.[3] There followed descriptions of vestments of black velvet, orphreys of 'nedle warke' depicting apostles and a set of white damask items with orphreys of red velvet with 'floweres of nedle werke'.[4] Examples of blue tissue and white damask with two archangels were listed, along with their donor's names. Other inventories describe those items that were sold. In London alone astounding quantities of lavish silk in its many forms were produced for ecclesiastical purposes. We can reasonably assume that this situation was replicated across the country to varying degrees.

During the period of *Opus Anglicanum* (English work), outstanding embroidery was produced mainly in London workrooms.[5] British ecclesiastic needlework was then at its most magnificent and universally admired. The bulk of this intricate embroidery was stitched with imported silk and gold thread, both equally exorbitant in price. Luxurious velvets of every colour were made of silk and imported from centres of excellence. Sicilian cloth of gold and silk, plus gold tissue from the Levant or Italy, were all very costly. During the Reformation iconoclasts wilfully ruined many of these beautiful things and even tiny hamlets did not escape the pillaging hordes, which destroyed many church interiors; Duffy portrays the Reformation as a people's tragedy that stripped away a beloved and familiar world of symbols. While much was destroyed, however, some textiles survived to give us a notion of what was lost, while others were cut and resewn into different forms. Thereafter the austere interiors of the puritans prevailed for centuries.

Ecclesiological Changes

From the 1830s controversy raged in the Anglican Church over different ways of arranging a church interior. Ecclesiologists looked back to the days of medieval splendour and were inspired. As building styles and techniques had evolved over four centuries, from the mid-eleventh century through to the second half of the sixteenth century, Gothic architecture had developed a number of variations. Early English, Decorated and Perpendicular were the main stylistic divisions in medieval Britain, when English stonemasons were some of the best in Europe. The principles that lay behind the construction and decoration of medieval church buildings were acknowledged as an expression of Christian belief that carried a spiritual message. In the nineteenth century there was a return to particular ecclesiological ideals that were directly reflected in church buildings and their fittings. Architects set about reviving the reverential magnificence that had been so gratuitously destroyed. The practice of vesting the altar was reinstated and, once again, silk came to the fore. Fine silks were woven with motifs specifically for church use on French and English looms. Silk damasks were particularly sought after for ecclesiastical work as the self-coloured patterns worked well as a base for lavish embroidery. They were overflowing with meaning: a calculated fusion of sensual cloth symbols and textures.

Gothic Revival architecture, led by Pugin from the 1830s, soon dominated church building and restructuring. As well as its overtly metaphorical, historic elements, Gothic architecture was flexible and adaptable to different sites. Yet not all architects accepted all of its forms, and heated discussions compared the virtues of the various forms against each other. Nineteenth-century architects selected from the various options according to their preference. Pugin and the journal *The Ecclesiologist* promoted Decorated Gothic, the exemplars of which dated from the twelfth century. Their influence was strong, and many eminent architects employed this early form in their buildings, although others were later to favour the lighter phase, English Perpendicular, from the fourteenth century. The architectural press carried vitriolic articles often attacking a particular architect for their choice. The Perpendicular was dismissed by *The Ecclesiologist*, Ruskin and George Gilbert Scott Snr as debased.[6] The latter's son, George Gilbert Scott Jnr, however, rejected these opinions, preferring the later phase.

Articles and illustrations in *The Ecclesiologist* emphasised the correct ways to embellish items and surfaces within a church, following Christian principles as perceived in Gothic buildings. Thereafter a number of eminent architects, including their mentor George Edmund Street, produced designs and wrote learned articles for publication. The lexicon of decorative images, with their sacred and secular symbolism, became a vital part of their architectural vocabulary, which they were determined to continue throughout their interiors. For many their buildings reflected their beliefs and they perceptively interpreted historic motifs with a contemporary response that fitted their own era. Generally, designs for embroidery had a lightness of touch, so that old symbols were seemingly invented anew, although they still required a degree of intensity to perform their ritualistic role. Some images were easily recognisable as Christian, yet others were not so readily categorised. Floral and fruit motifs, for example, did not always carry obvious Christian references in the way that the designer intended, which created an element of mystery combined with beauty.

The Seven Lamps of Architecture (1849), Ruskin's analysis of architectural concerns, promoted Gothic as the only valid form.[7] He advocated 'truth to materials' and the employment of decorative motifs inspired by nature. This vastly influential author deeply affected William Morris, among others, as he urged a return to the joy in hand labour, along with the reuniting of design with making. Using Gothic architecture as a model, Ruskin promoted a closer collaboration between architects and craftsmen, along with a greater unity of the arts, as had been the case in the Middle Ages. He upheld the study of nature as a source of inspiration for artist and designer alike, as well as the use of natural rather than man-made materials for the production of domestic objects. Ruskin's *The Stones of Venice* (1851–3) was an epic publication that was of great interest to Morris. As a young man still in his twenties he considered the chapter 'The Nature of Gothic' as 'one of the very few necessary and inevitable utterances of the century'.[8] It was a complete text in its own right, which had a significant impact on designers, craftsmen and socialists. Ruskin condemned 'the degradation of the operative into a machine', along with the loss of spontaneity and imperfection that were features of machine-making. He famously stated 'I believe the right question to ask, respecting all ornament is simply this: Was it done with enjoyment?' Scott Snr followed his principles, Street and William Lethaby were deeply influenced, and because of him Edward Burne-Jones designed embroideries for Winnington School for Girls in Cheshire.[9] Even Oscar Wilde came under his sway. Ruskin eventually became a friend of Morris when he joined the Society for the Protection of Ancient Buildings (SPAB). Their considerable combined forces helped fuel the massive revitalisation of the decorative arts, which flourished in the latter part of the nineteenth century.

Gavin Stamp, biographer of George Gilbert Scott Jnr, argued that 'the mid-Victorian decades were certainly a vital and creative period in English architecture'.[10] A group of young architects, inspired by Ruskin and Pugin, developed a neo-Gothic approach that was evidently contemporary. Street was their accepted leader and extraordinarily influential in a number of ways. His approach to his buildings was reinforced by his knowledge of the design of fittings, including textiles, and the continuation of craft practice. Along with Pugin, Street was a prolific designer of vestments and embroidered items for use on the altar. He planned them well because he had a good understanding of stitch and ancient models. As a result his buildings achieved a coherency that came from this integrity. They were 'eloquent with thought and feeling'.[11]

Although Morris spent only a short time at Street's Oxford office it was enough to galvanise his appreciation of architectural principles. He absorbed a great deal from him and became convinced that the role of the decorative arts was bound up with that of architecture, a view that many of his contemporaries shared. Morris took similar values from Pugin and Ruskin, which stayed with him throughout his life.

Richard Norman Shaw was also a protégé of Street, and, in turn, inspired and trained others. Sedding, another of Street's pupils, likewise trained young architects who designed decorative interior fittings. Gavin Stamp maintained that churches designed by Scott, Bodley, Sedding and others in the last three decades of the nineteenth century were 'intellectually sophisticated creations, cosmopolitan in spirit, which reconciled many strands within the Gothic Revival'.[12] These eminent architects interpreted Gothic buildings in their own ideological manner, instilling historic forms with a new vitality and creating churches that were recognised as some of the greatest buildings of their time. Their intertwined connections were responsible for a distinctiveness that permeated the decorative arts. They sought to revive craft skills and an understanding of materials and aesthetic harmony, which they perceived in the grand medieval cathedrals and churches. It is this extraordinary network of giants, standing on the shoulders of giants, which is explored in this chapter. One major outcome, which is particularly pertinent here, is that the altar was returned to its previous central space in the overall plan of the church. Once again it became the focus of worship, replacing the pulpit, which had taken that role when preaching was the dominant force. Following this change of emphasis there was a general opening out of the church interior to create a less restricted view of the altar. This was a logical step following the revived importance of ceremony and the priest's re-enhanced role. One result was a need for specific items to vest the holy table and, subsequently, substantial modifications took place in church decoration. The architect Edward Schroeder Prior estimated that half the money spent on churches in the second half of the nineteenth century went on decoration and ornament. This rapid development became the focus of an important debate for those concerned about the most appropriate ways in which to furnish a church interior.

Beauty and the Sacred Were One

As Gothic Revivalism flourished it stimulated a greater demand for elaborate textiles. They were significant because they were as much an expression of belief as any other aspect of a church interior. As Morris noted, textiles produced for these magnificent buildings reinforced the unity of the arts, as they used the same images for the same ends, the bond between history and decoration being so strong. They followed a long tradition, contributing a vital reinforcing element to rituals and the centrality of the altar. Buildings were enhanced by their finely worked details, often the product of the relationship between the architect and a collaborative team of workers from the region. Some textiles played an essential functional and ritualistic role when worn or used by the priest at the Communion table and were subsequently the focus of his activities and the congregation's gaze. As they were part of a coherent reiteration of specific imagery in the service, design and symbolism were at the heart of an architect's concepts for such compositions. Appropriately, all embroidered items were worked in rich, symbolic colours that changed according to the liturgical calendar. The opulent, reflecting textures of silk and gold clearly signalled rank and power. Beauty and the sacred were mutually reinforcing.

In May 1845 *The Ecclesiologist* carried a detailed and influential article titled 'Church Needlework and Altar Hangings'.[13] It began with a quotation from 'English Medieval Embroidery', an illustrated piece published in the *Archaeological Journal*, in which the depth of scholarship attached to this subject was made clear. The article in *The Ecclesiologist* gave considerable consideration to the proper hangings for an altar, revealing the relationship between the clergy and the textiles they used during a service. There were rigid rules governing almost every aspect of these textiles, including the selection of specific colours and the arrangement of vestments. An understanding of historic examples was considered necessary for anyone undertaking church needlework, although it was not easy to find appropriate patterns for large altar cloths as so few ancient pieces remained. The author focused on a study of ancient needlework specimens with a view to reviving this aspect of church decoration; the most common technique suggested for silk thread embroidery was 'long and short' stitch, which was versatile and useful for forms, draperies and flowers. Even advice on current types of cloth suitable for a church was given. The ground cloths for altar frontals were to be of silk velvet or cloth of gold embellished with needlework. The author acknowledged the difficulty of working with complex textured materials and suggested that embroidery should be worked on another cloth first, such as stout linen of pure flax, before being applied to the costly ground cloth. Descriptions of appropriate threads followed, with detailed instructions for using each thread type; the pros and cons of floss silk compared with twisted silk yarn were discussed at length. Jewels and spangles were valuable additions that increased the richness of effect. Needle types were given a separate section. Suppliers were listed, and Pearsall & Co. was recommended as the best supplier of silk threads.

Commissions for ecclesiastical needlework typically consisted of sets of items intended for use on and around the altar. All items carried multilayered meanings. Following the divisions of the church calendar, each set was produced in one of four liturgical colours: green, red, purple (or blue) and white (or gold). Embroidered items could include sizeable altar frontals, typically measuring between 1.8 and

2.7m (six and nine feet) wide and between 0.9 and 1.2m (three and four feet) high, with matching superfrontals, litany desk falls, pulpit falls, chalice veils and burses, all of which required costly silks and embroidery. Occasionally alms bags, bible markers, stoles and banners were provided. Embroidered bands, or orphreys, were shaped into borders, or a 'Y' or cruciform shape, and applied to chasubles and copes. Invariably the design and stitching of smaller pieces was more delicate than the work for the dramatic frontals as the former were not usually seen by the congregation. Demand grew for coverings for the altar, particularly for those that effectively used colour to create emotive power. The article's author observed that all the examples of nineteenth-century embroidery studied seem to have been stitched by more than one person, larger compositions generally being worked in many separate parts that were then assembled. It was thought obvious to all involved that the stitched flesh work necessary for figurative designs needed the greatest skill, whereas flowers, especially those used for powdering across a sizeable surface, were comparatively easy and recommended for beginners. Some indication that the creation of fitting designs for frontals was not easy was demonstrated by Pugin's apparent difficulty with this task, despite his leading a revival of better standards in church ornamentation.

Historical methods of hanging an altar cloth were also studied. This research indicated that a superfrontal from 15 to 20cm (six to eight inches) deep should overhang the main cloth. It could be plain or powdered with flowers, or embroidered with a flowing pattern, or even charged with a legend (lettering), and it must be fringed, usually in the same manner as its frontal. Silk fringing was preferred to gold, and should be of two bright colours alternating; if more colours were included, they were to adhere to a specific order. There followed a list of approved colours for fringes, which varied according to canonical rules.

The frontal itself could be of one colour or type of cloth, or divided into three compartments, the middle one being the largest if they were of unequal sizes. Only the middle section needed to be of the appointed liturgical colour; side panels could vary. The centre could contain a sacred monogram or cross. Vertical lines dividing sections could incorporate any amount of ornamental embroidery. The variations were thought to offer an endless variety of design possibilities, from the very simple to the highly elaborate. Ambitious figures and complicated emblems were to be avoided by all but the most competent. Good examples were to be found in *Instrumenta Ecclesiastica*, with its series of engravings, including a number by Street.[14]

The status of church furnishings was so high by the time of the Great Exhibition of 1851 that a special section was devoted to them. The only award – a gold medal – was given to the firm of Jones & Willis for its display of church decoration. Street's designs for ecclesiastical embroideries were included in this award. At the International Exhibition of 1862 the only medal for church furniture was again presented to that company, for which Street created many designs. They could be found in trade catalogues,[15] which extended to over 500 items, with every form of textile for every type of ecclesiastical interior. As well as supplying completed frontals and other embroidered items, the firm prepared designs and cloth for those who wanted to stitch their own. For women who could produce fine embroidery there were growing opportunities to make beautiful work for significant buildings. The 1862 exhibition was a noteworthy event for Morris, Marshall, Faulkner & Co., as the firm displayed an altar frontal designed by Morris. This is still in St Martin-on-the-Hill, Scarborough, designed by George Frederick Bodley. Like Street's winning design, it too was of red silk velvet. The design by Morris was more informal, with alternating pomegranate and floral motifs powdered across the surface. There is some affinity with Street's first frontal, designed for his church in north Staffordshire.

Businesses in a variety of forms sprang up to cope with the great demand for church furnishings. Specialised warehouses provided designs along with a supply of cloth, braids, fringes and other trimmings. The aptly named Vicars and Poirson Ltd, a firm based in Newgate Street, London, prepared designs for church embroidery 'for ladies own working'. There was, therefore, much activity coming from many different quarters when Elizabeth Wardle first tried her hand at church needlework.

Manuals of Stitch

Agnes Blencowe was an influential woman who, along with Street's sister, Mary Ann Street, founded the Ladies Ecclesiastical Embroidery Society in 1854. Blencowe designed embroidery and published on the subject. She ran the convent's embroidery workroom at St Mary the Virgin, Wantage, from 1866, which quickly became known for the fine quality of its work. Numerous sisterhoods were formed in the 1870s and many produced ecclesiastical embroidery. St Margaret's East Grinstead and the Sisters of Bethany (Islington), both established in 1876, became famous for their gold work. Others included the Church Extension Association, the Decorative Needlework Society and the School of Medieval Embroidery. Queen Victoria's embroiderer, Anastasia Dolby, became so interested in these developments that she published her *Church Embroidery Ancient and Modern* in 1867, with clear line drawings and technical instructions for needlewomen. A number of authors followed her and their books and journal articles guided both beginners and the experienced with diagrams and detailed explanations of techniques.

Some authors had wide experience and were willing to inform readers on more than stitching techniques. Letitia Higgin, among others, believed that architects 'were the most successful in producing designs capable of effective treatment with the needle, without carrying elaboration too far to be practical'.[16] She had no doubt that this arose from their practice of 'designing ornament for stone or metal-work, which required the same breadth and simplicity of treatment as decorative needlework; and also from the practice they acquire of obtaining just proportion between construction and decoration'. Embroidered ornament, moreover, often used the same motifs. Higgin was a needlewoman herself so understood exactly what was needed; she had the credentials to offer her opinion and did not hesitate to do so. In one article, 'The Revival of Decorative Needlework', she considered that 'Designers for needlework have much to learn before they are able to produce something which shall be capable of being worked so as to produce a good effect without costing an enormous amount of labour, and therefore, money.'[17] It was thought necessary that the function of each piece should always be understood by the designer, who should adapt drawings for the needle accordingly. Higgin firmly stated that in all cases when a drawing is transferred to the fabric it should be checked by the designer and 'worked under his direction and only by an embroideress who is a perfect mistress of her art'. Whether this was ever practical in the case of the Leek needlewomen is not known, as the architects concerned were all based in London. Possibly Leek embroiderers gained a degree of liberty and creative freedom to complete their work?

Architects and Embroidery in North Staffordshire

Many exceptional embroideries made for north Staffordshire churches in the mid-nineteenth century have survived in remarkable buildings. Their history overflows with personalities, including those of some of Britain's greatest architects, who made significant contributions to the region. Pugin, George Gilbert Scott Jnr, Street and Bodley received important commissions to work in the county. Each had their own notion of Gothic Revival architecture and understood the expressive power of decorative forms and each provided inspirational models to live up to. The distinctive results were the precedent for numerous outstanding embroideries made in the final third of the century under Elizabeth Wardle's direction.

Augustus Welby Northmore Pugin

Pugin's parish church of St Giles in Cheadle opened to great national acclaim in 1846. The *Illustrated London News* described it thus: 'Probably so perfect a church was never erected in England before.'[18] In this building we can see clearly that Pugin understands how colour and pattern works in practice. He produced designs for needlework from the 1830s and published *On the Present State of Ecclesiastical Embroidery* (1843) and *Glossary of Ecclesiastical Ornament* (1844), which influenced a generation of architects and designers.[19] He was, moreover, instrumental in reinstating the wearing of vestments. A number of his designs survive.

George Edmund Street

Just a few kilometres from Cheadle can be found Street's embroidered altar frontal and sedilia hanging, designed for the church of St John at Hollington. Stitched by Miss Hutchinson of Checkley, Staffordshire, between 1859 and 1861, they are the earliest known examples of Street's ecclesiastical textiles and are still in use in this lovely rural church. In these pieces we can see how his well-thought-through, historically conscious principles worked in practice.[20] Street, as well as being a High Church Anglican and a dynamic member of the Ecclesiologist Society, was a prolific designer of fixtures and fittings and understood that different types of traditional, collaborative craftsmanship in metal, wood, textiles and glass were essential for the coherent interior of a major building. This was a guiding principal for Street, who was seriously interested in the role of needlework in churches and in needlework practice. Many of his designs for churches were stitched by the Ladies Ecclesiastical Embroidery Society.

Coinciding with the building of Hollington church was Street's major scheme for nearby Denstone in 1860–2. This comprised a school, a vicarage and All Saints church. John Betjeman described it as 'the architect's favourite church of his own design'.[21] Street planned a number of internal fixtures, including four altar frontals, which employed the skills of exceptional craftsmen. The embroideries have been remounted onto modern cloth and are still in use in this magnificent setting. Street's designs were circulated in *The Ecclesiologist* and consequently lived on for some time. One example of their longevity can be seen in the parish church of St Edward the Confessor, Cheddleton, Staffordshire, where there is a frontal by Street of green silk damask with appliquéd motifs forming a chequerboard pattern. The design was produced around 1865, originally for the chapel of St Margaret's Convent, East Grinstead. This version of the frontal was purchased from the Devon House of Mercy in 1943, an occasion that produced a revealing piece about the embroidery in *The Leek Deanery Magazine*. The frontal was described as cheaper to buy as it was second-hand and was, therefore, a great saving in the war years. It was altered to fit the Cheddleton altar by Clara Bill, formerly of the Leek Embroidery Society, whose husband made a frame for it. A frontal to this design, but of different colouring, is displayed in the Lady Hoare Gallery, at Liverpool cathedral.

George Frederick Bodley

Bodley was the first pupil of George Gilbert Scott Snr and trained with him for five years. Later he rejected Scott's interpretation of Gothic and was instead more influenced by the works of Street and William Butterfield, and intellectually by Ruskin. But, as Andrew Saint recognises, there were overlaps rather than a clear-cut demarcation between one (Gothic) style and another.[22] When Bodley, with his architect partner Thomas Garner, was commissioned to design the lavish and magnificent Holy Angels at Hoar Cross, Staffordshire, in 1871, he was at the peak of his career. Michael Fisher acknowledges that 'there is no finer example of his work anywhere in England'.[23] Michael Hall, Bodley's most recent biographer, states that 'his conception of every element of a building as part of an integrated design places him at the centre of the Aesthetic Movement'.[24] Bodley, a talented designer of patterns, was intent on designing furnishings for his buildings. He made a study of textiles in fifteenth- and sixteenth-century paintings and recorded these in his 'diaper book'.[25] This detailed catalogue was used by Watts & Co., the company he formed with George Gilbert Scott Jnr, who became a close friend, and Garner. Bodley's reputation as a flat-pattern designer was such that he was one of only three experts in needlework design invited to form an advisory Art Committee at the Royal School of Art Needlework (RSAN) in 1875. As Lynn Hulse explains, they 'would convene once a month to oversee the artistic direction of the School'.[26] The RSAN's displays of needlework at the first World Fair of 1876 in Philadelphia included a red velvet pilaster designed by Bodley.[27]

Watts & Co. produced Bodley's design 'Bird' as a silk damask, which was often used by the Leek Embroidery Society. The design, taken from a medieval original, survives in a pattern book in the Watts & Co. archive.[28] 'Bird' was originally hand-woven in Sudbury, Suffolk, by the English Silk Weaving Company, a small firm that lasted only ten years. Still in production, and renamed 'Hilliard', it is now woven by the Gainsborough Weaving Company in Sudbury and is available from Watts & Co., which continues to be renowned as the leading ecclesiastical and artistic furnishers. 'Sarum', also a silk damask, was designed by Bodley in 1870. This was based on a textile painted on the figure of St Andrew, depicted on the noted Ranworth church rood screen in Norfolk.

Company records show that Thomas Wardle ordered at least nine different silk damasks from the Sudbury company.[29] Orders from Leek were typically for thirty yards (approximately 27m) at a time.[30] They were frequently selected by the Leek Embroidery Society for ecclesiastical projects. Why Wardle used silk weavers in East Anglia rather than those from Leek or even nearby Macclesfield is not known. Damasks, woven in a single colour with subtle contrasts of light and shade, had understated changeable surfaces that provided a suitably rich, yet subtle, background for silk embroidery. The rhythm of repeated woven motifs, which were often symbolic, added to the emblematic nature of the embroidered piece.

The growth of ecclesiastical embroidery had an obvious continuity with the development of craft revival, as reflected in the Arts and Crafts movement. Although entirely secular in its aims, the movement added another dimension to church building during the Gothic Revival phase. It was ethically driven, contemplative and idealistic with a strong work ethos, and questioned many modern developments, particularly where industry was concerned. Followers successfully promoted craftsmanship as a dynamic, collaborative force that had an important role in contemporary life, which attracted important architects, artists and craftspeople. While ecclesiastical work was independent of fashionable taste there were crossovers, as certain motifs, such as traditional Indian designs, sunflowers, pomegranates, lilies, marigolds and peacocks, had relevance to Gothic Revivalists, Aestheticism and the Arts and Crafts movement alike. There was, similarly, a constant cross-pollination between designs for fashion, domestic and ecclesiastical pieces, as so many designers looked to historical or Eastern examples for inspiration.[31]

Leek Embroidery and the Gothic Revival

By commissioning a relatively young group of distinctive architects the people of Leek were clearly willing to give rising stars a chance. Their buildings reflected the town's great sense of civic pride and the wealth that came from the local silk industry. These young, ambitious and creative people, who designed emblematic embroideries for their churches, were linked to each other through numerous networks. While their influential buildings are well documented by eminent authors, the textiles they designed for them are hardly known. Yet, arguably, they were an important part of the architect's aim to create the correct spiritual dimension for their schemes. It is this that is explored below: in this chapter these textiles are documented and revealed as varied and enriching. Elizabeth Wardle collaborated with this diverse group of distinguished men, each with a dramatically different approach to design. They needed very skilled needlewomen, such as her, to understand their vision and translate their working drawings into embroidery suitable for their elaborate interiors. Elizabeth was often acknowledged in the Staffordshire press as an exceptional needlewoman and organiser of others' work. As she became more widely recognised word spread beyond the local newspapers via a series of articles in national journals in which her skills were praised.

Embroiderers needed to be versatile in order to adapt their expertise to meet an architect's demands. We know that these collaborations succeeded on all counts, as the richly coloured and textured outcomes can still be seen in many public buildings. Although the compositions differed greatly, a study of the finished pieces reveals a number of features that mark Leek embroidery out as distinctive. Typical of this work is an intense, yet muted, colour palette, which complements the strong designs of most surviving frontals and related pieces. Other design elements found in frontals made in Leek were ornamental borders, with flowing, undulating motifs with an obvious rhythm. They were invariably stitched over an underlying block-printed pattern, which had the effect of guiding the stitching and producing regularity. Motifs were usually naturalistic, so were far removed from Pugin's more geometrical forms.

From Paper to Stitch

As far as we can tell most architects were detached from the process of creating the embroideries they designed. Apart from Streets' schemes, scarcely any original designs on paper survive, so it is difficult to know what was typical regarding directives from the architect to the embroiderers. Fortunately a number of important designs by Horsley were recently found in Staffordshire. They were in private hands, probably as a result of a particular aspect of Leek's embroidery history. As stitching often took place in women's homes, some working drawings may have remained in a domestic environment rather than a professional office or public collection. This newly discovered hoard is a unique set of connected items created by Horsley and Mrs Beatrice Ethel Warren, the Leek needlewoman who frequently stitched his designs for Staffordshire churches. Few, if any, records of this type exist, so these, which trace the various stages of production from start to finish, are of great historical importance.[32] Other drawings by Horsley are in the RIBA archives in London. The mass of paperwork generated by him and Warren indicates just what has been lost, as presumably other architects and needlewomen would have produced a similar volume of documentation for each frontal or hanging.

Most architects would initially have produced a scaled cartoon. If approved, that would be followed by full-sized drawings from which tracings could be taken by the embroiderer. Measured drawings of each motif might be made and all materials, including the expensive ground cloth, threads in their various colours, beads, spangles, edging cords, braids, fringes, linings and interlinings, then calculated accordingly. The expense of such extravagant materials needed to be factored in at an early stage. To date no reference to the architect's fee for his designs has been discovered.

Some surviving drawings by George Gilbert Scott Jnr have instructions regarding materials, colouring and technique. Research for this book has linked them to embroideries made by Elizabeth Wardle and other local needlewomen for specific Staffordshire churches, where the pieces remain today. Although drawings and designs on paper by Sedding and George Young Wardle survive in London archives, they do not include guidelines for needlewomen. Even though the Royal Academy of Arts, London, has detailed working drawings for other fixtures and fittings by Shaw no designs for embroidery by him have been found. If architects and designers were removed from the act of making they conceivably gave others the opportunity to interpret their work. It could be that some architects were unaware of the different outcomes that were available with needle and thread, or perhaps they just preferred to leave the choices to needlewomen, who had greater knowledge of the visual effects that were possible. The selection of a colour and texture of a rich ground cloth and the types of thread, surface and contrast that needed to be considered to fully realise the potential of a design on paper required experience. Decisions about these important elements may have been left to some individual needlewomen or at least to the person with overall responsibility for a workroom and the 'arrangement' of the composition. Elizabeth Wardle was acknowledged as having the ability to interpret a design, while many other Leek embroiderers would have been variously skilled.

Many embroiderers of ecclesiastical pieces were parishioners who worked on items for their own church. This is hardly surprising, as most people then were churchgoers and as women often formed the major part of congregations they were frequently involved in associated charity work. In this respect Elizabeth Wardle was typical, although not every needlewoman would have been capable of the same high standards. Her first known piece of ecclesiastical work reveals that she had remarkable expertise. This commission allowed her to use her fine skills to play an important part in the venue at the heart of her cultural life: her parish church. The degree to which most Leek needlewomen could freely explore different aesthetic outcomes is not, however, known.

A New Era

Elizabeth and Thomas Wardle would almost certainly have been aware of earlier outstanding embroideries in north Staffordshire churches. When newly married they lived at Leek Brook, close to the dye works where Thomas worked with his father.[33] Cheadle was about 13km (eight miles) away, Denstone and Hollington about 22km (fourteen miles). As both were closely involved with local church activities it is highly likely that they would have visited these impressive Staffordshire churches and viewed their contents. Thomas Wardle was organist, choirmaster and churchwarden for the medieval church of St Edward the Confessor at nearby Cheddleton and both he and Elizabeth taught at the Sunday School. That was during the period 1863–64, when George Gilbert Scott Jnr, working with local architect Robert Edgar, was modifying the church. Other projects there by Scott were in progress up to 1877.[34]

Cheddleton was one of the first independent restorations undertaken by Scott Jnr, although his father had surveyed the building. This seems to be typical as, even though he started his own practice in 1863, many of his early commissions came via his famous father.[35] He was described by some as the most brilliant of the Scott architectural dynasty and his contemporaries Sedding and Shaw regarded him as crucial in the debates surrounding Gothic Revival building. In 1891 Shaw said of him that 'many of us consider him to be our greatest architect'.[36] He was searching for beauty when he reinterpreted historical forms in his buildings and was known for careful restorations.

Elizabeth and Thomas Wardle would have understood perfectly what Scott and his contemporaries were striving for. They were searching for the same thing but in different ways. As Scott was reacting against his father's choice of architectural styles, Thomas Wardle was reacting to the intense industrialisation that was rapidly dispensing with craft skills. As a master craftsman Wardle was also in pursuit of beauty in everyday things when he returned to traditional dyeing methods. He promoted the use of meaningful designs, those that had a timeless quality stemming from a complete understanding of form and colour unaffected by fashionable taste. Many from other cultures were, furthermore, imbued with complex symbolism.

The collective forces required to create and furnish a church were numerous and they needed to be overseen by someone sensitive to the overall aims of the architect and the diocese. Thomas Wardle took responsibility for vital decisions quite early on in what was a complex collaborative scheme at Cheddleton. He was a devout Anglican who, as churchwarden, had formal duties and a decision-making role. He orchestrated the combined talents of architect and craftsmen in various media, including those working for Morris & Co. Both Elizabeth and Thomas Wardle had a strong sense of how things were made and made well. They were disciplined, precise and knew how essential it was for craftspeople to understand the nature of the materials with which they worked. As he was used to communicating with other craftsmen on a daily basis he knew about the need for necessary compromises and the potential for risks this involved. He became very involved with Scott's project for Cheddleton church, declaring it a 'conscientious partial restoration'.[37] There was, however, another dimension to his contribution. Wardle was an experienced geologist who was driven to look more closely at his environment and record it in detail. As a young man he made a major geological study of the region in which he grew up and which shaped his life. His brother-in-law, George Young Wardle, provided sheets of fossil illustrations when the research was published in 1862.

Clearly Thomas Wardle's Christian beliefs were not compromised by his scientific investigations, which contributed to the increasing knowledge of how the earth was understood. This research gave him currency in the growing field of geology, a useful attribute to have when extensive restoration programmes on historic stone buildings were underway. Ruskin likewise shared this interest in geology. Gavin Stamp argued that the crisis affecting English architecture prior to this was deepened by 'geological discoveries and scientific developments and by the materialist and determinist implications of Darwin's conclusions about natural selection'.[38] George Gilbert Scott Jnr gained a Fellowship of Jesus College, Cambridge, for a learned essay that addressed the challenges to Christianity brought about by science. He concluded that 'Science and Theology are aiming at the same point. The unity which the one vaguely suggests is clearly presented by the other.'[39] It would seem that, to Scott, both science and religion helped to explain the world. It is difficult not to speculate about whether Wardle and Scott ever debated these matters as they collaborated on the numerous alterations of Cheddleton church.

Scott, Wardle and Morris collaborated on replacement stone sculptures for the ancient standing cross in Cheddleton graveyard, with Morris providing the drawings. Wardle, who funded this restoration, was concerned that the correct stone should be used. He drew on his expertise to locate the quarries from which the Millstone Grit was cut for the original preaching cross and the matching stone was then carved in London. The cross was raised from its sunken position, where it had lain partially buried for some time. Wardle also fought to keep an original pillar from the medieval church against local opposition. He sought the backing of the architect and archdeacon to get his way, which indicates his level of commitment. To his lasting regret stonemasons chose an easier, softer stone to work with for the building's main refurbishment. He made his thoughts clear thus:

> How sad it seems that while we possess such abundant stores of splendid building stone – stone which the ancient church builders of the south and south-west counties would have been delighted to meet with, in place of the oolitic sandstones and limestones, some of which are cut up by handsaws – people should be running miles away to fetch soft and easy cutting stone for works intended to last for centuries – stone that is neither suited to the humid climate nor possessing that durability for which Millstone Grit is noted.[40]

Later Wardle funded the restoration of Norman crosses in St Edward's churchyard, Leek, after having brought in an expert from Cambridge to examine them. We can see from their actions at Cheddleton early examples of what was to become for the Wardles a constant mind-set. They were people of strong convictions and set high standards in church restoration and ornamentation, subjects that were to be highly contentious for some. This became an unceasing search to understand the nature of things they encountered on a daily basis, which gives us some idea of their characters.

Scott, Morris and the Wardles

Scott produced a number of needlework designs for the church at Cheddleton and we can still view what are thought to be Elizabeth Wardle's first ecclesiastical embroideries there. By 1864 she already had refined craft skills and her work was clearly accepted by an architectural practice of considerable merit. By then she was also the mother of four small sons, having lost three babies in infancy, but she nevertheless found the time and energy to produce acclaimed needlework. The *Leek Post & Times* celebrated the work 'which was executed by the ladies of the neighbourhood', stating that 'never before have we seen such needlework in this part of the world'.[41] Alms bags produced by her remain in the church today, along with three sedilia cushions stitched by Thomas's sister, Phoebe Wardle. Elizabeth's stitching on the alms bags follows the underlying pattern woven into cream silk damask. Both designs were worked in coloured silks and couched gold thread.[42] The cushions are of felted wool cloth similar to that used for the sedilia hanging at Street's first church at Hollington. The artichoke pattern for the cushions, stitched in silk and metal thread on an olive-green ground, had historical precedents.[43] It was also a motif regularly used by Morris and the design closely follows the curve of the carved stone seats.

During research for this book another embroidery in the church, a silk panel finely stitched in shaded silks, was identified as designed by Scott. Although we do not know who embroidered it, we do know that it is identical to a design Scott made for two chancel carpets elsewhere in the region. It was also adapted later for a table centrepiece created by the Leek Embroidery Society around 1914 and stitched in vibrant colours. Clearly Scott's design was flexible enough to be worked in a variety of techniques and materials for over fifty years. Scott worked on Cheddleton church sporadically for more than ten years, contracting Morris, Marshall, Faulkner & Co., founded in 1861, to provide stained glass and other items for the building. Along with Bodley he was one of the first architects to subcontract aspects of restoration projects to Morris's firm at a crucial early stage in its development. The firm, re-formed as Morris & Co. in 1875, produced decorative fixtures for ecclesiastic and domestic interiors. The mainstay of the young company was the production of stained glass, in which it excelled. Over time magnificent windows designed by Morris and Ford Maddox Brown, and a stunning three-light design of red-winged angels by Burne-Jones, were installed at Cheddleton by Morris & Co. Thomas Wardle commemorated his beloved sister Phoebe, who died in 1890, with a new window by the firm.

Scott also collaborated closely with Morris on a rare fifteenth-century Flemish relief sculpture, *The Lamentation of Christ*, a gift to Cheddleton church in 1866. He designed an oak casing with two side pieces for the sculpture, thereby turning it into a triptych with folding wings. Measured drawings for this, along with those for a 'Bishop's Chair', are in Scott's notebook No. 5, dated 9 September 1874.[44] Morris provided drawings of scenes from the Annunciation for the wings, which were painted by Charles Napier Hemy.[45] As Gavin Stamp reveals, it provided an exceptional opportunity 'to be able to design an altarpiece which fulfilled his ideals by incorporating a genuine piece of Medieval art'.[46] Scott, in a letter to the churchwarden – presumably Thomas Wardle – declared 'you are quite before the age in possessing such a work, as I do not know of any other church in England where such a thing is to be seen'. In the process of preparing the sculpture for its wooden frame the original medieval carving was restored and garments worn by the figures were painted over with elaborate patterns emulating complex Italian silks. Martin Harrison states that one pattern can be traced to George Young Wardle's sketches.[47] In all probability most of the painted patterns, along with the decoration on the pediment of the frame, originated from George Young Wardle's drawings of East Anglian rood screens. He filled many sketchbooks with similar details of painted screens and various ornamental features from Norfolk and Suffolk churches, which were used by Morris's firm in a number of ways. Elaborate painted textiles were prominent features of the ancient screens and he copied a lot of them. His depictions of angels from the renowned rood screen at Barton Turf appear in stitched form in four locations in north Staffordshire. Two versions, which were worked by the Leek Embroidery Society, directed by his sister Elizabeth, are discussed later (Colour Plate 5), and a further two were incorporated into altar frontals worked by the Society for Shaw's All Saints and Ipstones, discussed below.[48]

George Young Wardle initially worked for Morris & Co. as book-keeper and draughtsman before becoming manager of the firm. Among other things, such as managing the Merton Abbey site, he is thought to have produced working drawings for a prestigious embroidery commission, the 'Romance of the Rose', a large detailed frieze.[49] This was a period when Morris was closely involved with his clients, as described by George Young Wardle in his *Memorials of William Morris* (1897). Although there is no evidence to confirm this, it is highly likely that when Thomas Wardle and Morris first met it was to discuss their shared interests in the Cheddleton church. It is possible that it was George

Young Wardle who introduced them to each other, most probably in London, as Morris was based there and Thomas Wardle travelled regularly to the capital on business. Certainly Thomas Wardle had strong links with, similar aims to and an appreciation of Morris & Co. at a critical early point in its expansion.

The Cheddleton project took place during what was clearly a formative period for this enterprising and creative group of people, all of whom were passionately attached to their principles and visions. Like Morris, both Elizabeth and Thomas Wardle worked well with Gothic Revival architects, providing fabrics that fed into the craft-based ethos promoted by Ruskin and his followers. They combined Anglicanism with craft skills, an ethical business ethos, in-depth research and a willingness to collaborate. Scott, in addition, produced numerous designs for Morris's firm and was familiar with its shop in Red Lion Square. This was before he started his own furnishing firm of Watts & Co. in 1874, at which point he and Morris became business rivals. Ultimately, Wardle & Co. supplied dyed and printed textiles to both Morris & Co. and Watts & Co. even though the customers were in competition. Elizabeth Wardle also supplied Watts & Co. with stitched items.[50]

This gathering of like minds at Cheddleton must have been energising for all concerned. Elizabeth Wardle and Morris were then 31, Thomas Wardle was 35, George Young Wardle was in his late 20s and Scott was only 27. Thereafter their lives continued to intersect in exciting ways as they become major players in their different fields. All three Wardles became increasingly involved with renowned architects, designers and artists, in the process making a significant contribution to Gothic Revivalism, the Arts and Crafts movement and Art Needlework. The links between them and Morris, Scott and Bodley remained in a variety of configurations as they developed as acknowledged experts. Thomas Wardle's learned understanding of stained glass probably stemmed from this period.

Ultimately, Morris became a passionate critic of church restoration to the extent that he helped form the Society for the Protection of Ancient Buildings (SPAB) in 1877. Both George Young and Thomas Wardle were founder members of this influential group. SPAB evolved during the period when Morris was periodically visiting the Wardles' home in Leek during their intense collaboration to produce an outstanding series of hand-printed textiles. At this time Thomas Wardle was questioning the poor results of industrial dyeing methods and was reviving traditional dye recipes, which had all but disappeared from his father's dye works. This became a sophisticated enquiry using measurable data to make sense of the materials with which he worked, and led to global recognition and a number of innovations.[51] It also gave rise to his involvement with a network of entrepreneurial people across Europe that proved vital to the later success of the Leek Embroidery Society. Wardle was clearly a highly intelligent, observant, focused man, with boundless energy. Was it he who suggested Scott should undertake the church restoration at Cheddleton? The project at Cheddleton was certainly an interesting early indicator of Elizabeth and Thomas Wardle's approach to church decoration – the beginning of what was to become a pivotal and lifelong passion. Here was evidence of a great commitment to getting things right, a fitness for purpose, an understanding of materials, attention to detail, with a sympathetic use of historical precedents.

Some years later, in July 1892, *Cheddleton Parish Magazine* stated that two very handsome altar cloths were given as gifts in memory of Phoebe Wardle. Both were designed by the architect Gerald Horsley specifically for Cheddleton church. Horsley, a pupil of Shaw, visited the church to ensure that the frontals harmonised with their surroundings. The commissions for the two memorial frontals came only a few years after Horsley had produced a series of wall paintings for Shaw's masterpiece, All Saints, Leek, about 6km (four miles) away. The paintings include many figures and scrolls with text. All of Horsley's designs for needlework for the region thereafter contain these features. His interesting series of designs for his own church at Longsdon, Staffordshire, just a few kilometres from Cheddleton, incorporate the same strong elements. Phoebe Wardle was a devoted member of the Cheddleton congregation, a Sunday School teacher, an unpaid organist and teacher of the church choir. She was described as a loving and self-sacrificing member of the church who led a quiet life with a willingness to serve. She was also an accomplished needlewoman, as Horsley's designs clearly reflect. He produced cartoons for two frontals: a white and a green one. The latter, given by Elizabeth Wardle, has not been traced. Velvet hangings for the pulpit and stool, produced to match the green frontal, were also given by her. They do survive and may indicate the materials and design of the missing frontal. A white antependium for the Faldt Stool was worked by another Miss Wardle to match the white memorial frontal and given to the church at Easter 1894. The white frontal was given by Thomas Wardle's surviving sister, Ann Wardle. Both were produced by the Leek Embroidery Society, although the three Marys on the white frontal – Mary of Bethany, Mary the Virgin and Mary Magdalene – were stitched by St Margaret's Convent workshop, East Grinstead. This was managed by Isabella Sedding, sister of John Dando Sedding. The Society of St Margaret had a branch in Queen Square, London, very close to Morris's firm. The Wardles knew Sedding as a sensitive architect who had worked in Leek. Elizabeth Wardle created some of her earliest ecclesiastical embroidery to his designs, including the pelican frontal for St Luke's church. The Seddings almost certainly would have known of Phoebe's reputation as an embroiderer of note.

Working drawings for embroidery are often incomplete. They may lay out the overall composition and contain some detail and annotations, but they are an interim stage that requires the skilful hands of needlewomen to make them come alive with texture and colour. We do not know if any face-to-face dialogue about the three Marys frontal took place between Horsley and the two embroidery workshops, but comparisons made between the concept on paper and the finished work reveal that changes took place. The boundless possibilities related to the colour palette and textures needed to be managed and agreement over these elements must have been reached between both workshops. Doubtless the whole project was well planned, so that materials and timing were all optimised without losing the integrity of the architect's concept. Elizabeth Wardle, who directed the Leek Embroidery Society's input, must have discussed the frontal with her counterpart at St Margaret's, East Grinstead, to ensure that different component parts were harmonious when assembled. That it is uniform throughout suggests that one person directed the colouring of the overall scheme. But who was it?

Although now too fragile to use, the white frontal still hangs in the church at Cheddleton, mounted behind glass so it can be seen on a daily basis. The church continued to acquire splendid embroideries, including a superb violet velvet frontal with a superfrontal depicting passion flowers funded by Mrs Elizabeth Wardle. This is depicted in Colour Plate 6 and we can still see that it was beautifully stitched by Elizabeth Wardle and her daughters. Mrs George Wardle, wife of Thomas's brother, gave the hangings for the pulpit and litany stool, which were stitched by her eldest daughter, Eleanor. A Miss Wardle gave hangings for the reredos and sedilia. All of the pieces were designed to coordinate with the altar cloth and had the same 'richly worked flowers on them'.[52] The silk velvet was dyed its intense purple colour at Wardle's dye works. The velvet probably came from Lister's Mill in Manningham, Leeds, which was once the largest silk mill in Europe. Samuel Cunliffe Lister had his own mulberry plantations in India, from which he sourced the raw silk for his velvet production. The embroideries are a wonderful tribute to a remarkable couple, Thomas and Elizabeth Wardle, who chose this significant church at Cheddleton as the place to be buried.

Scott designed other textiles including 'Compton', which was produced as a stamped velvet in 1878. It had a clear historical precedent in numerous voided velvets produced in the Italian city states of Lucca and Venice in the fifteenth century. It was used in a deep rich crimson for four panels of an altar frontal for Cheddleton church, and again for a red frontal and superfrontal designed by Robert Edgar, a friend of Scott, for Compton School chapel, which were stitched over with coloured silk thread by Leek embroiderers. The frontal is now in Shaw's All Saints, Compton, Leek, which replaced the school chapel. This version bears a considerable resemblance to an example of embroidered silk velvet illustrated in *Merchants, Princes and Painters* (2008) by Lisa Monnas.[53]

St Leonard's Church, Ipstones, Staffordshire

After Cheddleton George Gilbert Scott Jnr was commissioned to do other work in the area. Between 1875 and 1877 he created a sanctuary and restored St Leonard's church, Ipstones, in north Staffordshire. Elizabeth Wardle stitched more of his designs for that church and the artwork of her brother George Young Wardle featured again. In this church alone we can see Scott's great versatility as a designer of embroidery, as all three frontals for his scheme are distinctly different. The needlework for St Leonard's resulted in an 'altar richly furnished with work executed by ladies of the neighbourhood'.[54] This work was displayed in the Exhibition of Modern Embroidery held in Leek in 1881. The catalogue names the needlewomen involved, thereby publicly acknowledging their skills. One frontal was stitched by Miss H. Beardmore, a frontal and two superfrontals were worked by Phoebe Wardle, while Elizabeth Wardle arranged and worked a superfrontal and frontal, assisted 'by several Leek ladies'. All items have now been identified and, remarkably, all are still in use. The sanctuary carpet, also designed by Scott and displayed at the 1881 exhibition, was stitched by fifteen local women.

One design, dated 1877, consists of stylised floral motifs placed within an ogival framework. The composition indicates that it was planned as a repeat pattern. It is illustrated in Gavin Stamp's *An Architect of Promise* (2002), where is it stated that it was originally for a dossal for the church of Ampney St Peter, Newport Pagnell.[55] The pattern appears to be based on complex cut-velvets from Renaissance Italy, which feature in paintings by Carlo Crivelli and other artists.[56] Colour Plate 7a illustrates a detail of the complex white silk velvet ground, which is inlaid with gold silk damask. The whole is overstitched with white, gold and contrasting blue silk thread, and an intermittent light touch of couched gold thread and groups of tiny spangles. Like Bodley, Scott researched ecclesiastical fabrics in the South Kensington Museum, as well as textiles depicted in paintings by Jan van Eyck, Hans Memling and Hans Holbein. This were not unusual; historic textiles were often a source of inspiration for nineteenth-century designers, and late fourteenth- and early fifteenth-century Italian silks were particularly admired all over Europe. The quality of the silks and dyestuffs was superb and a great many featured in manuscripts, carvings and paintings. Italian and Flemish painters portrayed huge varieties of Italian voided velvets and brocaded silks. The work of Crivelli, which is crammed with lavish cloths, was much admired by Thomas Wardle, who made a study of his and Giovanni Bellini's work in the National Gallery, London. A series of Wardle's hand-block-printed velveteens, inspired by Italian voided velvets, reflect this. Produced for sale by Liberty, they were used in both church interiors and domestic settings. The rich colourings and varied textural effects of the fabrics gave undeniably beautiful results in keeping with the sumptuous interiors of Gothic Revival buildings.

Scott's design for the Newport Pagnell dossal was arranged as an altar frontal for Ipstones church. The full-scale section of a repeat pattern design, in black ink on paper, was hand-coloured with a green and light brown wash. It is one of his designs for 'Church Decoration, Fittings and Furnishings' in the RIBA archive that reveal his understanding of embroidery threads and techniques. Some of his designs include directions regarding colour, sometimes referencing precise shades, along with instructions about types of silk thread, the exact number of gold threads to be employed for outlining and the placement of silk cord for emphasis. There are also notes referring to carpet designs but it is not clear whether they were to be made to his design. For Ipstones the green sections of the design on paper became a gold-coloured damask, although the white ground colour was retained. The composition was planned on the 'counter-change' principle, using a device that produced an intricate interchange of both colour and textures. This is clearly seen in Colour Plate 7a. Local needlewomen cut plain blue silk and gold damask into bold curving shapes and applied these to white velvet to form a frontal with a matching superfrontal. The frontal also has a number of orphreys, or vertical bands, which have different motifs but follow the same principles. The orphrey drawings have not been traced. Golden-brown velvet was cut to form acanthus leaf shapes for the orphreys, which were appliquéd onto blue silk to provide further contrasts. One of Scott's notebooks has instructions for a 'foliated scroll pattern, this pattern repeated all through'.[57] It was an appliquéd design, which also refers to 'alternating stripes' of silk damask and cut-out blue velvet, which could indicate orphreys. This undated design may refer to the same technique that was used for Ipstones but is not found elsewhere in the region. Another design by Scott, also illustrated in Stamp's book and adapted for Ipstones, has a large rose motif surrounded by a repeat pattern of meandering vine leaves.[58] The working drawing 'No. VI', dated June 1876, was intended for 'Embroidery for a super-frontal'. Scott's notes indicate that it was to be of 'red silk worked in gold passing'. There are precise directions for needlewomen indicating colouring, fabric and the placement of braid, cord and fringing. Regardless, the design underwent changes for Ipstones and a number of Scott's written instructions were not followed. Although the central rose motif was worked as directed, the rose was separated from the vine design and applied to rich red velvet to form a less crowded superfrontal. The green edging cord was omitted. The horizontal vine pattern was employed vertically instead, to form four pillar orphreys delicately stitched with silk thread onto the palest pink ribbed silk ground. Each orphrey has, additionally, a finely worked angel, some bearing tiny seed pearls, in an architectural framework added to its lower edge. They are identical to four of the many angels drawn

134

by George Young Wardle in East Anglia. The exhibition catalogue of 1881 describes the angels as the work of Miss Blackie of West Derby, Liverpool. To date no information about her has been traced.[59] As the angels are depicted with human faces and colourful feathered wings they offered opportunities for lavish embellishment. The orphreys were evenly spaced across the surface of an elaborate red brocade frontal for Ipstones. The detailed silk brocade was embellished with white, red and black silk thread.

George Young Wardle, as already mentioned, spent a considerable time in East Anglia making measured drawings from painted rood screens. They included designs of angels taken from the magnificent fifteenth-century screen in the church of St Michael and All Angels, Barton Turf, Norfolk. Other screens yielded details of a variety of elaborate medieval textiles. In correspondence sent from East Anglia to Morris, Marshall, Faulkner & Co. in 1863, he states he had sent some designs for Mr Bodley. According to Michael Hall, 'Bodley was to make greater use of them than Morris ever did.'[60] Could it be that George Young Wardle was referring to the angels that appear in Ipstones and elsewhere? The drawings of angels were certainly made great use of by the Leek Embroidery Society. Stitched renditions of his angel drawings can be seen in three other locations in north Staffordshire beside Ipstones.[61]

A third frontal in St Leonard's church also displays designs by Scott. The effects are strikingly different to anything else stitched by the local women who later formed the core of the Leek Embroidery Society. This frontal and superfrontal are unassuming in comparison to the more lavish silk pieces, which were invariably used for ecclesiastical work. The design comprises two simple outlined floral motifs derived from medieval precedents, stitched in wool yarn and dyed in muted shades of red, yellow and buff. Two separate drawings for these designs have only recently been identified as the source for the Ipstones frontal. Although they are in the RIBA archive there are no annotations to identify them with this Staffordshire piece. One motif is described in RIBA archive notes as a 'textile design for a painted pattern for the church of St Dunstan, Finstead, Kent c. 1878'. The composition indicates that it was intended as a repeat pattern. The other floral motif has no description. Like the others, the final frontal, with its order, balance and harmony of colours, was the result of pooled talents. The individual black ink drawings were provided by Scott and were placed into a balanced repeat pattern – a rhythmical line of shapes flowing in three directions – by someone unknown. If there was a working drawing by Scott showing the final concept, this has not been discovered. Another sequence of events, requiring multiple skills, needed to happen before completion was achieved: sketching, tracing, pouncing, decisions on colouring, yarn dyeing, stitching and various finishing stages. The finished embroideries are powdered across the entire surface of the frontal, the base of which is a heavy linen dyed deep indigo-blue (See Colour Plate 7b). The results are so harmonious that it is easy not to notice just how considered these pieces are. We do not know who had the monumental tasks of assembling the separate elements of the frontal into a coherent whole. The frontal was probably stitched by Phoebe Wardle, but Elizabeth Wardle was often referred to as an 'arranger' of designs. The result is close in feeling to Morris's 'Daisy' bed hanging for his home, Red House.

Such similarities are hardly surprising given that so many designers referred to historic examples as models of perfection. They studied carvings in buildings, viewed paintings in galleries and examined textiles in museums. Renaissance silks and velvets, medieval church decorations, tapestries, embroideries, Sicilian brocades, *Opus Anglicanum*, crewel work and Ottoman and Persian silks and carpets provided rich sources of stylised fruit and plant forms and sumptuous colourings. From these models architects, designers, needlewomen and textile printers such as Thomas Wardle drew inspiration. Loaded with sacred and secular symbolism, many medieval motifs translated happily into both ecclesiastical and domestic work.

St Leonard's church at Ipstones has smaller pieces stitched by Leek needlewomen for use on the altar, which have patterns based on traditional Indian designs. 'Indian Ceiling' and 'Poonah Thistle' are two that were hand-block printed in black outline onto hand-woven tussar silk dyed crimson by Wardle & Co. The patterns were densely stitched over with Indian tussar silk thread in shades ranging from palest pink to crimson and used to embellish a chalice veil and burse. The same patterns were employed for a cream festal frontal for All Saints church, Compton, Leek, along with seven others, while 'Allahabad Marigold' was stitched for Chester cathedral and other Indian patterns for St Luke's church, Leek, and elsewhere. It is only the small items used on the altar at Ipstones that bear overtly Christian motifs, such as a cross.

Susanna's Carpet

George Gilbert Scott Jnr designed a sanctuary carpet for Ipstones church in 1876. It was stitched in wool yarn by fifteen local needlewomen under the direction of Elizabeth Wardle.[62] Mrs Susanna Ingleby (née Sneyd) was one of those who contributed.[63] When she was twenty her father inherited Ashcombe Park, a substantial estate in Staffordshire that became the family home. Although she led a privileged life Susanna had no independent means. As far as we can tell, she was unlike most of the needlewomen involved, as she kept a diary and was a prolific letter writer. Her journals reveal interesting information about the process of making the Ipstones carpet. This is important as very little is known about people in the region and their day-to-day lives in the nineteenth century.

Chance survivals of diaries or memoirs are our only records of what most people thought about local events. Susanna's writings give a rare glimpse of everyday life with a strong sense of immediacy and reality and full of domestic detail. As her diaries cover only one person's point of view we cannot, however, assume that her experience mirrored that of all the women who worked on the carpet project. We can presume, though, that certain practical details would have been similar for anyone stitching a portion of it. Certainly, each of the women would have needed some basic stitching skills to produce their section.

John Sneyd, Susanna's father, was the minister at Ipstones church between 1833 and 1861, so she knew it well. When the church was renovated by Scott in 1876 she commissioned an east window in memory of her father. That same year she commenced a section of the carpet for the church, which she declared finished in April 1877. From her diaries we know that Susanna, then living at Basford Hall, near Cheddleton, started work on the carpet on 11 July 1876. Five days later she walked to Leek, 6km (four miles) away, and joined two others, Dora and Emily, 'at Mrs Wardle's to learn carpet work'.[64] The Sneyd family was friendly with the Wardle family, and there were strong links between them. The next day Susanna was 'up at 3: o clock to attend to patterns for the carpet'. The following day was much the same, as she rose very early to work on the pattern, which she needed to return to Emily. Working on the pattern presumably meant making a copy of Scott's working drawing for her use. Probably only one existed, as the original was seemingly passed from one needlewoman to another. On 24 July a carpet frame was delivered to Susanna so that she could begin stitching. We presume Elizabeth Wardle had by then taught her the relevant techniques in her Leek home. On 1 May 1877, almost a year after starting the project, she took the carpet to Elizabeth. Susanna visited her again on 30 July, when she viewed the carpet and '2 altar cloths'. In August the carpet was still in Leek. We know that the various sections were assembled as a carpet 'at the Tailors'; perhaps the tailor had a workroom big enough for this task.

This was during the era when Morris regularly visited the Wardle home. At least two letters between Morris and Thomas Wardle refer to carpet making at about the same time as the Ipstones carpet was in production. On 18 October 1876 Morris wrote, 'as to carpets Mrs Wardle shall have pull up frames whenever she wants them; and I will send down the book about Gobelin carpets, you will find the plates so good that I have no doubt you will be able to set up a frame.'[65] The book was sent on 17 November 1876, with a covering letter from Morris wishing Elizabeth Wardle 'all success in finding out how to do carpets' and offering to supply her with designs for these as soon as she was ready. Another source mentions a rug of tussar silk designed by Morris, which was displayed by Thomas Wardle at an exhibition in Berlin. To date this has not been traced.

A Scrap of Evidence

Although only a fragment of the Ipstones carpet now remains, saved by a vigilant member of the congregation, there is just enough to identify the pattern and techniques. The surviving section was closely worked in wool dyed in muted shades of green, pink and orangey-brown, with a natural-coloured background. The meandering design is of rounded flower heads and leaves.[66] It is similar to some designs made by Morris for his Hammersmith rugs. Pamela Inder and Marion Aldis suggest that 'it was probably worked in velvet stitch', also known as 'raised stitch'.[67] This is a simple technique in which the yarn is worked over a 'mesh' to create a loop, which is then cut to form a pile. The technique was mentioned by Thomas Wardle when describing carpets stitched by the Leek Embroidery Society in his *Handbook to the Silk Section of the Royal Jubilee Exhibition*, held in Manchester in 1887. He refers to 'Leek Church Carpets, worked by hand on meshes cut in pile, [communicants] kneelers for All Saints, Leek'. The kneelers have not been traced. The catalogue for the 1881 Exhibition of Modern Embroidery states that a sanctuary carpet produced for Ipstones church, which was worked by fifteen ladies to Scott's design, was on display.

Susanna's diaries give a unique insight into the hand stitching of a chancel carpet, revealing that she was part of this collaborative effort and that she produced about a third of it. Others involved included her sister Emily, Miss Challinor, Mrs Illsley and a Mrs Worthington, who died before she finished her section. Ten others remain anonymous. It was ready in time to complement the frontals stitched by Elizabeth and Phoebe Wardle and others at the reopening of the renovated church in 1877. Now that other, larger, parts of this design have been identified we have a better idea of what Scott's original scheme for the Ipstones carpet entailed. The range of different designs and fabrics still in use in this rural village church is extraordinary.

Richard Norman Shaw: St Matthew's, Meerbrook

Shaw, a pupil of Street and a close friend of Sedding, was an original and flexible architect who worked in a number of styles. He was acknowledged as prolific and influential, with no less a figure than Sir Edwin Lutyens describing him as 'our greatest architect since Wren, if not greater'.[68] As he built only sixteen churches, far fewer than either Street or Scott, he was known more for his grand public buildings and houses.[69] Shaw was responsible for many of the houses that were built in Bedford Park, London, one of the earliest garden city estates. As a result, thousands of people needed suitable furnishings to complete their vision of the ideal home. Arthur Lasenby Liberty found a huge and growing market for furnishings owing to the rise in middle-class homeowners. Many textiles sold by Liberty were produced by Wardle & Co.; Thomas Wardle transformed Morris's designs into printed cloth and supplied Liberty with numerous fabulous fabrics using India's silks. Elizabeth Wardle turned Shaw's only known ecclesiastical design into fine needlework. By the end of the 1880s Shaw was the leader in architecture, Morris in design, Liberty in retail and the Wardles in fine textile production.

Shaw was involved in various projects in and around Leek before embarking on his magnificent All Saints, Compton, in the town. This church is thought to be one of the best examples of Shaw's brilliance. Andrew Saint, in his masterwork on Shaw, explains that the architect was drawn to build in Leek through a series of contacts with leading families in the region: the Wardles, Condlyffes, Challinors and Sleighs, all of whom were influential in attracting major characters to the town. Shaw's initial contact resulted from a link between the Sleigh family and John Horsley, artist and father of the architect Gerald Callcott Horsley (a pupil of Shaw). It was thought at first that Shaw would modify the parish church at Cheddleton, but Scott's practice was given that project. Instead Shaw was commissioned to extend the church in the hamlet of Meerbrook, to the north-east of Leek, a project funded by the Condlyffe family. Shaw also designed 'Spout Hall' for Hugh Sleigh, a distinctive townhouse in St Edward Street, Leek, very close to the Wardle family home.[70]

According to Saint, Shaw took his early knowledge of church building from Pugin and Street. One of Street's first masterpieces, Denstone in north Staffordshire, was in the process of being built just as Shaw entered Street's office. The rural church of St Matthew's, Meerbrook, is, however, described by Saint as a 'most valuable early church', closer to Butterfield than to Street.[71] It was a major restoration carried out in two stages. The chancel (1868–70) was funded by the Condlyffe family, while the nave, designed in 1872 and executed in 1873, was financed by public subscription. Saint detects a subtle Japanese influence in some of the decorative features, including the 'masterly' altar frontal designed by Shaw. Shaw became interested in Japanese ceramics at this stage and used Japanese ornament sparingly in his interiors, although Saint argues that this was never more than a stylistic choice reflecting awareness of a world outside Europe. Here is an interesting example of the many links that existed between Aestheticism, which raised the profile of Japanese design, the Arts and Crafts movement and Gothic Revivalism, all of which were evident in a small Staffordshire town. Shaw, like others, aimed for structural unity in his buildings, but felt this was often difficult to achieve if too many different craft-speople were competing with each other. He followed the thinking of both Street and Pugin, who considered that decoration should be concentrated in areas of a church with the most important activity. The high altar was, of course, the focal point. The altar frontal that Shaw designed for Meerbrook is significant in a number of ways. It is thought to be the only design for needlework he produced, although over ten variants have been located. It is also noteworthy as it appears to be the first altar frontal on which Elizabeth Wardle worked. Such a prestigious early commission was a major leap for her from the smaller pieces designed by Scott for Cheddleton church. The Meerbrook frontal shows the scale of her ambition and her extraordinary development in just a few years. Again, there are interesting connections as Shaw learnt a great deal from the brilliant George Gilbert Scott Jnr, who in turn had designed Elizabeth Wardle's first known piece of ecclesiastical embroidery.[72]

'The Chief Genius of the Cloths'

The frontal design for Meerbrook church consists of disconnected formal features held together by scale, theme and colour. It comprises two panels of a complex woven fabric dyed deep blue and five panels of the gold-coloured 'Bird' silk damask designed by the architect Bodley. Dating from 1870, it is the first recorded use of this damask in the Leek area. With its charming, small-scale repeat pattern of plant and bird motifs it provided a perfect foil for elaborate stitching and was used many times by the Leek Embroidery Society.[73] The larger, central panel of the frontal bears a cross with a distinctive three-pronged foot and a motif containing a jewelled centrepiece with seed pearls. It is ringed by an outer circle of rays of light stitched with couched gold thread. The cross is formed from metal threads couched down with dark blue silk to create an extremely fine chequered pattern. The metal thread has tarnished. This was a common problem before major advances in Japanese metal thread production resulted in 'Jap gold' being made available in Europe, which revolutionised the lifespan of this complicated technique of laid and couched work.

The cross is surrounded by panels of elegant olive branches bearing flower-like whorls with distinct Japanese characteristics. They are stitched in blue silk and the centre of each has a cluster of French knots. The leaves are delicately worked in metal thread. Four narrow panels of gold silk damask bear scrolls of cream figured silk that loop through olive branches. Each of the scrolls has a different citation taken from the Song of Solomon, stitched in pale gold silk thread. The curving scrolls give the piece a degree of graceful movement, which offsets the strong, static cross. The border that runs along the top edge of the frontal has a design of olive branches and floral coils. Although differently arranged, they are stitched in blue to echo the motifs below. Narrower panels of deep blue cloth create a simple base for the elaborate silk stitching. All sections are edged with a slim chequered band of blue and gold braid, which serves to frame and clarify the units that make up this frontal. The superfrontal is composed of alternating rectangles of the same blue and gold fabrics. It is not embroidered, although it is edged with a blue and gold fringe. Similar fringing is applied to the bottom edge of the frontal. The result is a balanced, elegant composition in blue and gold that would have needed very skilled needlewomen to accomplish the fine couched gold thread work and the final assembly of the various sections.

Saint quotes the *Staffordshire Advertiser*, which states that 'responsibilities for the silks were Mrs Bodley and Mrs Sleigh worked under the superintendence of Mrs Wardle'.[74] Possibly twenty women, 'most of them living in Leek', were involved with the 'splendid new altar cloth, which has been worked in variously coloured silks, … from designs by Mr Norman Shaw'. A special toast was drunk to Elizabeth Wardle as 'the chief genius of the cloths' at the reopening of the restored church.[75] Also in 1870, a pulpit fall is recorded as worked by Miss Woolinscroft for Meerbrook church, although the designer is not named. Was it Shaw? Presumably the Mrs Bodley referred to was the wife of the architect, although it has not been possible to confirm this.

The group enterprise necessary for the stitching of a large, complex altar frontal meant that there were often subtle differences in the stitched motifs. All appear the same from a distance, as, overall, the stitching is beautifully controlled. When viewed at close quarters, however, it is possible to detect different women's 'handwriting', seen in the placement of a stitch or minor deviations in the delicate shading of a colour. Evidence of the maker was an important element of the Arts and Crafts ethos, with its focus on individuality and rejection of a world of increasing machine-made perfection. The human effort apparent in these attempts at perfection is a reminder of the potential for uncertainty in any handmade object. Meerbrook church has other lovely embroideries, including a Passiontide frontal with embroidered passionflowers, while an accompanying chalice veil is appliquéd with a small, finely stitched crowned head, the designer of which is unknown.

The 'Gladness of Colour': John Dando Sedding

In his *In Memoriam* Henry Wilson declared that Sedding was 'remarkable as a child for a love of flowers and all wild things, he gave early promise of future greatness by his strong passion for drawing, indulged at every opportunity'.[76] Following his older brother Edmund, John became a pupil of Street at his Bloomsbury practice. Shaw was then Street's principal assistant and only two years earlier Morris had been attached to the same practice. John worked with his architect brother until Edmund died in 1868. His reputation grew rapidly and, while he was a committed Gothic Revivalist, his output was always described as distinctive. He was renowned as a sensitive restorer of many old churches, preferring to work with local craftspeople he knew well. He was also known for his love of gardens and studied them from every perspective.

Whether Sedding was designing an altar cloth, a church or a garden, it was important for him to try something new. Although his work was fresh, Wilson thought it always had something of the solemnity, the earnestness, of old work about it. Sedding studied historic examples so that his designs were nourished by them and rooted in tradition. He never ceased to marvel at the natural world, 'its beauty, and the wonder and the power, the shapes of things, their colours, lights and shades'.[77] As a sense of creation was one of his greatest pleasures, Sedding's challenge was to embody that enthusiasm in his work, so that everything was tinged by his astonishment for natural beauty. This aspect of his personality made itself clearly felt in his distinctive embroideries. As Wilson said, 'I think he was more happy, when working for embroidery, drawing at the desk with a flower in his hand, turning it and twisting it in every possible way.'[78]

Both Sedding brothers created designs for needlework that were distinctly different from anything produced by Street, their influential master. It is likely that additional knowledge of techniques came from family members. John's wife Rose Tinling and their daughter Alice were distinguished needlewomen. His sister, Isabella Sedding, known as Sister Isa, was in charge of the embroidery workroom at the Society of St Margaret's, East Grinstead, for twenty-five years. She had the same artistic gifts as her brothers, through whom she met Morris and other leading members of the Arts and Crafts movement. This was thought to have influenced her renowned embroidery.[79] Ultimately John Sedding became known as the archpriest of the Arts and Crafts movement. He unceasingly promoted handcraftsmanship, aiming to stir a deep interest in the many crafts linked to architecture, which he felt were of lifelong value, as they had enthused him at an early age – he had been only fifteen years old when he fell under the influence of Ruskin. Sedding's uplifting lectures and visionary papers on the subject were legendary. His *Art and Handicraft* was published posthumously in 1893. His detailed paper 'Design' (1893), written after producing many schemes for needlework, reveals his thoughts on embroidery thus: 'Never was a time when the art and science of needlework were so thoroughly understood as in England at the present moment.'[80] This was not, however, the paean of praise it seems to be; rather, it was a cynical overview of what he felt was wrong with contemporary embroidery design. He continued,

> we are all in a terrible earnestness about the whole business. The honours
> of the British nation, the credit of Royalty, are in a manner, staked upon

the success of our 'Schools of Needlework.' And yet, in spite of all these favouring circumstances, we get no nearer the old work that first mocked us to emulation.[81]

This was not Sedding's famous mischievous humour at work; here he was conveying his deep disappointment in the many prominent architects and designers who were busy designing embroidery and, in his opinion, failing. He made it clear that it was not the act of stitching that was at fault. The problem lay with designs based on ancient work copied 'from the camphor-scented preserves at Kensington'.[82] He was convinced that museums, such as South Kensington, were not places to inspire. It was nature, experienced at first hand, that gave stimulus to anyone designing embroidery. He believed that a church should be 'wrought and painted over with everything that has life and beauty – in frank and fearless naturalism'.[83] That said, Sedding was acutely aware that direct copying from nature was not the complete solution where embroidery was concerned. He knew enough about techniques and materials to understand that their inherent limitations and benefits needed to be factored into a successful design from the beginning. For the best results, nature should be interpreted rather than realistically copied. He insisted that

> needlework is still a pictorial art that requires a real artist to direct the design, a real artist to ply the needle. Given these, and our needlework can be as full of story as the Bayeux tapestry, as full of imagery as the Syon cope, and better drawn. The charm of old embroidery lies in this, that it clothes current thought in current shapes. It meant something to the workers, and to the man in the street for whom it was done.[84]

Sedding's commission for a distinctive festal frontal for York Minster in 1869 demonstrated his love of nature in its colourful exuberance. It was stitched by the Society of St Margaret's, East Grinstead. Although his sister ran that important workroom he also used other convents, such as St Raphael's Sisterhood. In 1874 he set up an architectural practice close to Bedford Square, London, where he continued to make designs for embroidery, wallpaper, gold work, chalices and patens. After meeting Ruskin early in 1876, Sedding submitted sketches to him for comment. Thereafter they exchanged many letters in which Ruskin stressed the need to obtain the texture of surfaces as, without these, drawing was simply a diagram. Paul Snell's doctoral research acknowledges Sedding's important role as an embroidery designer. Snell considers that when Sedding designed a frontal for St Augustine's, Kilburn, in 1874, he 'clearly borrows scenes from Japanese porcelain, its end panels, with birds, insects and vegetation more familiar to a *Famille Rose* tea service than an altar frontal. The central panel conversely looks elsewhere for inspiration.'[85] Snell is convinced that Sedding's understanding of materials and needlework techniques gave his work a greater impact, as 'many features stand proud of the cloth, creating areas of recession and projection, and thus even greater richness; passionflower stamens project forth; tree trunks are rounded and gnarled; vividly coloured fruit swell outwards in their ripeness'.[86] But we may never know whether that was his influence or the embroiderer's interpretation, although Sedding engaged with the workmen he employed whenever possible and sought out the best craftsmanship for his schemes. We do not know whether he was ever in contact with Elizabeth Wardle about the two altar frontals that she stitched to his designs, although Thomas Wardle spoke of Sedding as a friend.

'Life and beauty in frank and fearless naturalism'

Sedding was commissioned to plan an extension for the church of St Luke, Leek, which lengthened the chancel by 3m (ten feet). He also devised a reredos of Caen stone and designed an altar frontal to celebrate the new addition, which were completed in December 1873. Even though this was a relatively early stage in his career, well before he had earned his reputation as a distinctive designer, Sedding had by then designed a number of altar frontals, each of which was noticeably different.

St Luke's parish magazine of September 1872 notes that 'a band of ladies have [*sic*] been for some time, and still are, busily engaged in embroidering an altar cloth to replace that which has been in use a quarter of a century and had grown dismally dingy'. They had been stitching for well over a year and although the superfrontal was completed before the chancel was finished the larger frontal was still not ready. There were various ways of funding these luxurious items in Leek: sometimes there was a public call for subscriptions, or a donation was made in memory of someone, or a local benefactor would pay for the work. In the case of St Luke's church, the completed superfrontal was put on display at 27 Stockwell Street to whet the public's appetite in order to raise money for the more costly frontal. People were invited to make donations, however small. A campaign was already in place, as the parish magazine reveals that members of some sixty families had contributed sums from sixpence upwards towards the cost of the frontal. Although this amounted to £10, considerably more was needed, as the materials alone came to about £25 (approximately £800 to £1,000 today). The superfrontal has not been traced but was described as being of a rich red ribbed silk with a central shield of white figured satin, which bore the sacred monogram in gold. The *Agnus Dei* and pomegranate motifs, also worked in gold, were placed on either side.[87]

The catalogue for the 1881 Leek Exhibition of Modern Embroidery lists embroideries for St Luke's church as a frontal and superfrontal designed by Sedding and a pulpit cloth, also by him, worked by Miss Pidcock (whose father was the first minister of the church) and Miss Clowes. Alms bags were stitched by Mrs George Wardle, wife of George Young Wardle, while a sanctuary mat was worked by several Leek women, although the designer is not named.[88]

The distinctive pelican design for Shaw's frontal was noticeably different to anything previously stitched by needlewomen of the town. Sedding's rectangular composition, placed centrally, portrays a pelican 'In Piety' and her young. The format has some affinity with designs Sedding produced for churches elsewhere, as rectangular and square arrangements appear in a number of his needlework schemes. The pelican, a symbol of regeneration, sacrifice, devotion and piety, was often used in Christian art, usually as a mythological device. The centrepiece, thought to have been worked by Elizabeth Wardle, is stitched in fine detail. As Colour Plate 8a reveals, the birds are depicted in soft natural shades of grey and white with black features and outlines, while some sections are padded and raised. The mother bird has embedded almost the whole of her distinctive beak into a slit in her breast, which has a soft smudge of red. A nest holding the young birds is streaked with light dashes of green and red. The pelican and her young are placed within an intricate architectural framework of turrets, spires and castellations, all outlined with black silk thread. This strong scene is surrounded by supporting stylised pomegranate and stellar motifs powdered across the frontal's surface. Derived from symbolic medieval precedents, they are worked mainly in laid and couched gold thread and coloured silks. They serve to emphasise the drama of the birds and their bold setting. The result is dramatic and emblematic. A narrow stitched border based on a traditional Indian pattern was possibly applied to the frontal later.

Elizabeth Wardle had been involved with only one frontal prior to the one for St Luke's. Whichever part of Shaw's Meerbrook frontal was her work, it would have been quite different to the pelican scene she stitched just two years later. Each architect presented a variety of challenges to her and other needlewomen, and we can see from this piece that she rose to meet them at a very early stage in her needlework career. The pelican frontal was the only one known to have been signed by the eleven needlewomen who stitched it, most of whom represented prominent families in the town. As Elizabeth's signature appears above the pelican scene, we can reasonably presume that this was her section.[89]

It was usual for many women to work on a frontal. Different levels of skill, from the very basic to the most demanding, were regularly required to complete such a complex item. Individual motifs or small sections could be stitched in the hand at home, then appliquéd to the large ground cloth by a needlewoman with the necessary skills for this vital task. Different parts would be assembled on a large frame by someone with experience to ensure that the frontal hung flat in front of the altar, without the weight of one part pulling against another. Backing cloths, braids and fringing would be applied to help the finished piece hang well. Some frontals were permanently attached to rigid frames designed to lean against the altar, while others had different systems, including one type that suspended the frontal from rods. Two matching pulpit falls on green silk damask were stitched to Sedding's designs for the church of St Luke. These are more conventional, as both have motifs of pomegranates and stars similar to those powdered across the pelican frontal. They appear to still be on the original silk damask, whereas the frontal embroidery has been remounted onto a much later paler silk backing.

Sedding often designed naturalistic, emblematic bird motifs such as ravens and owls, or fantastical, almost dreamlike creations. His plant symbols, such as thistles, were often untypical of other architects' ecclesiastical designs. One extensive working drawing for an altar frontal is particularly interesting in that it features a number of emblematic wild things with menacing connotations: stinging or biting subjects such as a stag beetle, bees and what could be a hornet, as well as two large owls in natural colours placed on ivy leaves and flowers including Himalayan poppies and deadly nightshade.[90]

Other needlework for St Luke's has recently been identified as designed by Sedding. It includes a purple Passiontide superfrontal, matching orphreys for a purple frontal and four alms bags.[91] Colour Plates 8b and 8c show the embroidery designs to be bold in form and colouring, strikingly combining meandering floral motifs, mainly exotic lilies, with an occasional inscribed scroll and unusual scatterings of prominent dots stitched in richly contrasting coloured silks. These floral motifs are far removed from the humbler wild flowers that Sedding favoured and instead have much in common with Italian frescoes of the fourteenth and fifteenth centuries. Sedding's use of flamboyant arabesques, with their distinctive spiralling, sinuous foliage, flowers, fruit, birds, animals and insects, can be linked to Renaissance precedents or possibly Indo-Persian designs.[92] This combination of strong motifs and dramatic colouring makes these works distinctly different from any ecclesiastical needlework in the vicinity before or since, even Sedding's other designs for the church of St Luke. The ground cloth used for the frontal is Bodley's silk damask 'Bird', dyed a deep shade of violet. Two alternating motifs stitched in silk thread are powdered across the entire surface of the damask.

The catalogue for the 1881 Leek Exhibition of Modern Embroidery lists a superfrontal designed by Sedding for Compton School chapel and stitched by Miss Ward. It is likely that this is the purple Passiontide superfrontal described above, which would have been removed from the smaller Compton chapel when it was replaced by Shaw's All Saints in 1885. Additional published evidence in the form of secular embroidery described as a table centrepiece links the design to Sedding. A black and white photograph of this appeared in *The Queen* in 1888 and clearly reveals that the design for the Passiontide frontal was also used as a border that surrounds another Sedding design: a rectangular block-printed panel with a pattern of four lilies. The centrepiece was created by Elizabeth Wardle for an exhibition in London in 1893, shortly after the architect's death. A quotation from Matthew Arnold's 'Memorial Verses April 1850' – 'Art Still has Truth, Take Refuge There' – was embroidered onto the border. This border is possibly the only known pattern by Sedding that was employed for both sacred and secular purposes. The central pattern was initially hand-block printed in strong colours by Wardle & Co. onto a green cotton ground intended as a furnishing fabric, probably for Liberty. When adapted for embroidery, the lily pattern was block printed onto an undyed, hand-woven tussar silk ground that was stitched in delicate shades of tussar silk. This form was illustrated in *The Gentlewoman's Book of Art Needlework* in 1892, without a border, and was described in the first volume of *The Studio* as a 'splendid example of Leek work'.[93] It is an intriguing example of the adaptability of block-printed designs produced by Wardle & Co. and the ingenious use of so many of these by Elizabeth for different categories of embroidery.

In one Arts and Crafts Exhibition Society catalogue, Sedding yet again singled out embroidery for discussion. His article firmly reinforced why he was against the unimaginative copying of historic forms. 'No more museum inspired work! No more dry as dust stock patterns … But instead we shall have designs by living men for living men – something that expresses fresh realisation of sacred facts, personal brooding: skill in nature, in use of form and gladness of colour.' He felt just as strongly about architecture, arguing that contemporary buildings needed new thought.

Further Leek embroidery for St Luke's church includes a festal frontal with an *Agnus Dei* motif surrounded by a crown of thorns and a circle of plants such as roses and pomegranates. There are matching pulpit falls and other pieces for the altar, with grapevine and rose motifs applied to a white silk damask ground. They have been attributed to Sedding, although I have doubts about this: they are beautifully stitched but quite conventional in design.

A red frontal also stitched for the church of St Luke has the same central cross motif as that designed by Shaw for Meerbrook. It is the only known example of the distinctive cross placed between two rose trees, while the corresponding superfrontal has the word 'HOLY' alternating with the emblematic motifs of tulips and roses across its width. There is a matching pulpit fall with an elaborate pomegranate motif stitched with laid and couched silk and gold thread.[94] The design is remarkably similar to a pulpit fall in St Edward's parish church, Leek, of green silk damask with lavish use of couched gold thread.

Shaw was thought to have designed a chancel arch for St Luke's, which was never built, and we know he thought highly of Sedding. This might explain why Shaw's design for needlework features in this church. It was remodelled just after Shaw's work for Meerbrook, only a few kilometres away, was completed.

St Luke's church also has fine examples of traditional Indian patterns incorporated into ecclesiastical pieces. Tussar silk fabrics were block printed with the designs 'Champa Chrysanthemum' and 'Gya' by Wardle & Co. Initially devised for Liberty & Co., as lengths of block-printed repeat patterns they were adapted for use as borders for stitching in richly coloured tussar silk threads by members of the Leek Embroidery Society. They were employed as orphreys for the red altar frontal, pulpit falls and other items. An old monochrome photograph reveals that the embroideries were originally mounted onto velveteen block printed with a pattern based on Italian Renaissance voided velvets, which has been replaced. A further frontal of dark blue wool has stitched and appliquéd motifs taken from the block-printed pattern 'Ancient Gothic', which was combined with red orphreys stitched with a stylised meandering vine-leaf pattern.[95] There are pulpit and litany falls, alms bags and bible markers featuring the same motifs to accompany the larger pieces.

The small rural church of St Anne, in Millersdale, Derbyshire, has four altar frontals thought to have been stitched by Leek needlewomen in 1879. They are striking and clearly designed specifically for that church. They are little more than superfrontals in terms of their size, probably because the altar is richly carved and meant to be seen rather than covered by a cloth. The design of a repeating lily flower and undulating stem for the green frontal is remarkably similar to a design by Sedding now in St Luke's, Leek. In 1875 Sedding completed a major restoration of nearby Tideswell church, Derbyshire, known as the Cathedral of the Peak. A fine set of embroideries was produced for that church by Leek needlewomen. There is no record that Sedding designed these pieces, but if he did not, then we do not know who did.

Sedding was a founder member of the Art Workers' Guild in 1884 and its master in 1886 and 1887. Horsley and Lethaby, who both supplied features for Shaw's All Saints church, Leek, were also deeply involved with the Guild, as was Thomas Wardle. They formed a significant group of brilliant men who made a lasting impression. Ironically, it was a number of Shaw's pupils who encouraged the development of the Arts and Crafts Exhibition Society, founded in 1887. They insisted on an interdependence of the crafts, which led to a rift between them and Shaw, their former mentor, who promoted the architect 'as an isolated designer of masterpieces in the mould of Inigo Jones or Wren'.[96] Walter Crane was the first president of the Guild and the committee included Morris, Burne-Jones, Lewis Foreman Day and Sedding: all men with firm connections to the Wardle family.

From the beginning embroidery was a conspicuous feature in all displays by the Arts and Crafts Exhibition Society. Following a stringent selection process the first exhibition, held in the New Gallery, London, in 1881, included needlework by the Leek Embroidery Society and printed and dyed textiles by Wardle & Co. These were shown alongside work by Jane and May Morris and Mrs Walter Crane, among others. It was such a success that another exhibition was arranged for the following year in larger rooms. In 1889 Thomas Wardle's textiles were singled out by *The Artist* as splendidly sumptuous, with glowing dyes of the richest hues being used with masterly purpose and to a worthy end. The same journal also reported on the amount of embroidery on display. By 1893 greater care was given to selecting fewer embroideries of a higher standard. The Leek Embroidery Society was again invited to show its work, along with May Morris and the RSAN.

'The great church of his maturity': All Saints, Compton, Leek[97]

All Saints church was designed by Shaw in 1884, built between 1884 and 1886, and opened to great acclaim in 1887. It was an architectural landmark. John Betjeman regarded it as one of the finest churches in Britain. The church was planned on Tracterian principles, something that Shaw took from his tutor Street.[98] When discussing the overall plan and interior, Betjeman is keen to emphasise how the eye is directed to the high altar, on which all lines of the building converge. It was here that 'artists in Leek have given their best stained glass, Embroidery, textiles and paintings', which, according to Betjeman, made it 'one of the wonders of England'. None of Shaw's other magnificent churches 'equals in richness and in splendour of proportion, All Saints, Leek'.[99] The pulpit and font for All Saints were designed by Lethaby, who founded the Central School of Arts and Crafts and was a close friend of Shaw. He also designed a massive reredos for the chancel. Saint declares that the fittings 'herald Lethaby's undoubted arrival as a designer of genius'.[100] They were surrounded by dramatic wall and ceiling paintings by Horsley, also a major architect in the Gothic Revival movement who designed embroidery. Although originally of plain glass, the nine-light window was filled with Morris & Co. stained glass at a later date. It, too, would compete for the congregation's attention. Into this glorious, colourful and intensely patterned chancel were placed beautiful embroideries stitched in Leek. They were, and still are, examples of extraordinary expertise that could hold their own in this magnificent setting.

All Saints contains a variant of Shaw's frontal design for Meerbrook, although the distinctive cross at the centre of the composition shows minor changes.

While there is no bejewelled centrepiece here, the laid and couched gold work is magnificent. Additional variations include a greater diversity of fabrics and different motifs and embroidery techniques. The colour scheme is unlike the original, although colour contrast is still important to the balance of the composition. For All Saints a striking combination of intense red tones and muted greens was planned. Instead of the plain blue panels of the original frontal, there are crimson velvet orphreys embroidered with an emblematic honeysuckle motif. Other frontal panels have the same olive branches as Meerbrook, complete with whorls, scrolls and lettering. Minor revisions at All Saints relate to the olive branches, which are stitched in a muted palette and applied to a velveteen block printed with the design 'Salangore'. This pattern was one of many popular designs that Thomas Wardle printed for Liberty. Here, in sombre colours, it is scarcely noticeable beneath the stitching. Rectangular panels of embroidery are divided by narrow bands of embroidery, sometimes two side by side. The bands were block printed with motifs derived from traditional Indian designs. The superfrontal design underwent more changes and is distinctly different from the one at Meerbrook. It is richly embroidered with alternating pomegranate and sunflower motifs applied to rectangular panels of russet-red velvet across its width. Additional block-printed, embroidered borders complete the scheme. William Kineton Parkes, librarian and principal of the Nicholson Institute, described the frontal as designed by Shaw in an article he produced on the Leek Embroidery Society that was published in the first volume of *The Studio*.[101] A matching litany desk fall and pulpit fall utilise the cross and olive branch motif, but with softer tones of blue on a white ground. Everything is finely stitched, while the textures are varied and do not overpower the design. The colouring may have been something Elizabeth Wardle organised, as she was particularly known for her expertise in that regard.

The collection of Shaw's drawings and correspondence held at The Royal Academy reveals that details of 'fixtures and fittings were laboriously worked out through a three-way correspondence between architect, client and craftsman'.[102] Whether Shaw was involved with the reconfiguration of his first frontal design for All Saints is not known, although we do know it was stitched by women of the Leek Embroidery Society. Given that he was famous for his finely detailed drawings of decorative features, which gave clear guidelines to craftsmen working on his designs, it is reasonable to presume that he would have been consulted about any changes to this major project. As Shaw set high standards for himself and others, we may suppose that embroideries produced for the focal point of his church would be particularly worthy of his attention, in that they embodied a symbolic as well as a liturgical function. As the high altar is emphatically the core of All Saints church, it would be astonishing if the frontal, which has been described as a masterpiece, was not altered to his modifications, or at least with his approval in consultation with Elizabeth Wardle. Shaw was convinced that interior schemes should be planned by architects as a coherent whole and not be subject to donations, no matter how well-meaning, that could change the balance of a carefully conceived arrangement. Unquestionably, a great deal of attention to detail was lavished on his outstanding interior for All Saints.

It is interesting that Shaw's design for a frontal cross, devised specifically for Meerbrook, appears more often in other churches than any other motif designed by an architect and stitched by the Leek Embroidery Society (Colour Plate 9). A version was also produced for the parish church of St Edward, Leek. This medieval church had undergone multiple changes over the centuries and so was not the result of any one architect's vision. Street had remodelled it between 1865 and 1867. Bodley supervised further alterations at the end of the nineteenth century and George Gilbert Scott Jnr's designs for a chancel carpet and kneelers were stitched in 1907. Windows by Morris & Co. were installed at various points. The 'Shaw' frontal for St Edward's employs the same symmetrical composition and the same number of cloth panels with the distinctive cross in its central position as the original. Bodley's 'Bird' damask, also used for the Meerbrook frontal, was again employed for St Edward's, although dyed a rich terracotta shade and used throughout, including for the superfrontal. It is embellished with the same embroidered motifs as at All Saints, although strong colour contrasts are not brought into play here. There are more subtle emphases, as the silk stitching echoes the terracotta of the ground cloth with some understated highlights of a richer red in parts. Olive branches are stitched in muted hues of soft green, and gold thread is applied with a light touch. Green and gold are echoed in the narrow bands that edge the various panels. Four slender velvet orphreys of crimson velvet are embroidered with a honeysuckle motif, as at All Saints, to supply a well-judged contrast.

As at All Saints, the superfrontal consists of alternating sunflowers and pomegranate motifs, although here they are applied to silk damask, not velvet. Colour Plates 10a and 10b show the fine details of these emblematic motifs. Narrow embroidered borders are used to divide the panels. They are of a neoclassical, interlocking ring design, block printed and stitched to echo the soft green and gold of the olive branches. This border design appears often elsewhere – a typical example of the Embroidery Society's multiple use of the same design, a benefit of block-printing. Shaw's cross holds its central place as before, and is yet again a superb example of fine raised gold work. As Colour Plate 10c shows, the texture of the laid and couched gold thread was carefully calculated to reflect even the slightest play of light across its surface. Floral and fruit motifs were again stitched with silks lightly embellished with gold thread, then appliquéd to the silk damask ground cloth. Each motif was edged with a slim silk cord, which emphasises the outline while hiding the stitches used to sew it in place.

Fruit and floral motifs were drawn from a lexicon of ancient, emblematic Christian designs. The clinging nature of the honeysuckle indicates steadfastness, while the olive branch is, of course, a universal symbol of peace. The sunflower represents faithfulness for Christians, owing to its natural habit of following the sun daily as it arcs across the sky. It also exemplifies the connection between earth and the heavens. The sunflower motif was one that Shaw used in a number of settings in various materials. It was also favoured by followers of the Aesthetic movement and most famously was adopted by Oscar Wilde, the great promoter of the house beautiful. Indeed, there were many crossovers as designers and architects found themselves involved with Aestheticism, Gothic Revivalism, the Arts and Crafts movement and Art Needlework simultaneously.

The pomegranate was everywhere. It was used as a motif in early English embroideries, printed textiles, woven silks and tapestry. Pomegranates were loved by carvers of stone and wood, by painters of allegorical subjects and by wallpaper, ceramic and stained-glass designers. This much-valued symbol, with its ancient precedents, was a constant source of delight in so many of the embroideries produced in Leek. The fruit's beautiful rich red colouring and the curving form of its hard outer case topped with a miniature crown lent itself to lavish and varied interpretation. Its emblematic history reveals that it was ubiquitous in the ornamentation of ancient Greece and was employed in Moorish buildings as often as in medieval Christian settings. The blood-red seeds packed tightly within added other layers of meaning. For Christians the fruit generally symbolises the one true church, which contained many things, but it is also a generic symbol of faithfulness and fertility for many cultures. Shaw's design for a ceiling panel of a house (1878) incorporated both sunflower and pomegranate motifs.[103] Tom Wardle Jnr produced 'Pomegranate', a design printed by his father as both a chiné print and a cretonne, which was embroidered over to form a litany desk hanging.

Versions of Shaw's cross have been discovered in various other locations. In all cases it was embroidered using fine laid and couched gold thread, usually with a basket-weave texture devised to reflect the light. Apart from the four churches in the Leek area, more churches in Staffordshire, at least three in Cheshire and one in Khartoum have been recorded as having a cross to Shaw's design.[104] One particularly individual interpretation can be seen in the church of St Luke, Leek, and what is possibly the final variant was produced for a church in Cheshire as late as 1927. The distinctive cross placed at the centre of the frontal is one of the few overtly Christian symbols stitched by the Leek Embroidery Society. Invariably the cross is accompanied by vertical pillar orphreys that employ a beautiful pomegranate and peony motif, a design registered by Wardle & Co. at the Public Record Office. It was then common practice for the manufacturer rather than the designer to do this, and we do not have the designer's identity. A hand-block-printed version of the design, in black on plain white cotton cloth, has recently been discovered, indicating that it was intended for multiple use as an embroidery; the whole point of cutting an expensive wood block for hand printing, a time-consuming and costly business, was to enable numerous copies to be made.

Shaw's modified frontal design was, moreover, often utilised in conjunction with a superfrontal, with a distinctive design of stylised floral motifs. The motifs were taken from the design 'Certossa', registered by Wardle & Co. in 1884. This was a hand-block-printed repeat pattern of stylised palmettes placed within a strapwork arrangement. Several individual motifs were taken from this design and rearranged on a horizontal axis suitable for a superfrontal format for a number of churches. It is yet another example of the Leek Embroidery Society's adaptation of a secular repeat pattern for ecclesiastical purposes through the use of the flexible block-printing technique.

Other frontals were adapted to grace the focal point of Shaw's outstanding interior for All Saints, including a number of pieces displayed at Leek's Exhibition of Modern Embroidery of 1881. A frontal and superfrontal were described as designed by George Gilbert Scott Jnr and worked by Miss Ward for Compton School chapel, a small mission chapel that preceded Shaw's design for All Saints at Compton. The items are now identified as a crimson stamped-velvet frontal, which has a section of the design stitched over with coloured silks in the medieval tradition. The pattern, known as 'Gothic', was designed by Scott for Watts & Co. and was in use by that company from its launch in 1874.[105] It was possibly taken from the painting of St John, on the painted rood screen in Ranworth church, Norfolk. It is conceivable that George Young Wardle made the original drawings on which Bodley's pattern was based. The crimson velvet panels in the frontal alternate with a pink silk damask, a fabric also sold by Watts & Co., although it was imported from Japan.[106] The same 'Gothic' pattern can be found as panels of an altar frontal at Cheddleton. There the velvet is also dyed deep crimson, although it is not embroidered over.

Other embroidered items for All Saints were produced after Elizabeth Wardle formed the Leek Embroidery Society. They include a glorious cream and gold festal frontal with matching superfrontal, which was on the altar when the church was consecrated. The *Leek Post & Times* attributed the design to Mrs Thomas Wardle, stating that it was worked by the ladies of Leek assisted by the sisters of the Society of St Margaret's, East Grinstead. It was described in the newspaper thus: 'This work is of great magnificence, the prevailing tone is white with gold thread chastely used.'[107] As the frontal is still in use we can see that it is a subtle arrangement of nine equal-sized panels echoing the nine-light window above. The panels of cream tussar silk were hand-woven in India, then block-printed in Leek with nine different repeat patterns based on traditional

Indian designs. Designs were numbered in sample books, although some were given names for retail purposes. 'Champa Chrysanthemum', 'Tanjore Lotus', 'Allahabad Marigold' and 'Indian Ceiling' were all incorporated into this 2.75m (nine foot) frontal. The patterns were stitched over with cream tussar silk with occasional flashes of blue and green, which created a delicate 'opal' colouring. All panels were subtly highlighted with fine gold thread. Alternate panels have an applied stylised lily based on medieval precedents; each is worked in couched gold thread, with copper tones and coloured silks. Every one of the nine patterns used for the panels was originally produced in Leek for Liberty & Co. as a printed tussar silk fabric.

The superfrontal representing the Garden of Eden incorporates nine angels placed into an architectural framework, alternating with rose bushes bearing pink flowers. The angels were based on drawings by George Young Wardle copied from the rood screen at St Michaels and All Angels, Barton Turf, Norfolk. The fifteenth-century screen is considered to have some of the best surviving examples of English rood-screen painting. Many sacred images were defaced during the Reformation and although some damage was inflicted on this screen it was minimal compared with that inflicted elsewhere. Each of the nine angels is different and is placed within a niche stitched in gold. Each carries a distinctive attribute and is wearing garments and accessories specific to its particular role. The angels were stitched at the St Margaret's Convent workshop at East Grinstead for the sum of £18 18s and mounted by Miss Beardmore. Invoices reveal that the total sum for the frontal and superfrontal amounted to £71 1s 4d. The few existing documents from the convent workroom do not mention what degree of artistic freedom was allowed in the choice of colouring and texture of each angel. East Grinstead was renowned for producing fine work and the angels were, unsurprisingly, stitched to coordinate with other parts of the frontal and superfrontal. Doubtless Thomas Wardle would have supplied the silk yarn and cloth that was used throughout. Stone Convent was also paid for work on the superfrontal for All Saints, although we do not know what aspect of the work was done there.

While the Leek Embroidery Society collaborated regularly with distinguished architects it is less well known that they also collaborated with at least two convent workrooms, in each case on distinctive figurative pieces. St Margaret's Convent workshop at East Grinstead later produced the three Marys for a frontal at Cheddleton church designed by Horsley. It is interesting to consider why such a renowned embroidery society was prepared to enter into partnership with other workrooms. Although Elizabeth Wardle was always a collaborator, this raises questions to which there are not yet answers. There are, of course, a number of reasons why it might have happened. Pressure of time due to a full order book or the lack of a pair of experienced hands able to stitch flesh and fine couched gold work to a tight deadline are the most likely explanations. These very demanding techniques needed the most skilled needlewomen. The true craftswoman would have aimed to create only the finest work for such a prestigious building and, as noted, the cream frontal was on the altar when the church was dedicated – so, was it a genuine commitment to producing the best, which only collaboration could achieve? It is worth remembering that just a short time before Elizabeth Wardle had supervised the production of a facsimile of the Bayeux Tapestry as well as completing other major ecclesiastical commissions, and in 1886 she had also lost her son Francis: all major events that must have had a huge impact.

An elegantly designed purple velvet Passiontide frontal and superfrontal and a glorious stole, depicting angels, were created for All Saints church by Tom Wardle Jnr, son of Thomas and Elizabeth, and finely stitched by his sister Lady Margaret Gaunt (Colour Plate 12; they can still be seen in the church). Tom was a student at Manchester School of Art on the advice of Morris, after which he attended art college in London. Art journals regularly published his successful patterns and he was acknowledged as a textile designer of note. Further textiles within the church include a set of magnificent litany desk falls, designer unknown, dating from 1891, when the chancel was decorated. One has an exceptional design of a golden pot of lilies stitched by Tom's sister, Lydia Wardle, onto red silk cloth. As a pot of lilies is traditionally associated with the Annunciation one is always seen in paintings of this subject. The pot in this particular version has very Persian characteristics. There are also embroidered cross orphreys used to decorate two copes, with matching stoles, maniples and bible markers, along with a funeral pall designed by Horsley. All of this hugely diverse work, mostly on a large scale, was either designed or stitched by members of the Leek Embroidery Society supervised by Elizabeth Wardle or by other members of the Wardle family. Elizabeth's embroidery was exhibited at the Arts and Crafts Exhibition Society events, along with designs by her son Tom. It is highly likely that at least some of the pieces designed by him for All Saints church were among those exhibits.

The *Leek Post & Times* reported the consecration of All Saints in great detail and described a chancel carpet as the work of the women of Leek. This, along with the kneelers mentioned earlier, has not been traced.

The Parish Church of St Edward the Confessor, Leek

Between 1865 and 1867 Street was responsible for major alterations to the parish church of St Edward the Confessor, Leek. In keeping with ecclesiastical changes, the rebuilding of the chancel and the extension of the south aisle opened up the interior to emphasise the centrality of the altar rather than the pulpit. This was a busy period for Street, as it came closely after the building of his churches at Hollington and Denstone and the production of magnificent embroideries for both. St Edward the Confessor was a significant church for the Wardle family: Thomas and Elizabeth Wardle were married there in 1857 and, after their move to Leek in 1866, they worshipped at the church, at which eight of their children were baptised.

The church continued to adapt to changing views and circumstances. Thomas Wardle was closely involved with installing a series of stained-glass windows when Bodley was the consultant architect for an additional renovation. Because of his long-standing interest in the subject, Wardle was deferred to when he strongly recommended Morris & Co. as the best supplier of stained glass. This was not only for the strength of its designs and colouring but also because the firm had excellent craftsmen in its Merton Abbey workshop. A series of letters dating from 1898 between Wardle, Bodley and Morris & Co. reveal the discussions that took place. They disclose that, although Wardle respected Bodley's report on the church, he wished Morris and Co. to provide the stained glass. Bodley had been closely linked to Morris's firm in its early years, until a rift developed between them. However, pressure from Wardle in the 1890s, shortly after Morris's death, meant that the two rival companies worked together once again on the stained-glass project in Leek. The letters reveal Thomas Wardle's long-standing admiration for Morris, and that he wanted only the best for the parish church where he and Elizabeth were married. Wardle persuasively argued that

> we ought to go to the best art possible, and the best art in painted-glass this century or almost any other has produced, is that which has been designed by Sir Edward Burne-Jones and executed by Morris & Co. whose works at Merton Abbey are considered the best in the Country, and where the best talent is employed in the manufacture and putting together of the glass.[108]

Wardle visited Bodley in London to discuss the situation further. He reasoned that 'Burne-Jones has left behind him a great number of cartoons designed for glass, any of which would be better in my opinion than any other glass we could have.'[109] Since Morris's death Bodley had supervised the colouring of the figures and ground work relating to Burne-Jones's cartoons, which he thought 'among the best of the existing drawings for glass'.[110] Clearly the highest standards were demanded for all decorative forms in Leek's churches.

Over time a series of beautiful frontals, superfrontals, falls and other items of needlework were created for St Edward's church by the Leek Embroidery Society, where they were used in a magnificent setting. Four frontals with matching superfrontals are now retired from use and mounted behind glass. They are on permanent display and can still be viewed in the church. The purple Passiontide frontal is composed of four panels of Indian tussar silk block printed with two different repeat patterns featuring floral motifs, one of which, 'Strility', owes its origin to traditional Indian motifs. It was hand-block printed onto two of the panels. They alternate with purple velvet orphreys embellished with richly embroidered passionflowers, which are repeated on the silk velvet superfrontal. All motifs were overstitched with tussar silk thread dyed in shades from palest lilac to deep purple. Gold thread is used sparingly. The velvet and yarns were dyed by Wardle & Co. The glorious red frontal features the central cross designed by Shaw originally for Meerbrook church. Other features from the original are retained, but added to with fruit and flower motifs, as at All Saints. Beryl Patten and Judy Barry describe it thus: 'this piece in its subtle use of colour is a celebration of the art of the dyer, weaver and embroiderer'. The matching superfrontal is considered to have 'careful shading, subtle gradation and harmonies of colour-choice, both in the motif and in the two vertical stripes on either side, confirming the high levels of craftsmanship associated with Elizabeth Wardle and the Leek Embroidery Society'.[111]

A green altar frontal was presented to the church in October 1895 by Elizabeth Wardle. Fourteen women worked on this frontal, which was designed by John Scarrett Rigby, supervised by his father-in-law, George Young Wardle.[112] The challenging composition was inspired by Gothic precedents. Four seated kings, each with detailed garments and strong facial features, are placed within an architectural framework with perspective. This is possibly the only example of the use of perspective in any work by the Leek Embroidery Society. Patten and Barry state that 'the drawing of the figures and overall handling of the composition details suggest the hand of an assured designer'.[113] This piece is densely stitched with subtle tones of silk thread. 'The skill displayed in working the design by the embroiderers, noticeably in the fluid treatment of the drapery and the handling of the architectural detail results in a successful collaboration between designer and maker.'[114] As the frontal is no longer in use it is now framed and wall-hung in the parlour of the church. Although it is claimed to be the first figurative work completed by Leek embroiderers there were a number of angels stitched before this date.

A white frontal in the church is unusual in that it is designed by three people. The architect Horsley designed the censing angels, while John Scarrett Rigby created the central form and Miss Lizzie Allen, an embroiderer from Leek who trained at the local technical school, designed the phoenix for the superfrontal. This mythical bird arising from flames symbolises resurrection. Like the green frontal, this is now mounted and wall-hung in the church parlour.

Six angels, embroidered by Miss Winterbottom of the Leek Embroidery

Society, are mounted onto one horizontal panel and hung in the church (Colour Plate 5). Typically, they have human-like faces, double wings, belts and elaborate jewelled crowns. Just a few stitches, mainly split stitch and couched gold thread, created the many different textures seen in the fine facial features, feathers and embellished garments, which are subtly highlighted with gold. The stitching, which is extremely delicate, and the distinctive mount and frame suggest that the piece was prepared for exhibition. The angels were probably based on drawings of the nine orders of angels made in 1864 by George Young Wardle from East Anglian rood screens. Similar ones can be found in churches and elsewhere in East Anglia.

Metal thread features extensively on other pieces in this church. Gold thread, which symbolises sovereignty and reflects the glory of God, is difficult to manipulate. It requires great expertise to obtain the variety of textured effects that can be seen at St Edward's church, which are of particularly high standard. Not every needlewoman was capable of achieving this. Although it is possible to see gold thread applied with a comparatively delicate touch on the festal frontal, on other pieces it is purposely dense, to create a sumptuous effect. The patterns and textures seen in Colour Plate 11 were produced when metal thread was laid and couched down with thread, and sometimes placed over cord to form a raised section.

The church also has many smaller pieces for use on the altar and a number of lovely alms bags. Unsurprisingly, perhaps, the Wardle family was involved with the production of a chancel carpet for the church: Lydia, daughter of Thomas and Elizabeth Wardle, supervised its production; Arthur, their son, dyed the wools; and their niece, Eleanor Wardle, was responsible for the colouring. Sixteen members of the Girls Friendly Society stitched the carpet in eighteen sections, which, when finished, measured 4.5 × 2.75m (approximately fourteen by nine feet). It was given to the church in 1907. The design was based on a carpet designed by Scott Jnr originally for Ipstones church thirty years before.

Gerald Callcott Horsley: 'a still, grave, blazing centre', amid a surrounding 'racket'

Horsley was a pupil to Shaw at the time when Lethaby was his chief clerk and there was a long waiting list of those wanting to be apprenticed to the practice. Horsley went on to become a major architect and one of the many who designed interior fittings for his churches. Saint suggests that in Horsley the spirit of Ruskin was asserting itself, as he was committed to the equality of craftsman and architect and the involvement of the workman in decorative design. His father, John Horsley, was one of the successful Cranbrook painters, who was able to win Shaw a number of important commissions through friends and clients. This was possibly how the link between Shaw and the Sleigh family of Leek was made.

Horsley provided an extensive series of outstanding wall and ceiling paintings for Shaw's All Saints, Leek, which include a number of stately elongated forms and lettering. They were completed in 1891. In addition, the church has a distinctive funeral pall designed by him. In contrast to the elaborate wall decoration, it is fittingly subdued, of plain wool cloth panels of alternating deep blue and scarlet with embroidered motifs at each corner. A quotation from the Book of Wisdom is worked in stitch. Applied narrow bands of embroidered flowers based on a traditional Indian border pattern divide the sections. This is likely to be the work of the Leek Embroidery Society, as Elizabeth and Thomas Wardle had strong links with the church. Other embroidery in the building was certainly from that source. Although no embroideries were designed by Horsley for Ipstones church, he did produce a modification of the chancel along with a chancel screen and an external sculpture of the crucifixion for the east end.

Horsley's work in the parish church of St Edward, Leek, includes the two censing angels for the white frontal, while Cheddleton church has his very beautiful altar frontal depicting the three Marys, which was commissioned by Thomas Wardle in 1891 to commemorate his sister Phoebe. The composition features three elongated, subdued, elegant female figures placed against a background of oversized lilies with vigorous coiling stems and strong flower heads, all following a pronounced diagonal axis. There is a lower border of snowdrops and other simple flowers, possibly pansies. Each end panel has stylised pomegranates densely stitched in silk and gold thread. The original working drawing, now in the RIBA archive, reveals that Horsley provided some indication of the colouring for this work, along with other directions for needlewomen. The drawing, 'Scale 1 – a quarter full size', has a central gold canopy containing a declaration and a narrow gold border, as well as some other gold highlights and a light wash of red on the cloak of the Virgin Mary. There is no other colour, although the architect notes where he wishes blue or red for garments. He specifies a 'fine white figured silk' for the ground cloth and 'fine old red velvet' for panels at each end of the frontal. There are no instructions referring to technique. The finished piece, however, does not have the central canopy, the lettering has been moved from a middle position to form an upper border, the banner held by the left-hand figure has had the word 'Truth' replaced by 'Love' while 'Peace', repeated three times in the lower border, is replaced by the names of the three Marys, and there are blue panels, not red, at each end. It is reasonable to suggest, given the Wardle family's great experience of ecclesiastical needlework and its commissioning of the piece, that family members would have been closely involved with the design of this memorial composition.

The finished piece has a muted colour palette of soft blues and greens against a white damask ground, delicately highlighted with gold. On the left side Mary Magdalene wears a garment with a diaper pattern similar to one in the carved triptych on the main altar. This pattern was possibly taken from a drawing made by George Young Wardle in East Anglia. As Horsley visited the church before he composed the frontal he would have seen the triptych, so this could be a conscious link. Although the three Marys were stitched by St Margaret's Convent at East Grinstead, the rest of the frontal was worked by members of the Leek Embroidery Society. Here is an interesting example of the collaboration that occasionally occurred between the Leek Society and convent workrooms. It must have been a matter of particular expediency to have had such an arrangement in place. We can see from other surviving pieces that, by this time, around 1888 to 1891, Leek needlewomen were capable of stitching a variety of textures and techniques. They were, however, especially busy producing numerous other ecclesiastical pieces at that time. Unfortunately, the crucial information is lost to us. The frontal can still be admired today in the church at Cheddleton, where it is on permanent display. We can see how delicately stitched it is, and in a more subdued palette than the frontals designed by Horsley for his church at Longsdon just a few years later and a short distance away.

Horsley was commissioned to build St Chad's at Longsdon, north Staffordshire. Illustrations of the exterior and interior appeared in *The Builder* in 1906 and clearly show that his designs included extensive wall and ceiling paintings similar to those for All Saints, Leek. They were not, however, completed for Longsdon. The altar frontal seen in one of the images was finished, although the design was modified. Horsley produced four designs for frontals and matching superfrontals for his church and would have taken its strong architectural features into account. The results are distinctive and powerful, and convey a deeply Christian message. The intensity of this is captured in the confident composition, matched by dense raised stitching and vibrant colouring. There are at least seven frontals by Horsley in the north Staffordshire region, plus a partial design of another frontal, one funeral pall (possibly two), and a framed and mounted image of an angel. A large dossal known to have been finished has not yet been traced.

It is fortunate that several of Horsley's working drawings for needlework still exist, giving some insight into his priorities. There are complete studies for a number of frontals: some full size, others that are approximately one-third size, and a series of outlines of details. Numerous tracings of limbs, hands, feet and faces produced by the embroiderer have survived. A watercolour of a crucifixion scene is in full colour on heavy cream laid paper, although other pencil and ink drawings have no colour washes. In some instances there are written instructions indicating the placing of a colour or fringing, which are clearly intended for the embroiderer. In the case of the Longsdon embroideries one person, Mrs Warren, stitched all of his work. Figure 17 shows her in what appears to be a formal studio portrait. In another photograph, taken in her old age, she is seen still stitching.

What becomes clear from viewing the drawings and the finished embroideries is that Horsley's designs have a number of distinctive features. Still forms surrounded by volume and movement dominate his compositions. Typical of Horsley is a sense of extraordinary energy achieved by his preference for

Figure 17   Mrs B. Warren, embroiderer

robust branches, bursting skins of plump fruit and full-blown flower heads. Often there are elements that are disproportionate to the whole, so that it is not uncommon to see realistic figures placed against gigantic, vigorous plants. He uses quotations in many of his pieces, enforcing the Christian message. We know from surviving working drawings that he took great care to sketch out lettering in full size. 'I have trodden the wine press alone' is in bold, carefully formed script, for example. His capital letters frequently have decorative details that create the effect of illuminated manuscripts or jewellery. The Passiontide frontal for St Chad's features an ancient, symbolic 'True Vine' motif, which shows Horsley's ability to create a powerful composition. Colour Plate 13a shows the crucifixion scene, which is applied to a purple velveteen ground cloth. It is full of strong juxtapositions: the fragility of the pale, lifeless, male body is exaggerated by being placed against the force of flourishing plant growth. Horsley merges the raised arms of the crucified Christ with the stems of a vine, which becomes a sturdy sinuous plant extending out towards the edges of the composition. On either side of the natural-coloured flesh and the agonised expression of the crucified Christ is a riot of colour, as branches laden with swollen fruit offer a continuation of life ever after. The disproportionately large bunches of grapes are about to burst their skins as their heavy flesh is so ripe. The intensity of the rich purple of the fruit is in contrast to the subdued realistic tones of the branches and leaves of the vine. Two small, fragile, kneeling angels at the foot of the cross reach out their arms to offer wine glasses (chalices) to the crucified Christ. Over-sized tulip plants at each lower corner give balance. The result is a symmetrical composition containing vitality and strength.

Powerful plant forms also dominate the green frontal for St Chad's. The original green ground was dyed by Thomas Wardle to Mrs Warren's specification. As the embroiderer she chose the colours and shading for the whole piece, which was completed in 1906. At the centre is Christ, wearing a simple white robe that stands out against the rays of dense gold against which it is placed. Horsley contrasts the passive figure with a forceful pomegranate tree that fills the rest of the composition. It, too, is laden with ripe, plump and richly coloured fruits, stitched to create strong, three-dimensional forms. The frontal is labelled with the virtues, which are scattered throughout the tree, their lettering worked in gold thread against a white ground. A further contrast is visible in the two orphreys at each end, which are of a more conventional, subdued design and colouring.

Longsdon's white festal frontal has a central mandala form containing a gold chalice against rays of gold (Colour Plate 13b). The effect of massed gleaming threads draws the eye to this still middle point. The rest of the frontal consists of a realistic, conventional rose growing over a trellis framework. The naturalistic thorny branches are curved to create a strong and symmetrical rhythm to the composition. Mystic roses and fat buds are raised to give a three-dimensional effect and are stitched in shades of red, from the palest of pinks and peach to rich crimson. Couched gold threads are used sparingly for a delicate emphasis.

Horsley also created a version of the Passiontide frontal for All Saints, Hanley, Staffordshire, a church extended by the architect and just a short distance away from St Chad's. It is now mounted behind glass and wall-hung. His design for a festal frontal for the same church was also stitched by the Leek Embroidery Society. It features a central mandala with a seated Christ against rays of gold, surrounded by a dramatic composition of large golden crowns and realistic palm branches, repeated and placed on a white damask cloth. These powerful, spiky images are in great contrast to the still central form. The more conventional orphreys at each end are similar to those used for the purple frontal at St Chad's. A chancel carpet, also a Horsley design, includes the crown and branch motifs. Handmade of tufted wool, it survives but in poor condition.

In every example it is clear that, while Horsley employed traditional Christian motifs, the results he obtained were decidedly modern. This is reinforced by the bold stitching techniques used throughout. At her home, 'Southfields', in Leek, Mrs Warren stitched all the frontals to Horsley's designs for St Chad's, the Passiontide frontal for All Saints church, Hanley, and a red frontal now in Zanzibar cathedral, East Africa. She was spoken of in contemporary reports as a member of the Leek Embroidery Society and her materials were all produced by Wardle & Co. Warren was talented in a number of ways: she was a writer, singer and public speaker as well as a fine needlewoman. She was the second daughter of the Charles family of Pelsall Hall, descendants of ancient Staffordshire and Shropshire families, and was closely linked to the Longsdon church, as her husband was the first vicar of St Chad's from 1900. We know that she was still stitching into her late old age, assisted by her daughter Hermione Grace, although she was confined to her home for over twenty years.

Horsley and Warren formed a very creative partnership and clearly she developed a technique that was sympathetic to his aims. There is no record of how she acquired her embroidery skills. Like other Leek embroiderers, she favoured just a few simple stitches. Long and short stitch dominates her work, along with laid and couched metal threads. The motifs in Horsley's compositions were stitched by her in such a way that heavily applied threads were layered to build up three-dimensional forms as well as creating exquisite banks of dense, shaded colour, which further emphasised the shapes. The profiles she produced stood proud of the backing cloth almost in the manner of Elizabethan stump work. She made clever use of the lustrous qualities of tussar silk threads and their texture so that the play of light and shade has a great effect. Rich, but not bright, colour fades to the palest hints and the thread is worked in such a way that the fruit and flowers look enticingly real, yet there is an ethereal quality to them that is perfectly judged, given their surroundings. A number of Horsley's ecclesiastical pieces have thickly applied gold threads in the form of crowns, crosses, letterforms and so on, while others have very little, if any, glint of gold, relying solely on colour for their sumptuousness. The distinctiveness and elegance of his details can be seen in Figure 18.

Horsley's work depicts distinctly human forms with realistic facial expressions. Although the concept is unmistakably traditional there is a strong Pre-Raphaelite influence apparent in the elegant figures, which no doubt presented the embroiderer with challenges. At close quarters we can appreciate the superb needlework, especially the subtle rendering of flesh and the folds of garments. All shapes are clearly delineated and the ornamentation is certainly suited to the wide, flat plane of a frontal. Despite the deliberately different scale of various motifs, the overall effect is unified and harmonious. This is helped by a particular use of colour, which binds each large composition together. In Horsley's working drawings there are occasional annotations, but they indicate no more detail than the words 'red' or 'blue' could convey. As there are multiple

Figure 18   Design (detail) by G. Horsley.
Photograph: Michael Pollard. Courtesy of Pamela Jones

shades of any given primary colour this could suggest that he was prepared to let the embroiderer select the best one to complement the overall composition. The wrong shade could ruin a carefully balanced arrangement while a number of clashing shades could be disastrous.

The light-filled interior of Longsdon church must have posed a significant challenge to both Horsley and Warren, as the frontals could easily have been lost in this generous space. Bold frontal compositions such as Horsley's had a practical value in that they could be seen clearly by the congregation from a distance. Although the fine quality of the needlework is not apparent from afar, the fact that the stitching technique created raised elements is an important

Figure 19   Design on paper for an altar frontal (detail), G. Horsley.
Photograph: Michael Pollard. Courtesy of Pamela Jones

aspect of the compositions' success. Such motifs were more visible from various places in the large airy interior and the delineated component parts are not lost in a chancel full of competing detail. The sense of vibrant colour is immediate.

The largest frontal stitched by Mrs Warren, 2.75m (nine feet) wide, found its way to Zanzibar cathedral. Her son, the Rev. Hugh St John Percy Warren, was then at the Teacher Training College in Zanzibar. The frontal depicts a detailed scene of the Annunciation by Horsley, who died before it was finished. A detail of the working drawing (Figure 19) indicates that alterations were made to the kneeling figure of the Virgin Mary, which were completed by the architect's assistant, Fox. This complex composition was stitched onto rose-pink silk damask. Although it was originally intended for Longsdon, Warren was apparently so unhappy with the new vicar's attitude towards her fine needlework that she sent it out to Zanzibar instead. This means that St Chad's is lacking a red frontal by Horsley and Warren to complete the traditional set of four. In 1990 it was returned to Britain to be remounted onto rose-coloured silk brocade supplied by Watts & Co., after which it was sent back to Zanzibar cathedral, where it is still in use. Once again there are kneeling figures, lettering and disproportionately large plants, which form a scene radiating out from a central dove motif.

These are virtuoso examples of a needlewoman and an architect bringing out the best in each other's chosen medium of expression. Warren had command of challenging craft skills and a complete understanding of tussar wild silk, which brought out its intrinsic beauty. The stitches she used are simple, but layering and dense packing of the lustrous thread shows a skilful handling of an unruly yarn, with an ability to fluff out of control. Horsley had the architect's discipline of line and form and an acute appreciation of scale and rhythm. He also understood that male and female forms, when used well, often with realistic expressions of sorrow and pain, give added drama, which serves to remind the congregation that these scenes are designed to bolster faith and elicit strong reactions. While they were exquisitely worked they were not just pretty pictures, but could be, for example, carefully considered scenes of grief. Anyone who doubted that ecclesiastical needlework could reach such sublime effects need only look at Horsley and Warren's work for St Chad's at Longsdon.

Colonial Commissions

Frontals stitched in Leek and supplied to other colonial parishes include a gold altar frontal for Grahamstown cathedral, in South Africa. The designer is unknown but there is a strong resemblance to a frontal design by Edmund Sedding featuring peacocks that was published in 1856. The Grahamstown frontal has four panels each containing a peacock with a dramatic fanned-out tail, finely stitched in rich colours. The ground cloth has the design 'Cortessa' block printed by Wardle & Co. and the motifs are outlined in gold thread. The superfrontal bears the inscription 'King of Kings and Lord of Lords' interspersed with foliage. Densely embroidered with silks and gold thread, it is similar to one in St Edward's, Leek, designed by George Young Wardle and his son-in-law, John Scarrett Rigby. The overall effect is sumptuous and striking.

A red velvet frontal was created by Leek needlewomen for St Mary's church, Port Elizabeth, South Africa. The design 'Ancient Gothic' was block printed onto velveteen to form an all-over repeat pattern in an effective use of a textile design regularly produced by Wardle & Co. that was particularly suitable for churches. It is based on a historic example, with no particular Christian symbolism attached to it. In this case it was given a rich effect through the application of gold outlining for each motif. Four pillar orphreys embroidered with angular motifs were placed across the surface at regular intervals. The superfrontal had a series of emblematic doves appliquéd across its width. The frontal was on open display in Leek in order to raise funds by public subscription to cover its costs, which amounted to £35. It was shipped to South Africa in 1896.

Twenty-eight women worked on the altar frontal for the Gordon Memorial church in Khartoum, Sudan. Funds to cover the £21 cost were raised by public subscription. At least eighteen people subscribed, Thomas Wardle among them. The frontal was sent out to Lady Wingate, wife of the Sirdar of Sudan, and acknowledgements were received from the royal palace, in Khartoum, in 1905. The design features Shaw's distinctive cross applied to a richly embroidered ground cloth. Four pillar orphreys were embroidered with a honeysuckle motif, which was also used for a similar frontal for the parish church of St Edward, Leek. The superfrontal is of a design that frequently appeared in conjunction with Shaw's crucifix. While we know the cost of this frontal there are no documents that mention the architect's fee for that design or any other.

The Leek Embroidery Society stitched an exquisite frontal designed by the architect John Loughborough Pearson in 1887 for Shrewsbury Abbey, which he remodelled. The composition consists of a repeated angel motif, alternately pink or blue, placed within an architectural niche on a horizontal plane which stretches across the width of the piece. It is still in use.

Anonymous Designers

Not all of the ecclesiastical pieces produced by the Leek Embroidery Society were designed by eminent architects. They were, nevertheless, stitched with the same materials, care, skill and sensitive selection of colour. Some are specific to a particular building, such as the wonderful banner in the parish church of St Peter ad Vincula (now Stoke Minster), Stoke-on-Trent, designer unknown. It has a tiny motif of a potter at his wheel, probably because Josiah Wedgwood is buried in the churchyard. The Staffordshire knot and other local references in the complex design still resonate. Others employed the range of hand-block-printed fabrics produced by Wardle & Co., a great number of which were originally destined for prestigious retailers such as Liberty, made to be sold by the yard for various purposes. Because they were hand-block printed the patterns could be adapted in a variety of ways by versatile printers. An all-over repeat pattern could be utilised as one long length, providing a complete patterned piece for an altar frontal. There are numerous examples of this. A frontal for Croxden church, Staffordshire, for example, has a richly dyed crimson silk printed velvet as the ground cloth, with a very beautiful result; a bold 'net' pattern, based on a traditional Indian textile design, formed the base of the repeat pattern, which was stitched in gold. The floral motif within each ogival shape was embroidered in shades of pink silk by Mrs Cruso, a local benefactor and wife of a Leek solicitor. It is still in use. A matching pulpit fall of crimson velvet has the pattern 'Champa Chrysanthemum' in pinks and gold. Alton church, Staffordshire, has a similarly designed frontal with an all-over lily pattern in pink silks and gold thread. Other block-printed designs were used as panels in frontals. The design 'Salangore' was hand printed onto velvet for the red frontal for St Edward's church, Leek. Also for St Edward's, two repeat patterns were employed for the Passiontide frontal.

In her *Handbook of Embroidery* Letitia Higgin stated that the work of the Leek Embroidery Society retained a distinctive regional character within the national Arts and Crafts movement. There were specific features of Leek work that resulted from the soft sheen of the silk thread used and the rich colourings, complex gold work and unusual designs. Although each architect had strong stylistic differences, they commissioned Leek embroiderers who had a particular ability to employ tussar silk floss threads in the assured way that they did. The special dye palette that natural dyes and wild silks provided, along with scintillations of colour, contributed to a recognisable way of working within the variety of designs. The Arts and Crafts movement prized diversity and individuality, things that most of the architects discussed here practised and promulgated themselves.

An altar frontal was in place on the high altar whether a service was taking place or not and could be viewed in numerous ways. As the congregation would see the cloth from a distance, which in a large church could be quite far away, scale was important. Shaw's All Saints, for example, was designed to seat a congregation of 750. Architects employed certain design strategies to fill the sizeable space needed for a frontal. They were designed to inform and evoke splendour. Fine details would not be visible to many, but the overall composition would be important and the harmonious balance of colour and texture would come into play. Some frontals were, of course, more embellished than others depending on their function in the church's calendar. Although smaller items used to vest the altar might not be noticeable to the laity, they could be closely observed by the clergy. Chalice veils and burses were important parts of the ensemble traditionally used by a priest, who could see tiny details, understand the relevance of the iconography and possibly register the superior quality of the materials. Other considerations came with vestments, of course. The clergy would probably not notice the features while they were actually wearing them but would when they were robing. Stoles, however, would be more easily visible to them. The congregation would observe the transformation that the robes created as they changed an ordinary person into someone able to perform the service. This was achieved through the richness of colour and the emblematic sheen of fine silks and velvets, with details of gleaming gold thread, some of which was very lavish. Fabrics woven with precious metal thread would also reflect and refract the light. It was used in order to glint in candlelight or be animated by the light streaming through stained-glass windows. Added spangles would give glittering notes. All combined to emphasise the sense of ritual.

The motifs and their relationships to one another would have been understood by individuals learned in Christian symbolism. Many compositions were employed for polemical ends and there were recognisable narratives for anyone who could decode them. For those who could not, the pieces were simply beautiful, calculated to amaze, to be a reflection of faith, a heaven on earth. Music added a further emotional element. Theologically speaking, iconographical interpretation has been constant since the Middle Ages, a time when the church had enormous power and religious beliefs were represented in lavish ways in various media and to high standards of craft skills. Some frequently used symbols, such as stylised lily and pomegranate motifs, can be traced back to medieval examples. Paintings, illuminated manuscripts and textiles all picked from the same store of symbols. A knowledge of their meaning today extends our comprehension of them as considerably more than wonderful craftsmanship. Whether or not they reveal the objectives of the designer is not, however, always possible to discover. It is also impossible to say if the laity had the same depth of understanding as the clergy. The craftsperson may have had no input into the choice of an architect's motif, although it would seem that they did have some degree of liberty when it came to colouring or stitching it.

The production of a harmonious altar frontal was the work of a team of many skilled individuals. Contributions came from designers, weavers, printers, dyers, thread makers, needlewomen and braid, fringe and spangle makers. Those who assembled the various parts so that it would hang just right and fit smoothly across the front of an altar table had a very challenging task to perform. On completion such works were often placed in exceptionally prestigious buildings, where they had to compete with a number of other equally beautiful and skilfully crafted pieces. As they were – and sometimes still are – working textiles, with a daily function to perform, this meant they were often in close proximity to hot candle wax, spilled wine, pollen from flowers and the wear and tear caused by bodies repeatedly brushing against the textured surfaces. Not least among the depredations they endured was the act of moving these heavy, bulky and elaborate pieces to and from the high altar. Frequent movements in and out of their storage chests meant that loose threads and heavy fringing often snagged. Damp vestries and leaking roofs have also taken their toll on fragile fabric. Indeed, the fact that so many ecclesiastical pieces made in Leek have survived is extraordinary.

Plate 1a   Elizabeth Wardle stitching.
The embroidered frame is the design
'Allahabad Marigold', tussur silk
thread on tussur silk hand-woven
cloth. Photograph: the author

Plate 1b   'Ajanta', block-
printed silk ground with silk
and gold thread embroidery.
Photograph: Maria Killoran.
Nicholson Museum
& Art Gallery

Plate 1c   Skeins of coloured silk dyed in Leek. Photograph: the author

Plate 2a   'Tanjore Lotus', tussur silk thread on tussur silk
hand-woven cloth. Photograph: Michael Pollard

Plate 2b   A block-printed repeat pattern, tussur silk thread on green tussur silk. Nicholson Museum & Art Gallery

Plate 3a Blotter, silk velvet, tussur silk embroidery on tussur silk ground. Photograph: the author

Plate 3b 'Indian Poppy', block-printed silk ground with silk and gold thread embroidery. Photograph: Michael Pollard

Plate 4a   Journey to Normandy, Scene 1. Copyright Reading
Museum (Reading Borough Council). All rights reserved

Plate 4b   Journey to Normandy, Scene 2. Copyright Reading
Museum (Reading Borough Council). All rights reserved

Plate 4c   The prisoner, Scene 1. Copyright Reading Museum
(Reading Borough Council). All rights reserved

Plate 4d Planning the invasion, Scene 2. Copyright Reading
Museum (Reading Borough Council). All rights reserved

Plate 4e The crossing (ships at sea). Copyright Reading Museum
(Reading Borough Council). All rights reserved

THE GIFT OF ELIZABETH LEEKE WARDLE.

BORN AUGUST 18ᵗʰ 1877 – DIED APRIL 20ᵗʰ 1946.

Plate 5   A panel of six embroidered angels, Parish Church of St Edward the Confessor, Leek. Photograph: Richard Knisely-Marpole

Plate 6   Passiontide altar frontal, St Edward's Church, Cheddleton, Staffordshire. Photograph: the author

Plate 7a   Velvet and silk altar frontal (detail), Ipstones Church,
Staffordshire. Design by Scott Jnr. Photograph: the author

Plate 7b   Linen with wool yarn, altar frontal (detail), Ipstones Church,
Staffordshire. Design by Scott Jnr. Photograph: the author

Plate 8a   Pelican frontal (detail), St Luke's Church, Leek. J.D. Sedding. Photograph: the author

Plate 8b   Passiontide superfrontal (detail), St Luke's Church,
Leek. J.D. Sedding. Photograph: the author

Plate 8c   Alms bag, St Luke's Church, Leek. J.D. Sedding. Photograph: the author

Plate 9   A variant of R.N. Shaw's design for a frontal for
Meerbrook Church. This was produced for the Parish Church of St Edward
the Confessor, Leek. Photograph: Richard Knisely-Marpole

Plates 10a & b Sunflower and pomegranate motifs, superfrontal, Parish Church
of St Edward the Confessor, Leek. Photograph: Richard Knisely-Marpole

Plate 10c   Cross designed by R.N. Shaw, Parish Church of St Edward
the Confessor, Leek. Photograph: Richard Knisely-Marpole

Plate 11   An example of gold work,
Parish Church of St Edward the Confessor, Leek.
Photograph: Richard Knisely-Marpole

Plate 12   Silk stole (detail), All Saints Church, Leek.
Design by Tom Wardle Jnr. Photograph: the author

Plate 13a Passiontide altar frontal designed by G. Horsley,
St Chad's Church, Longsdon, Staffordshire. Photograph: the author

Plate 13b Festal altar frontal designed by G. Horsley,
St Chad's Church, Longsdon, Staffordshire. Photograph: the author

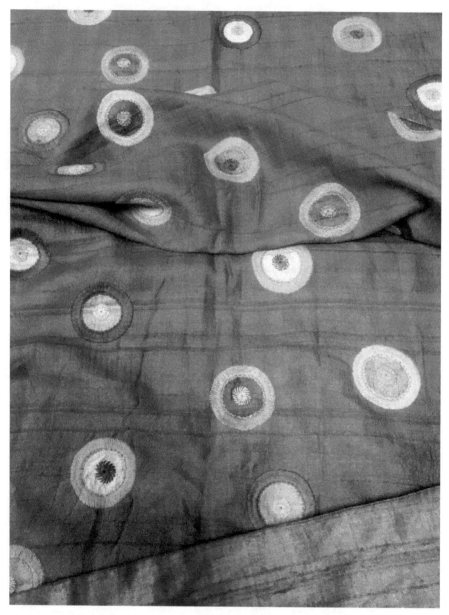

Plate 14   Indian tussur silk dyed with indigenous natural dyes
from India. Kolkata, 2014. Photograph: the author

CONCLUSION:
REDISCOVERIES AND
REVELATIONS

… to those of us in the Crafts Council of India who work with crafts and textiles and attempt to improve the lot of the artisans who nurture traditional skills, access to India's rich textile heritage via these meticulous 19th-century records is like a journey into the past and to certain breath-taking skills the Indian subcontinent seems to have lost forever.

Kasturi Gupta Menon, 2013[1]

The motivating principles that dominated the Wardle family's drive for perfection were the understanding of materials, the role of the designs they used and the perfection of lasting colour. While this was acknowledged in their day it is only comparatively recently that we have come to comprehend exactly what that meant in practice. The significance of fresh evidence found in Britain and India in the twenty-first century illuminates what was achieved in the nineteenth century. This gives this history a new vitality as well as indicating why it still matters. It is now no longer an untold story but a strong, evidence-based account of a remarkable time and place.

Thomas and Elizabeth Wardle's children continued to produce renowned textiles and the Leek Embroidery Society was acknowledged for its fine work well into the twentieth century. Dyeing and printing proceeded at the Churnet print works for a range of well-known clients, including Bernat Klein, Laura Ashley and Jacqmar, until 1968, when what had become the largest family-run dyeing and printing company in Britain was taken over by the multinational giant Courtaulds. It is likely that it was at that juncture that many important documents relevant to this history were lost, as hardly any company records

171

have survived. In 2009, the centenary of Thomas Wardle's death, four exhibitions in noted venues celebrated his life, along with lectures, publications, walks and talks.[2] They shone a light on the wide range of his achievements for the first time. What was not known at that point was that there was still more to discover, as some amazing finds would soon reveal.

As related in earlier chapters, Thomas Wardle was someone whose creative energy and commitment attracted a great deal of talent to his home town. He achieved astounding success in all that he set out to do, mastering difficult raw materials and publishing numerous learned accounts of his research. New evidence confirms that his intensive study of India's wild silks and dyestuffs was intended to improve day-to-day working knowledge in the dye house, whether that was in England, across Europe or in India. His analysis and application of his results was vital to the success of the Leek Embroidery Society and almost certainly stimulated its launch. It is likely that it was his research that was responsible for the remarkable condition of the surviving embroideries that were created using the materials that he transformed. This, along with creativity, common sense and diligence, was at the core of the Wardle family's success, rather than some elusive, inherent genius. The ability to push boundaries led to an extension of traditional skills, a wider choice of materials, a mastery of colour and a new and unsurpassed depth of understanding relating to India's wild silks. This set a whole new agenda for embroidery then and since. Although it was apparent that India's designs and materials were a catalyst for both Elizabeth and Thomas Wardle at that time, this has barely been acknowledged elsewhere.

While India's dyes had been admired for centuries they had never been subject to systematic analysis before Thomas Wardle began his study. We now know that his research, featuring a variety of commonly used natural fibres, produced over 4,000 dyed yarn and cloth samples. Crucially, the research included a number of wild and cultivated silks from across the subcontinent. Despite intensive searches by this author, the results of this inquiry remained forgotten until the last decade of the twenty-first century. At least two similar sets of samples thought to be in Britain have seemingly disappeared. The search for them continues, although there are currently no records that reveal details of their past or present whereabouts. I had almost given up when in 2009 came news of an important find in India: the discovery of the samples Wardle had sent to Calcutta (now Kolkata), which were thought to have been lost. To date they are the only samples known to have survived and are from 'the sixth and final instalment of the report',[3] which almost doubled Wardle's previously published results. They are now in the archives of the British Survey in India (BSI) in Kolkata. Dr Himadri S. Debnath came across them in an overlooked part of the Indian Museum, Kolkata, when he was joint director of the BSI, and realised the significance of this long-neglected research. The impact of the discovery was immediate and we instantly came closer to understanding what Thomas Wardle had achieved long ago in Leek. They are the direct evidence of his vast experience and his feel for colour and the transformative role that dyestuffs can have. These samples help us to understand why his contemporaries admired him: the legacy that he constructed then still has currency today. The volumes reveal a learned body of work built on a comprehensive series of facts. This was more than sinply recording detail – they shed new light on the complex and versatile process of dyeing in the nineteenth century. His tenacity and meticulous notations are everywhere, demonstrating his comprehension of the materials arrived at through his master dyer's sensibility. The records are a treasure trove for scholars of natural dyestuffs and fibres and they tell us a great deal about Wardle and his years of research. Even the private Wardle is evident, as he reveals his admiration for India's dyers and love of particular colours in his related publication.

The thousands of cloth and yarn samples are the results of his research made tangible, and his success can be measured in numerous ways. We can see in the samples what drove him on, what animated him and also what he could not possibly have known: just how well his results have stood the test of time, even in India's unforgiving climate. His years of work now have another life, as India's dyers have been inspired by his results, as have European makers, who view the samples as a valuable resource. The culmination of years of research in the nineteenth century now benefits different cultures in the twenty-first. They may be distant from each other by thousands of miles, but they clearly have craftworkers and markets that have a great deal in common. In both, unassuming materials are expertly converted into symbols of rank and power. The connections between craftworkers and markets in India and Europe have now been celebrated in numerous, fresh ways, which introduced them to wider audiences. As Kasturi Gupta Menon, honorary president of the Crafts Council of India, said of Wardle's research: 'It is the most comprehensive and complete documentation on this subject.'[4] The press of India reported: 'At last we could finally view the incredible range of subtle colours he obtained.'[5]

Due to the importance of the discoveries funds were made available for the initial digitisation and conservation of this precious heritage. Although digitisation is completed, the conservation of the fragile volumes has yet to take place at the time of going to press. If action is not taken before too long Menon is convinced that 'India will lose forever the only extant document that reveals the palette of colours Indian dyers could produce with subtle combinations of dyes and mordants.' She considered that it was comparable to 'creating a brilliant digitized image of the Taj Mahal while allowing the actual monument to disintegrate and collapse'. She continued, 'Preserving the samples is also thought essential as organic chemists can use them to provide an in-depth scientific analysis which might be able to unlock dyers' methods and ingredients used in the past.'[6]

Thomas Wardle's alliance of science and art continues to be celebrated and valued in Britain and India today. Following the rediscovery of his samples a SUTRA conference, titled 'Raksha', or 'protection', organised by Amrita Mukerji, was held in Kolkata in 2010.[7] At this very vibrant international event scholars, including historians, practitioners, conservators and botanists, met and shared their collective knowledge. One part of the event, 'Vriksha' (meaning plants, trees and shrubs), aimed to promote awareness of natural dyes by not only paying particular homage to Wardle's records but also covering many other aspects of the subject.[8] Pramod Kumar curated a stimulating display that included a selection of the Wardle volumes situated alongside beautiful watercolour illustrations from the Botanic Gardens in Kolkata and a superb collection of textiles from Old Bengal. The conference, which included music and traditional Indian dancing, was opened by the noted film-maker Sandip Ray, indicating just how important it was to India's different creative sectors.

SUTRA hosted another international symposium, 'The Colours of Nature', in Kolkata in February 2014.[9] It was the second such event in India to honour Thomas's Wardle's research and once again the symposium attracted an appreciative and varied audience and speakers from around the world. A selection of his dye samples was exhibited in an associated exhibition, 'Natural Dyes: Destination India', curated by Dr Bessie Cecil, who visited Leek in 2015 to see where they had been produced. The displays highlighted and celebrated the range and depth of Wardle's research. India's dyers and printers could again view Wardle's results, which retain potency for them today. One member of a noted family of tenth-generation cloth printers explained to me how Wardle's results had inspired him to try different dye recipes. Many others are now motivated to better understand their heritage and replicate the range of colours he achieved. More global cloth suppliers are undertaking this type of work as the international fashion market demands more natural dyestuffs. India's journalists covered the finds in detail and wanted to know more about Wardle in the process. Nationally available English-language broadsheets that were well aware of the significance of sophisticated craft skills to the nation's economy – *The Times of India*[10] and the *Telegraph*, based in Kolkata – covered the Wardle story.[11]

Thomas Wardle's impressive dedication to the dye analysis project becomes immediately obvious when the samples are viewed. The care taken to mount and comment on each one of them is extraordinary and possibly unique. There are on average ten cloth samples per page (70 × 45cm, two feet by one foot four inches), and each page features a particular dyestuff trialled on a range of silks, cotton and wool. Each sample, roughly the size of a large postcard, is separately stitched into place and positioned between layers of grey card, which supports it. A small tab of blue tape is attached to every one, allowing easy removal from between the pieces of card. The samples are annotated with plant names, usually in Latin, along with their place of origin. There are various code numbers, which may relate to detailed notes and occasional marginalia. Thread samples are mounted differently. It was a thorough, integrated system that would have allowed for long-distance interaction about particular minutiae. Yet, we do not know who had the crucial task of fixing the samples in this way; it must be presumed that this was done in Leek by those who could identify each one. The samples' display seems to be a collaborative pragmatic gesture, done with others in mind. The pages with their sandwiched samples were bound into fifteen volumes with hard green covers; each has tooled and gilded lettering on the spine stating *Specimens of Fabrics Dyed With Indian Dyes by Thos Wardle*, clearly indicating the prestigious nature of this project. Every single sample, let alone the overflowing volumes, indicates the endless hours spent achieving the colours, which still retain their beauty long after they were despatched from Leek to India in 1885. No doubt the colours have lasted because they were bound in volumes away from the light, yet the fact that they then survived the extremes of India's climate for this length of time is remarkable and unexpected.

The volumes were sent to India in order that the information they contained could be made available to India's dyers. They represented Thomas's Wardle's determination to share what he knew to be possible and, importantly, how it was possible. He realised the potential before anyone else because he understood how different mordants and dyestuffs interacted, although the mordants he used were not revealed in the published results that accompanied the samples. This withholding is commonly known as the 'mystery' of dyeing, an ancient tradition that protects each dyer's livelihood, as it prevents rivals from copying dye recipes. Wardle's research, nevertheless, demonstrated how craft could help commerce through understanding. In an age in which textile products were increasingly similar globally Wardle's research was an aesthetic and commercial masterstroke that significantly expanded India's silk export trade to Britain and Europe. Wardle's aesthetic sense, his deep knowledge of dye chemistry, his entrepreneurial skills and centuries of the dyers' craft had combined in his Leek dye works with astonishing outcomes. The delicacy of some colours, the carefully calculated shades and the slight shifts of luminescent colour reflected from the undulating surface of the silk threads reveal just how well he succeeded.

After years of experimentation Thomas Wardle's admiration for India's dyes remained undimmed. In his report he wrote that too little was known in commerce about the 'comprehensive and beautiful range of natural dye stuffs India possesses – colours of every hue and tone and amply sufficient for all artistic and commercial requirements'.[12] We can still see today that the range of reds alone was magnificent, from a delicate pink obtained from root bark from Madras to deepest crimson and purple from cochineal and lac. Scarlet came from manjit and madder sourced from Bengal. Different dye recipes created rich full reds of crimson, vermilion, terracotta, copper, coral, ruby, garnet and every shade of pink through to the palest rose quartz. Indigo dyeing, although a notoriously temperamental process, was thought to be worth the extra effort, as the numerous blues it gave were unsurpassable. When combined with yellow dyestuffs such as weld or turmeric, indigo resulted in many tones of green. Galls from Punjab, pomegranate rind from Oudh and walnuts from Europe produced a variety of bluish or greenish blacks.

The scientific, commercial, imaginative and practical skills honed in Leek were applied to India's troubled silk industry with equally productive results. The government of India, which commissioned the research, was, however, reluctant to cover the increased costs of the extended final phase and Thomas Wardle was out of pocket as a result. The samples in Kolkata bring into focus much of what we can still see today in England. They provide an important backdrop to the surviving pieces in churches and collections as they indicate clearly the astonishing dedication involved in achieving the perfection of enduring colour.

During preparations for the 2014 Kolkata symposium another Wardle collection came to light in Rajasthan. Once again it was possible to view in India a newly rediscovered collection of textiles produced in Leek. This particular collection consists of a series of repeat patterns that had been hand-block printed by Thomas Wardle and donated by him to the Albert Hall Museum, Jaipur. The Museum, which opened in the late nineteenth century, was similar in its aims to the South Kensington Museum in London. Local residents had the opportunity to see what were recognised internationally as designs and goods of the finest type. Examples of Wardle's patterns, including a series of velveteens, are still on permanent display in the Museum's elaborate setting, alongside lace from Nottingham and ceramics from Stoke-on-Trent (Figure 20). These two collections alone confirm that Leek was a centre for active inquiry. Ultimately Wardle was knighted for his visionary research into India's silks and dyestuffs, and for the rest of his life he worked tirelessly for the English and Indian silk industries as a provocateur. There was, however, a general collapse of the British silk industry in the 1930s as this beautiful but expensive fibre was gradually replaced with cheaper man-made substitutes globally.

The limited nature of the evidence has caused a degree of speculation about the Leek Embroidery Society and about Elizabeth Wardle in particular. This

Figure 20   Albert Hall Museum, Jaipur, 2013. Photograph: the author

history challenges some publications that simply got it wrong. Some twenty-first-century authors in a hurry to publish have resorted to fact-free interpretations based on recycled secondary sources. In a number of instances this dynamic and creative craftswoman has been reduced to a distorted stereotype. To frame her life as one of oppression or illness, as has happened, is to take the heart out of her achievements, as it rejects a more nuanced appreciation of her life and work. The glorious embroideries she helped create have sometimes been barely mentioned, yet they are her legacy. Owing to recent finds, we now know that a broader range of designs, materials and colourings has survived than was first thought to be the case. They reveal that Elizabeth Wardle was a remarkably talented and productive woman whose work was globally acknowledged for over thirty years in her lifetime. For the most part the fine condition of the embroideries shows that they have stood the test of time; some are now more than 150 years old, and are a remarkable testimony to the dyer's and stitcher's craft.

In the summer of 2013 an important textile festival was held in Leek. The ten-week event celebrated the town's remarkable heritage of creativity, which was once central to its vitality and is now carefully conserved. A comprehensive exhibition titled The Extraordinary Leek Embroidery Society: Textiles, People, Places was the focal point, which confirmed the significance of the Embroidery Society and its heritage. It was held in the Nicholson Institute, a fine Arts and Crafts building in the town centre, and attracted over 6,000 visitors. Many of the pieces that were on view 132 years before in the 1881 Exhibition of Modern Embroidery were again displayed alongside others produced since. What was

177

once a contemporary, living craft has now become the reason behind exhibitions, guided walks and workshops. The project pulled together a great number of local volunteers determined that their regional heritage should be more widely celebrated. The sense of place was profound, as thousands of visitors experienced in impressive local buildings a rich array of historic textiles demonstrating the variety of work Leek embroiderers had created. Displays covered various stages of the Society's development over more than sixty years, highlighting the very high standard of craft skills achieved in both secular and sacred work. From the small alms bags of 1864 to a large processional banner of 1911 from Stoke, it was possible to witness a sustained level of excellence in one location.

A small collection of embroideries donated to the Nicholson Institute by Lydia Wardle, daughter of Thomas and Elizabeth Wardle, provided important information. She had assembled the items in 1933 in frustration that so little of the Wardle history was then known in Leek. To these items was added newly discovered work for the festival displays. As many of the exhibits had been cared for by private individuals, some of whom were linked through family ties to former Leek embroiderers, they had never before been seen by the wider public. All are interesting in their own right, but when displayed alongside so many other pieces of Leek embroidery they took on additional meaning, as designs and colouring constantly reinforced each other. Relationships between the pieces, in both tangible and intangible ways, proved as important as the sum of the individual items and their histories, and, in turn, could have some bearing on whether or not they are preserved for future generations to enjoy. This is one of the joys and benefits of curating an exhibition and can have an immense effect on how the items are perceived. For example, in some cases one design was reproduced on a number of different ground cloths and in different colourings, demonstrating the flexibility of the block-printing process and the creative freedom of the needlewomen. Such pieces became differently animated by being placed next to one another, in a way that was never possible when items were only ever viewed individually.

The great range of materials and the diversity of designs, techniques and colouring that characterised the work of the Leek Embroidery Society, and which prompted many published articles in the late nineteenth century, was revealed in the variety of exhibits, finally allowing a true understanding of Thomas and Elizabeth Wardle's combined achievements. Every piece can now be understood as the product of interlocking influences and each had a purpose in either the domestic or ecclesiastic sphere. Picture frames, cushion covers, chair backs, a tea cosy, a letter rack, a nightdress case, portiere borders and a number of fire screens were on display alongside five altar frontals and other ecclesiastical pieces, plainly indicating the roles of decorative objects in widely different interiors.

Importantly, the needlewomen's skills came across as being alive to the characteristics of the materials they used and the colours they selected. This is was all the more apparent when original working drawings were on view next to finished pieces. Recently identified rare cartoons by the architect Gerald Horsley were displayed in public for the first time. Colour and texture were noticeably absent from these, which were produced for a variety of ecclesiastical embroideries. This emphasised the role of the needlewomen, who brought these marks on paper to life with textured silks and gold thread. Designs for large altar frontals were seen alongside tracings and needlework samples by Mrs Beatrice Ethel Warren. As they were displayed together with the completed pieces, they demonstrated the whole sequence of creative techniques from concept to final article.

The exhibition illustrated how three main design traditions had provided inspiration for Leek work. Historic Indian and Persian textile traditions were prominent; other historic influences included Renaissance velvets and Sicilian silks. Contemporary designers were represented by Morris, Sedding, George Gilbert Scott Jnr, Bodley, Shaw, George Young Wardle and Tom Wardle Jnr. It was a roll call of the most eminent, whose embroidered designs were on view side by side, probably for the first time, their local significance placed alongside their importance in terms of major national movements. For the most part they are now returned to private collections, and the exhibition was, therefore, important in that it confirmed the extraordinary range of designs, colourings and techniques produced in this small town. It was also possible to see just how enterprising the Leek Embroidery Society was, as so many of the designs, including a large number from India, were ingeniously adapted to work as both ecclesiastical and domestic pieces.

Alongside the main exhibition, churches in the region displayed their embroideries in the buildings for which they were designed. A printed trail guided visitors to eight churches where striking embroideries still fulfil their original role by adding beauty and symbolism to the interior. Designs by Bodley, Horsley, George Gilbert Scott Jnr, Sedding, Shaw, Street, George Young Wardle and young Tom Wardle were again admired in their great variety and, importantly, their original settings. Their condition is remarkable, the brilliant effects that the Wardles achieved having survived the ravages of time and use: their colours are still vibrant, the gold work dazzles as it always has and more is now known about their makers, designs and the wide range of skills that were necessary for their creation.

Visitors came from across the globe to see the exhibition. Embroiderers from Australia had travelled especially for this event, while sixty-five people from three generations of Indian families from Sheffield and Chesterfield were thrilled to find exquisite examples of their heritage in a small Staffordshire town. As a

BBC Radio 4 programme cleverly pointed out, they were part of the *British Raj in the Peak District*.[13] The exhibition, and associated talks and walks, offered an opportunity for reflection; countless comments in visitors' books praised the exhibits and stressed the need for a permanent display of the magnificent work, confirming that the event was long overdue. Since then even more examples of Leek's work have been identified, reinforcing the fact that a researcher's work is never done. Celebrations will continue in other forms in the future.

Owing to twenty-first-century discoveries it is now possible to trace the development of the Leek Embroidery Society from its earliest phase, before it was formalised, through to the final stages in the twentieth century. The previous chapters and extant pieces show that Elizabeth and Thomas Wardle established and developed a truly remarkable enterprise for which the large number of surviving textiles offer a significant body of evidence. In a world of increasing mass production this creative couple proved there was still room for a family-run business to thrive on craft skills as long as good design and fine materials remained a priority. Their imaginative initiatives preserved and developed traditional skills in north Staffordshire and demonstrated how they could work in parallel with the world of expanding commerce without compromising their integrity. High-quality design and finely honed techniques were at the heart of their success and consequently became a part of everyday life for many others, both as makers and consumers. Like Morris, they shared their skills and ideals to create useful and beautiful domestic pieces in their workshops and homes to be enjoyed in households across Britain. This allowed craft skills to grow in importance alongside industrially produced goods. Thousands of people could have experienced their work in towns and villages every day if they so wished, as the pieces were made by the community for everyone. The Wardle family gained international attention and popular and critical acclaim through its perceptive combination of local talent and international awareness.

Tracking down, documenting and interpreting the various finds has been rewarding, revealing and thought-provoking. As many of the pieces have survived we can see today exactly what residents and visitors to Leek saw all those years ago on a daily basis. They indicate to some extent the essence of the community from which they came, even if the modern visitor may not always understand the iconography and ceremony that was once involved. In addition to an obvious mastery over materials and techniques, the work reveals a diverse aesthetic at the core of the embroidery enterprise. It was then, and is now, a celebration of needlework skills in all their diversity. The Leek Embroidery Society was more than a family business; it raised the status of needlework nationally and internationally, and this needs to be acknowledged. There is strong evidence that a regional idiom became a significant element of a number of national movements, and India's remarkable raw materials and wealth of traditional designs were undoubtedly major aspects of this.

This all confirms that Leek, the home of the Society, was not stranded in moorland isolation; it was a town of considerable confidence and much civic pride, well connected to mainstream ideas and the world at large. The town was an outward-looking centre of excellence with a strong cultural infrastructure, which was essential to the spirit of the place. It supported and developed a high concentration of craft skills and a critical awareness of good design in the face of fierce global industrialisation. When market forces desired new products Leek was able to respond as indigenous craftworkers and traditional techniques were flexible enough to develop items for global markets. Local craftworkers' combined skills grew organically to provide the foundation for high-profile commissions to and from major architects. The scale and focus of the town, with its embedded resources, made this possible: on the one hand there was the traditional silk industry, and on the other there was contemporary design of the highest order; these overlapped in a mutually reinforcing way. When this was then merged with the social and cultural life of the town the wider impact was an improved economic life for its citizens, which came from the greater sustainability of local businesses in north Staffordshire. Simultaneously, local needlewomen gained opportunities for considerable artistic expression through their involvement in prestigious community projects, the result of commissioning the most eminent Gothic Revival architects, with the highest ideals, to build in the region. The list of renowned figures who were working in one small area of north Staffordshire is a remarkable record of the greatest in the field. That they were responsible for at least two new churches, five major restorations, various minor adjustments and at least one domestic building was extraordinary. They all drew on medieval ornament that embraced elements of nature using a familiar historical lexicon. Many large cities would not have witnessed such high-level activity.

It is astonishing that every one of the architects involved designed embroideries for their churches, which were then stitched by Leek needlewomen. Implicit in this glorious work are stories of creativity, vision, traditional skills, understanding of materials, faith, ritual, intense hard work, collaborations, the global and regional silk industries, women's history and the British Arts and Crafts movement, Gothic Revivalism and Art Needlework. They live on still in a number of remarkable buildings, the result of an intricate blend of the sacred and the secular, trade and craft, art and science. Unpicking the multilayered collaborations has established that the element of commercial enterprise did not in any way compromise theological integrity. No doubt this was down to careful management by the Wardle family, who were both entrepreneurial and active Christians.

181

A number of Thomas Wardle's publications have recently been republished as facsimiles of the originals in the United States. They are considered to be culturally important as they are seen as part of the knowledge base of their time, more proof of how seriously Wardle's breakthroughs are taken on the global stage.

Although very little is known about the many designers who must have produced work on paper to be converted into interesting printed textiles, recent developments have highlighted the work of Lana Mackinnon, who produced work on a number of occasions for Sir Thomas and Arthur Wardle, as the family firm became known. Her work was exhibited at the important 'Britain Can Make It' exhibition in London. One of her designs is a block-printed silk handkerchief given as a present to Wardle clients in 1947 (Figure 21a). It

Figure 21a   Printed silk, design by Lana Mackinnon, 1947.
Courtesy of Nicholas Gilmour

Figure 21b   Printed fabric designed by Lana Mackinnon, 2017.
Courtesy of Nicholas Gilmour

features the designer in the act of block-printing, with two of her designs for the Leek company hanging behind her. They have recently been reproduced and look strikingly contemporary (Figure 21b).[14]

As new light has been cast on both the making and meaning of ecclesiastical textiles, embroideries in churches, along with their associated documents, provide important insight into a variety of intersecting lives. We now know that the production of many exceptional pieces was not simply a matter of providing decorative interior fittings as an afterthought, completed after important architects had returned to their London office. On the contrary, evidence reveals just how necessary was the needlewomen's role to finishing an architect's emblematic interior scheme. Inevitably, however, our view of historic objects changes over time and textiles intended to be perceived in a specific, liturgical way may be judged differently by researchers and others today. All too often craft skills are taken out of their nineteenth-century context and reassessed using a twenty-first-century awareness. Embroideries designed for ecclesiastical and ceremonial use in the nineteenth century can be regarded solely as crafted and/or aesthetic objects if there is no comprehension of their original ritualistic and communal context. Their creation would, nevertheless, have required the same understanding of materials, skills, thought, choices and creativity practised today.

Knowing the needlework's symbiotic history is important, as it emphasises the diversity of interaction that was involved in its production. Men and women from Leek pooled their talents and formed partnerships with London-based architects to make major projects happen. Designs from India and Europe were particularly inspirational and worked wonders when adapted with local materials for different purposes. Raw materials were shipped from across the globe; Japan provided sophisticated gold thread and some finished pieces stitched with this ended up in Africa.[15] They are tangible evidence of many people united in a common attempt to produce beautiful and useful things for a specific, ritualistic purpose.

Tracing the life cycle of individual pieces, from original designs to their final destination and ultimately long-term survival, has undoubtedly raised their level of significance in a number of fields. There has been a tendency more recently to think of ecclesiastical items as simply decorative pieces, which has led to a lessening of their wider importance. Yet this was work that was taken seriously and created with integrity. As more opportunities to produce fine ritualistic textiles developed, their value was reinforced. The architect's role in raising the profile of needlework, with the related rise in the standing of Art Needlework, cannot be overestimated. The designs were by men who lavished great care on the symbolic weight of every aspect of their schemes and it was their clear intention that the intangible notion of the sacred was to be embodied in stitch as well as stone. There is a self-referential logic to their embroidery designs that echoes their function and emphatic focal place in the building. This created an obvious sense of harmony intended to bolster belief. That this happened in parallel with developments in the Arts and Crafts movement was no happy accident. Both sacred and secular textiles were key elements of this ethical movement that valued beauty in everyday things, and members of the Wardle family played major parts in that history also. Their lives spent doing research through making led to a better understanding of materials and techniques. The status of hand embroidery and textile design rose dramatically during this era, reinforced by overlapping links to the Gothic Revival movement. As Morris and other high-profile designers were to discover, Leek was a prime place for their visions to be realised as glorious textiles. A further interesting aspect of this was the consistent ways in which new interpretations repeatedly revitalised historic designs. In turn, the town attracted the greatest talents, who became involved with Leek in various ways. The distinguished designer Walter Crane was there when the cornerstone of the Nicholson Institute was laid in 1892 and for a time he was its principal.[16]

Conditions in Leek combined to produce fabrics that were simultaneously local and international, traditional and modern. They were made by a community that offered the best craft skills and the finest materials with which to create fine embroideries intended to be used by that same community and elsewhere. Children of craftworkers gave birth to children of craftworkers, many of whom participated in communal patronage as individual members of congregations and were often involved with the funding, creation and use of pieces in a major public space. Through the pieces they created we have a vision of a close community. For many, churches were the grandest buildings they would ever enter, filled with fine specimens of the decorative arts as a matter of civic and personal pride. They became familiar and cherished objects for the citizens of Leek and today they attract many visitors to the town.

Needlewomen contributed to the narratives regularly observed by congregations in some very elaborate settings. Their work was sited alongside items in other materials designed by the highest-ranking architects and designers. This raised the profile, both locally and nationally, of those embroiderers who produced the work. It is now clear that through their skills women took a more active part in local life than had previously been recognised. Elizabeth Wardle was one of a number of highly successful women whose work has only recently been scrutinised. Although to date embroiderers have generally been studied as an homogeneous group, their personal lives, motivations, skills and creative styles varied enormously. It is time for their work to be accepted as on a par with that of their male counterparts working in design and architecture at that time.

The facsimile of the Bayeux Tapestry, completed in Leek in 1886, came into its own again in 2016, when the 950th anniversary of the Battle of Hastings was celebrated. Events at Reading Museum, organised by the Textile Society (UK), the Society of Antiquaries, London and Winterthur, USA, looked at the lasting significance of this remarkable achievement and the life it led on its various tours. In 2018, President Macron caused a media storm when he announced that the original Tapestry could travel from France to Britain. Once again this impressive work is subject to massive interest and its significance debated at length. As a result, Leek's facsimile has been rediscovered all over again as it is featured across the media.

All of this confronts issues related to amateur versus professional status. How was this to be measured in the circumstances that prevailed in Leek? The professionalisation of embroidery was a far from straightforward concept. Although it was referred to, it was not always clear what credentials were required in order to be considered a professional, and the whole notion seems to rest on random definitions by researchers. How many pieces and of what size needed to be worked for a needlewoman to gain professional status, or was something else at play here? The perception of professionalism was even more complex for women, as so few could devote their entire time to developing their work. Whether it was achieved through commercial success or by other means was not obvious. If it was a matter of tuition and examination, then that must have restricted college access to those living nearer to major educational centres. The idea of recognition being gained through the production of the finest examples is riddled with issues related to subjectivity. This history of the Leek Embroidery Society does not provide simple answers, as so many different conditions were operating at any one time.

When she died in 1902 Elizabeth Wardle's work was recognised globally. Obituaries were carried by newspapers and journals as far away as Australia, with details of her many skills and achievements. They were aware of Leek embroidery in the Antipodes through the international exhibitions held there that included Wardle exhibits. Some pieces still survive there in private and museum collections. Elizabeth Wardle was mourned as an embroiderer of exceptional work and as someone who applied her expertise to India's wild silks by responding to the material and maximising its potential. She was also known as an excellent tutor of others through her practice-led Society. By attracting commissions from distinguished architects she had the ability to enhance their buildings without detracting from other features in a highly decorative chancel. Her expertise as an organiser, colourist and stitcher of embroidery was highlighted again and again, and many parts of the country had examples of her work as witness. What is less well known was that she was a woman with a strong sense of public duty, associated with many charitable institutions for which she worked extremely hard and which brought her into regular contact with a variety of people. She was described as a warm, generous and broad-minded woman who particularly abhorred narrow ideas in public life. She was frequently consulted upon the subjects that interested her and was involved with numerous committees. After her death it was discovered that she had regularly donated profits of the Leek Embroidery Society to various charities.

This evidence-based history challenges some twenty-first-century publications that have depicted embroiderers as invariably passive and exploited, oppressed seamstresses sewing seams – assertions that would have baffled Elizabeth Wardle and her contemporaries. Although her life defies these stereotypical portrayals a number of authors have attempted to squeeze complex embroidery history into a narrowly defined occupation that is invariably seen as unfair towards those engaged in it. They are seemingly unaware of a great many achievements within the field, as they rarely mention the work that was produced; yet, in so many cases, this work is the ultimate triumph. The concept of the suppressed seamstress or bored housewife who plies a needle is a seductive and persistent one, but it has denied the public acclaim that many creative women undoubtedly experienced and represents a lost opportunity to record how they earned a living by using their demanding skills in a number of spheres. Elizabeth Wardle never wavered and there were seemingly no barriers to prevent her enjoying worldwide acclaim, but she has been misperceived in the twenty-first century – her stellar career has been ignored and she has been pigeonholed as a repressed woman, a slave to domesticity. She has even been subjected to misplaced, evidence-free psychoanalysis based on her appearance in a photograph[17] and described as someone who scarcely knew her own mind.[18] This is a past that needs to be more carefully interrogated. There are many capable, ambitious, skilled women who need to be rescued from their rescuers, who have downgraded embroidery history for far too long. In the worse cases, crude mythologising is used to pad out anecdotal comment and the authors' theoretical preoccupations. As we have proof of many women's fine skills these dramatic flourishes can now be seen as surplus to requirements.

There is now a clear need to tease out myth from reality, correct over-simplified impressions and restore their rightful agency to many talented people by presenting a more balanced appreciation of a lifetime's work. The story of Leek and its Embroidery Society is important as it acts as a counter-point to received wisdom regarding nineteenth-century women's capabilities and demonstrates that needlework was not a single entity; rather, it was finely nuanced and embraced a number of different areas of activity. It should also be pointed out that Elizabeth Wardle epitomised what many women still strive for today.

A Call to Action: Whose Responsibility?

The challenge in the twenty-first century is to consider how best to preserve this magnificent textile heritage in ways that will be meaningful and representative to those who produced it, used it and have cared for it ever since. They are not products of obligation or monotony and, as there are a multitude of histories embedded in these pieces, there are a number of things to consider if they are to be preserved for future generations to enjoy, learn from and be inspired by.

Those whose ancestors created these beautiful things and the many others who have celebrated this work in various ways ever since, as part of their national and international history, may have different ideas about what this might entail.

The production of every piece is testimony to human agency operating at a variety of levels, from the recognition of the piece's symbolic function to an individual's refined craft skills to the collective action of a small town and the global silk industry, among other things. This connected creativity is now better known and vital to our complete understanding of the pieces, as it fixes them firmly in the society that made them. As we can see from this history, churches had a strong community role that bound people together, as well as being agents of art and ceremony. Craft practice and aesthetics were part of many people's lives, whether they were makers or members of a congregation, or both. A knowledge of the wider communal context is crucial and should lead to a greater understanding with regard to exhibiting the work and planning conservation and preservation. This last point is a matter of growing concern for ecclesiastical textiles in particular. Who decides what the most important factors are? And, without relevant contextual knowledge, how does anyone decide what should be saved or discarded?

Arguably, textiles are the most vulnerable items in a church interior. Owing to the nature of their raw materials they have a finite life, and they are susceptible to damp, light, insect damage and general wear and tear. Embroideries produced in Leek have stood the test of time and generally are looked after carefully by volunteers who are dedicated to their preservation. Some are in use on a regular basis; others, retired from active service, are framed and mounted so that they can still be enjoyed daily. Others are not on constant view but are regularly displayed and valued.

Fieldwork in north Staffordshire brought me into contact with the people who care for ecclesiastical embroidery today. While identifying new pieces made in Leek was a great delight, it also alerted me to an increasingly worrying situation that needs to be addressed. It is an undeniable fact that congregations are in severe decline across the country; many parish churches, particularly those in rural areas, are facing uncertain times and there is a serious and escalating problem of church closures nationwide. It is probably inevitable that the following decades will see an increase in this. As a consequence there are a number of redundant embroideries, some of which are now homeless, calling into question the future of other historic work. Many fragile textiles are at considerable risk if they are stored in unheated, damp churches. Without policies to protect them these superb treasures will gradually disappear. There are also connected issues relating to suitable storage and the high costs of conservation. This proved to be of sufficient concern to the Textile Society (UK) that it was agreed that I could organise a seminar, funded by the Society, dedicated to the future of historic ecclesiastical textiles. *Who Cares* was an oversubscribed event, held in London in 2015, and described as 'long-awaited' and 'much needed'. The Leek Embroidery Society provided a model case study of what could be done to raise the profile of this particular history through exhibitions and publications, highlighting the importance of this particular heritage to many thousands of church visitors. As a result, more people than ever are interested in saving this heritage for the future.

Although this is acknowledged by many institutions whose remit is to monitor and assist with Britain's endangered ecclesiastical heritage, vulnerable textiles come low down on the long list of priorities. It is an urgent issue, however, and many people are rightly anxious about the prospects and visibility of these beautiful pieces, many of which are often under-appreciated and unknown except to specialists. Across the country fundamental questions are being raised about future storage, conservation and preservation. There are agonising collective decisions to be made over which of the historic items should be saved, as not all are viable in the long term. Congregations and friends of churches should ready themselves for some challenges ahead. They will require a vision and a great deal of creative thinking in order to find solutions to a countrywide problem. Funding of these delicate items is, as ever, a major consideration, and a recognition of the need to support those who care for these works is critical. As this history shows, these wonderful pieces are significant regionally, nationally and internationally. Surely it is the responsibility of us all to ensure their survival?[19]

WHERE TO FIND THE WORK OF THE WARDLE FAMILY

Apart from the ecclesiastical pieces, many of which are still in the churches for which they were made, the work of the Wardle family can be seen in various places beyond Leek, as listed below.

Birmingham Museum and Art Gallery
The Gallery has original designs by William Morris that were converted into printed fabric by Thomas Wardle in Leek.

Cartwright Hall, Bradford
Cartwright Hall has a large tussar silk hanging commissioned to celebrate Thomas Wardle's achievements. It was designed by Shenaz Ismail and made in Karachi in 2012. Her design contains the book title *Silk and Empire* woven into the structure.

Department of Economic Botany, Kew Gardens, London
The Department holds skeins of embroidery yarns dyed by Thomas Wardle.

Edinburgh and Glasgow Museums
The Museums have a small selection of items, some donated by Thomas Wardle.

Gawthorpe Hall, Padiham, Lancashire
Gawthorpe Hall has a selection of finished and unfinished embroidered pieces

and dyed silk threads from Leek, and a photograph of Mrs Wardle with local embroiderers.

Goldsmiths College, London
There are a few examples of ecclesiastical embroidery in the Constance Howard collection.

Leek Library, Staffordshire
The Library holds a selection of documents and publications related to the Wardle family.

The Museum of London
The Museum has a dress made from a fabric with an Indian-inspired pattern block printed in Leek.

Reading Museum
Leek's facsimile of the Bayeux Tapestry is on permanent display at the Museum. It still intrigues, although the embroidered panels seen today have been through a long and strenuous peripatetic life, which, unsurprisingly, has caused some wear and tear. The various attempts to clean and restore the panels have also taken their toll, which is to be expected. Some colours have faded, probably because they have been constantly exposed to light and have endured numerous washings, which released dyestuffs from the wool threads. Consequently, the facsimile does not look exactly as it did when it was assembled in Leek in 1886. Some recent commentators, aiming to compare it with the original, have relied on photographs in publications or online, as it is impossible to take the Leek facsimile to France to make a true appraisal. Yet photographing textiles is a notoriously tricky business despite the latest camera technology and can give an unsatisfactory result where colour reproduction is concerned. Different ambient lighting can change a colour tone, reproducing that on a computer can change it again and the printing process for publications can distort the subtlety of a colour range even further. Refined comparisons are almost impossible to achieve and conclusions lack solid evidence to sustain them. All of these circumstances need to be taken into account when assessing the facsimile's impact today.

RIBA Collection (V&A) London and the Staffordshire Record Office
Both hold working drawings for embroidery by Gerald C. Horsley.

Shrewsbury Abbey
The abbey has a magnificent altar frontal designed by the architect J.L. Pearson.

Staffordshire Museums Service

There are a number of secular items held at the Nicholson Institute and in storage.

Sunnycroft, Wellington, Shropshire

This National Trust property displays its Leek embroidery collection in a domestic setting.

The Victoria and Albert Museum, London

The V&A holds a number of block-printed designs produced by Wardle & Co., which provided popular patterns for embroiderers, and an uncompleted 'kit' with associated threads. It has completed embroideries stitched with wild silks from India, some of which were unearthed when the textile collections were moved from the South Kensington site to the new Clothworkers' Centre, Olympia. They were probably donated when Thomas Wardle installed a collection of India's wild silks for permanent display in the Museum in the 1880s. The Museum has two versions of the hand-coloured photographs of the Bayeux Tapestry, which was exhibited at the International Exhibition in South Kensington in 1873. They may be the very ones that were lent to the Wardles to be copied in Leek. The quality of the photography is remarkable, as it is still possible to see repairs and individual threads of both the ground cloth and the embroidery. The Prints and Drawings Department has drawings by George Young Wardle.

The Whitworth Art Gallery, The University of Manchester, Manchester

The university-owned Gallery holds Elizabeth Wardle's sewing basket, with threads and a few small pieces of embroidery. The Gallery also has a comprehensive selection of hand-block-printed piece goods produced by Wardle & Co., a number of which were used as a base for needlework. There is an important series of block-printers' trial books, which, likewise, provides an invaluable source of information on many repeat patterns used by the Leek Embroidery Society. The gallery also has a collection of Indian silks formed by Thomas Wardle to display in the Indian and Colonial Exhibition, London (1886) and the Royal Jubilee Exhibition, Manchester (1887).

William Morris Gallery, Walthamstow

The Gallery has original designs, printing blocks and finished textiles designed by William Morris and printed by Thomas Wardle in Leek.

Antipodes
Auckland Museum, Auckland, New Zealand
The Museum contains some items of Leek embroidery.

Europe
The Museum of Decorative and Applied Arts, Budapest, Hungary
The museum owns eleven samples of velvet printed in Leek by Thomas Wardle. They were bought directly from the Morris & Co. shop in Oxford Street, London, by the museum's director Jenő Radisics in 1896.

Rijksmuseum, Amsterdam
The Museum holds a finely stitched version of the 'Indian Poppy' design.

India
The Albert Hall Museum, Jaipur, Rajasthan
Thomas Wardle donated to the Museum a collection of block-printed textiles that he produced in Staffordshire.

The Indian Museum, Kolkata
A unique collection of thousands of dye samples created by Thomas Wardle in Staffordshire was donated by him to the Museum.

Private Collections
Numerous private collections across Britain and Europe contain various domestic pieces that we know were printed in Leek. It is not always possible to know, however, who stitched these pieces. While the printed designs, colouring, cloth and thread may be traced to Leek and seem similar to the work of the Leek Embroidery Society, they could have been produced by any number of individuals who purchased the same printed designs, possibly in kit form, and stitched them using the same range of stitches and threads as Leek needlewomen.

NOTES

Preface

1. Two previous publications concentrated on different aspects of the Wardle family: *Silk and Empire* and *Dye, Print, Stitch: Textiles by Thomas and Elizabeth Wardle*, both by Brenda King.
2. Edwards and Hart 2010, p. 40, n. 38. As recently as 2010 the prolific Wardle family was dismissed in a sparse footnote, which simply named Thomas Wardle, in a publication that claimed to rethink Aesthetic and Arts and Crafts interiors c. 1867–1896. Gere fails to mention the family in *Artistic Circles*, although the publication focuses on design and decoration in the Aesthetic interior.
3. See Linda Parry's numerous publications on William Morris.
4. Ann Jacques publication *The Wardle Story* (1996) was the first to recognise the family's importance. As relevant material had not then been located it lacks numerous contexts and in-depth discussion of the textiles and there are no colour plates.
5. Bannerjee 2014 and Mukerji 2014.
6. Morris 1893, p. 38.
7. Menon 2013.
8. Lister *et al.* 2017.
9. King 2009b.
10. Wainwright 1981, pp. 1–3.
11. Work still needs to be done on Street and Sedding.
12. I am grateful to Linda Eaton of Winterthur, USA, for her help with locating press reports.
13. Hicks 2006, pp. 181–5, and Cluckie 2008, pp. 95–7.
14. Cecil and Dasgupta 2014, p. 16.

Introduction

1. John Ruskin's letter regarding the first Morris memorial. The book of the opening of the William Morris Labour Church at Leek, 1897, was published for the church and sold by the 'Clarion' office, 72 Fleet Street, London.
2. King 2005.

3. King 2005. This publication explores Wardle's invention of a new cloth from recycle waste as well as his expansion of the use of India's wild silks.
4. Thomas Wardle reported that by 1884 there were few cottage handlooms to be found. Some yarn twisting continued as a domestic occupation for women and children.
5. Morris 1886, p. 6.
6. Ibid.
7. The book of the opening of the William Morris Labour Church at Leek, 1897.
8. A number of Rigby's designs are in the V&A, London.
9. Day 1900, p. 1.

Chapter 1: The Wardle Family and its Circle

1. Mackail 1899, I, p. 331; Mackail reprints a letter dictated by Morris just before he died.
2. MacCarthy 1994, as quoted on p. 349.
3. Mackail 1899, II, p. 316.
4. Harvey and Press 1993, p. 99.
5. See Watkinson 1997, p. 20.
6. Harvey and Press 1993, p. 124, n. 16.
7. Walton 2014, p. 166.
8. Mrs Warren stitched a number of ecclesiastical embroideries designed by G. Horsley.
9. They can be found in the V&A.
10. Parry 1996, p. 20.
11. Jacques 1996, p. 4.
12. A letter from J. Wardle to a client, now in a private collection, confirms this.
13. King 2013, pp. 20–27.
14. Ibid.
15. Bandyopadhyay 2009.
16. King 2013, pp. 20–27.
17. Watkinson 1997, p. 21.
18. Harvey and Press 1993, p. 99–103.
19. Parry 1996, p. 22.
20. King and Spring 2001, pp. 4–19.
21. King 2013, pp. 20–27.
22. Wardle 1887.
23. Harvey and Press 1993, pp. 186–7.
24. It became known as 'Sir Thomas and Arthur Wardle, based at the Churnet Works'. Gilbert Wardle became managing director of Joshua Wardle Ltd, Leek Brook; Bernard Wardle had his own printing company, with a branch at Pale Meadow, Shropshire; while Tom Wardle became an eminent designer.
25. Lara Mackinnon did designs for Thomas and Arthur Wardle Ltd. She is one of the few twentieth-century designers we know anything about. The image of a textile shows a hand block printer at work, with some of her designs displayed on the wall behind. They were reproduced recently. I am grateful to Nicholas Gilmour for this information.
26. Marsh and Sharp 2013, pp. 84 and 407.
27. Harvey and Press 1993, p. 29.

28. The relevant correspondence is now at the Staffordshire Record Office.
29. Saint 2010.
30. Higgin 1886 a.
31. Harvey and Press 1993, p. 57.
32. Watkinson 1997, p. 20.
33. Mackail 1899, II, p. 60.
34. Ibid.
35. Harvey and Press 1993, p. 167.
36. Wardle 1883.
37. Harvey and Press 1993, p. xii.
38. Linda Parry Archive. The William Morris Gallery, Walthamstow, London E17 4PP.
39. Hall 2014, p. 138.
40. It is in Charterhouse Square, close to the Barbican, London. It reopened in 2017 after extensive renovation.
41. Goodall 2017.
42. Greystones, a prominent historic house in the centre of Leek, bears an early SPAB blue plaque stating that the building was saved with the help of W. Morris, through SPAB, in 1884.
43. Mackail 1899, II, p. 167.
44. Aplin 2015.
45. MacGowan 2007, p. 139.
46. From 'An Address on English Art and Industries', given to students at Burslem School of Art, Staffordshire, 1887.
47. King 2005, pp. 141–2.
48. From *The Leek Post and Times*, 30 March 1915.
49. T. Wardle, Local History section, Leek Library.
50. 'Wardle, Sir Thomas (1831–1900), Silk dyer and printer and promoter of the silk industry', p. 663, *Dictionary of Business Biography*, vol. 5: *S–Z*. Butterworths, London 1980, pp. 661–65.
51. See King 2005, p. 77.

Chapter 2: The Business of Stitch

1. At the time of writing blue plaques were being prepared to mark the Wardle residences.
2. King and Spring 2000, p. 1.
3. Kay is mentioned in letters dated 8 October and 2 November 1875.
4. Wardle 1881, Preface.
5. They included items purchased at £5 each in December 1880. This was quite soon after her initial experiments with stitching tussar. More were acquired in 1881, while in 1884 a large piece of tussor on tussar needlework was purchased for £12. This was possibly a piece that was exhibited in Berlin.
6. Anon. 1881.
7. Ibid.
8. See Morris 1893, p. 18 for a description of long and short stitch and p. 23 for couching methods.
9. Anon. 1881.
10. Ibid.

11. Thomas Wardle gave a paper 'The Wild Silks of India Principally Tusser', to the Royal Society of Arts, London, in 1879.
12. Hulse 2010, p. 1.
13. Ibid.
14. Higgin 1880, p. 14.
15. Ibid.
16. Ibid.
17. Watkinson 1988, p. 28.
18. Parry 2013, p. 26.
19. Ibid., p. 31.
20. See Marsh and Sharp 2013, p. 84, Letters 58 and 59. I am grateful to Lynn Hulse for directing me to this publication.
21. Marsh and Sharp 2013, p. 407, letter no. 468.
22. Parry 2013, p. 29.
23. Kelvin 1984, Volume 1, letters 11–12, 1876.
24. King 2005.
25. Ibid.
26. In 2014 a number of the embroidered tussar examples were discovered in the Indian Section of the Victoria and Albert Museum during the relocation of textiles to the new Clothworkers' Centre in Olympia. I am grateful to Dr Sonia Ashmore for this information.
27. Morris 1989, pp. 16–17.
28. Ibid., p. 17.
29. The caves are currently undergoing restoration.
30. An example of 'The Nubian', printed onto velveteen, was donated by Thomas Wardle to the Albert Hall Museum, Jaipur.
31. King 2009a, pp. 57–8.
32. The *Fine Art and Industries Exhibition*, St James Hall, Manchester, December 1882, in the *Manchester Guardian*.
33. Ibid.
34. At the same exhibition Messrs Wardle & Co. was awarded a diploma of honour for beauty, colour and design in its specialities.
35. Samples of wallpapers based on Wardle & Co.'s textiles are in the Nordiska Museet, Stockholm.
36. Letters from Thomas Wardle, 1882. Local Studies Collection, Leek Library.
37. King 2009a, pp. 57–8.
38. Morris 1893, *Dedicatory Note*.
39. Couched gold thread from Japan was a new product that did not tarnish. It consisted of gold-coated paper wrapped around an orange silk thread.
40. In 1884 there were references in the *Leek Post & Times* to Elizabeth Wardle's support of local embroiderers who wished to sell their work through emporia.
41. Higgin 1886a, p. 122.
42. This pattern was a particularly popular one, initially printed by Wardle & Co. for Liberty of Regent Street.
43. Higgin 1886b, pp. 139–40.
44. Ibid., pp. 141–3.
45. Ibid.
46. Jacques 1996, p. 51.
47. Anon. 1888.

48. Ibid.
49. Ibid.
50. Anon. 1898, p. 198.
51. Parkes 1893, pp. 136–40.
52. Masters 1892, p. 63.
53. Ibid., pp. 70–71.
54. Ibid., p. 71.
55. Ibid., p. 67.
56. Walton 2014.
57. The Alan Bednall archive, http://www.bednallarchive.info/localhist/staffshistjurnl. htm (accessed 2 April 2009).
58. The Technical Instruction Committee expanded in 1892. In 1900 an extension for the County Silk School was built in Leek.
59. Morris 1893, back cover.
60. A flyer advertising this event was displayed in an exhibition devoted to Wilde entitled *Insolence Incarnate* at the Petit Palais in Paris in September 2016.
61. 'Oscar Wilde at Leek', *Leek Post*, 1884.
62. Staffordshire Pasttrack, https://www.search.staffspasttrack.org.uk/Details.aspx?&Res ourceID=29559&PageIndex=9&SearchType=2&ThemeID=208 (accessed 2 January 2019).
63. Walker 2011, p. 128.
64. In 2017 this church received a grant from the National Churches Trust to restore its roof. This should provide a better environment for the embroideries than the damp conditions that prevailed before.

Chapter 3: Stitching Narrative – Leek's Facsimile of the Bayeux Tapestry

1. Wardle 1886, Preface, pp. 3–4.
2. Bruce 1856, p. 6.
3. Ruskin 1906, p. 160.
4. Hockney and Gayford 2016, p. 88.
5. Ibid., p. 89.
6. Staniland 1991, p. 40.
7. Ibid., p. 57.
8. The few panels on display in the Medieval Gallery and Renaissance Galleries of the V&A are more sober and the ground cloth is of an uneven colour.
9. Staniland 1991, p. 35.
10. Engravings and casts are still held in the archives of the Society of Antiquaries, London.
11. Anon. 2008, p. 150.
12. Ibid.
13. Ibid.
14. Hicks 2006, p. 160.
15. Ibid.
16. Ruskin 1851–3, pp. 226–7.
17. Ibid., p. 234.
18. Watkinson, R. 1988, p. 27.

19. MacCarthy 1994, p. 94.
20. Wardle 1886, Preface.
21. King 2005.
22. K. Barker, Conservator's Report for Reading Museum, November 1992.
23. Ibid., p. 4.
24. Bruce 1856.
25. The watercolour drawings were hand-coloured photographs. See Wardle, E. 1886.
26. The nine surviving offspring were aged approximately 7, 9, 12, 13, 14, 15, 18, 19 and 21.
27. Bruce 1856, p. 6.
28. Holland was a type of cloth.
29. Jacques 1996, p. 62. Each woman stitched her name below the section on which she worked.
30. Barker 1992 (see note 20).
31. Conservation work undertaken in 1992 revealed that panels were not lined up correctly when joined together. The conservator noted that some blue borders were longer than the panel and excess was taken up. These anomalies could relate to extensive cleaning and repair of severe damage undertaken in 1927. After a third washing, relining and remounting the panels were hung as separate sections in Reading Museum.
32. See King 2009a.
33. *Boston Daily Journal*, December 1886.
34. *New York Tribune*, 1887.
35. Schoeser and Rufey 1989, p. 51.
36. It is likely that this method of display was used elsewhere as it would adapt to any space. 'The Bayeux Tapestry. A "Tragical-Comical-Historical-Pastoral", as Polonius would Say'. *'The Springfield Republican'*, Springfield Massachusetts, 20/03/1887.
37. Jacques 1996, p. 64.
38. *Leek Post*, 23 March 1928.

Chapter 4: Stitch Meets Stone

1. Duffy 2012, p. 102.
2. Ibid., p. 91.
3. Ibid., p. 113.
4. Ibid.
5. The V&A's well-received exhibition *Opus Anglicanum* made this era better known and admired.
6. Stamp 2002, p. 3.
7. Ruskin 1849.
8. Miller 2012, p. 6.
9. Hulse 2010.
10. Stamp 2002, p. 6.
11. Wainwright 1981.
12. Stamp 2002, p. 7.
13. Anon. 1845, pp. 97–197.
14. Schoeser 1998, p. 55.
15. Ibid., p. 48.
16. Higgin 1886a, p. 125.

17. Ibid.
18. Fisher 2006, p. 63.
19. Schoeser 1998, p. 45.
20. Street promoted the use of strong motifs, particularly those from the late fifteenth century, organised in an orderly manner. The sedilia hanging shows two alternating stylised floral motifs appliquéd onto plainly woven olive green felted wool cloth. The altar frontal of cream wool has more intricate geometrical motifs based on Gothic precedents and is worked in cream and gold with strong red and blue highlights.
21. See Fisher 2006, p. 75.
22. Saint 2010.
23. Fisher 2006, p. 28.
24. Hall 2014, back cover.
25. Schoeser 1998, p. 58.
26. Hulse 2010, p. 21.
27. Hall 2014, p. 272.
28. See the Watts & Co. website, https://www.wattsandco.com (accessed 2014).
29. The designs were: 'Blenheim', 'Gloria', 'Hart', 'Henry VII', 'Medallion', 'Ridley', 'Sarum', 'Thistle' and 'Valence'.
30. Silverware to Bodley's design was acquired for the Compton School chapel, Leek.
31. See King 2005.
32. An archive in Oxford holds designs and completed work by Ninian Comper.
33. Thomas Wardle became a partner in his father's business in 1852.
34. Edgar was a local architect who knew Scott previously. He designed Compton School chapel, Leek.
35. Stamp 2002, p. 210.
36. Ibid., p. 8.
37. T. Wardle, 20 April 1876, reprinted in *Cheddleton Parish Magazine*, 1890.
38. Stamp 2002, p. 5.
39. Quoted in Stamp 2002, p. 5, taken from G.G. Scott, 'The Argument for the Intellectual Character of the First Cause as Affected by Recent Investigations of Physical Science. Being the Burney Prize Essay for the year DCCCLXVIII'. Unpublished thesis, Cambridge University, 1870, p. 82.
40. Jacques 1996, p. 28.
41. Ibid., p. 58.
42. Morris 1893, p. 27. As May Morris stated, couching was a method 'admirably suited for decorating materials which are to be displayed flat'.
43. Scott's design for the cushions, originally intended to be a curtain, has recently been identified in the Jones and Willis archive, the Wolfson Centre, The Library of Birmingham.
44. Now in the RIBA archives, the same notebook has references to nearby churches, such as Leek, Bakewell, Waterhouses and Tideswell, as well as Hardwick Hall, Derbyshire.
45. Parry 1996, p. 132.
46. Stamp 2002, p. 212.
47. Harrison 1996, p. 132.
48. Similar angels were embroidered for a cope for Lincoln cathedral.
49. Elletson 2011, p. 19.
50. Thanks to David Gazeley, director of Watts & Co., for this information.
51. King 2005.

52. *Cheddleton Parish Magazine*, no. 53, May 1890.
53. Monnas 2008, Fig. 189, p. 174.
54. Stamp 2002, p. 382.
55. Ibid., p. 286.
56. See the image of St George, detail of an altarpiece for the cathedral of Sant'emidio, Cappella del Sacramento, in Monnas 2008, p. 171, in which the background cloth has a design that is close to that utilised by Scott.
57. Now in the RIBA archives.
58. Stamp 2002, p. 382.
59. West Derby could indicate the large diocesan region, not just an area of the city of Liverpool. With thanks to Vicky Williams for this clarification.
60. Hall 2014, p. 58.
61. They are the parish church of St Edward, Leek, All Saints, Compton, Leek, and the Nicholson Institute, Leek.
62. The same design was adapted for a chancel carpet stitched for the parish church of St Edward, Leek, where it is still in use. It was adapted for two silk thread embroideries: one is now in Cheddleton church, the other is held by Staffordshire Museum Service.
63. Inder and Aldis 1998. Her twenty-eight diaries and other surviving documents from family members reveal a certain amount about her and her needlework. Thanks are due to Inder and Aldis, who produced a small, invaluable publication from their research.
64. Inder and Aldis discovered that Emily was Susanna's elder sister and Dora was their niece (see Inder and Aldis 1998, p. 3).
65. Typescripts of William Morris's letters, Staffordshire Record Office, accession no. 618/36.
66. The fragment was saved by Mrs Barbara Fishburne.
67. Inder and Aldis 1998, p. 15.
68. Betjeman 1970, p. 104.
69. Saint 2010, p. 10.
70. Ibid., p. 332.
71. Ibid., p. 302.
72. Ibid., p. 300.
73. It was produced by a small Suffolk company, East Anglian Weavers, in Sudbury, Suffolk, and is still in production at Gainsborough Weavers, Sudbury, although renamed 'Hilliard'. I am grateful to Sue Kerry for this important link. Watts & Co. still supplies this damask.
74. Saint 2010, p. 303, n. 19.
75. Jacques 1996, p. 57.
76. Wilson 1892, p. 1.
77. Ibid., p. 5.
78. Ibid., p. 6.
79. Schoeser 1998, pp. 111–15.
80. Sedding 1893, p. 406.
81. Ibid., p. 407.
82. Ibid., p. 408.
83. See 'Arts and Crafts Architects', Holy Trinity Church, Sloane Street, London SW1X 9DF, http://www.vam.ac.uk/content/articles/a/arts-and-crafts-architecture (accessed 28 February 2018).

84. Sedding 1893, p. 411.
85. Snell 2006, p. 209.
86. Ibid.
87. Thanks to Val Harrison for supplying the parish records that are the source of this interesting information.
88. Mrs George Wardle was the wife of George Young Wardle. She was tried for the murder of her lover in Scotland in 1857. The case was 'not proven' after a notorious trial that received great publicity.
89. The stitched signatures read from left to right: Ann Sutton, Mary Young, Elisabeth Pidcock, Sarah Needham, Mary Elizabeth Sutton, Ann Clowes, Elizabeth Wardle, Rose Worthington, Alice Worthington, Fannie Shute, Catherine Whitles. The list ends with *Me Fecerunt*, 'my work'.
90. RIBA archives, DR10/6 1977.2.
91. A purple frontal of the 'Bird' damask has been stitched over in places, following the underlying woven pattern, a technique often used in Renaissance Italy. There is a matching pulpit fall that also uses the 'Bird' damask.
92. For example, frescoes in the side chapel of the Duomo, Verona, Italy.
93. Parkes 1893, p. 140.
94. A red brocade with orphreys of Leek embroidery for this church was priced at £25.
95. This pattern was block printed onto velvet and used for a Swedish royal palace. See King 2005.
96. Saint 2010, p. 347.
97. Ibid., p. 315.
98. Following Tracterian principles, there is a direct east–west trajectory from the marble font in the centre of the west wall of the nave to the high altar.
99. Betjeman 1958, p. 335.
100. Saint 2010, p. 335.
101. Parkes 1893, p. 138.
102. Wainwright 2014, p. 1.
103. Saint 2010, p. 189.
104. All Saints, Compton, Leek, St Edward the Confessor and St Luke's, Leek, St Luke's, Endon, St James's, Sutton, Cheshire, St James's and St Paul's, Marton, Cheshire, St Peter's, Prestbury, Cheshire, The English Church, Khartoum.
105. It is described in documents as a Utrecht velvet, with the design worked in coloured and gold thread.
106. I am grateful to David Gazeley, director of Watts & Co., for this information.
107. *Leek Post & Times.*
108. Correspondence between Wardle and Bodley, 1898. Staffordshire Record Office.
109. Ibid.
110. Ibid.
111. Patten and Barry 1996, slide 19.
112. Rigby was a textile designer with a national profile who shared a studio with his brother, also a designer. He married 'Kitten', daughter of George Young Wardle and Madeleine Smith.
113. Patten and Barry 1996, slide 28.
114. Ibid. Patten and Barry 1996 includes a reference to parish notes of 1888, which refer to this frontal.

Conclusion: Rediscoveries and Revelations

1. Menon 2013, p. 16.
2. Exhibitions were held in the William Morris Gallery, London; the Whitworth Art Gallery, Manchester; the Silk Museum, Macclesfield; and the Nicholson Institute, Leek. *Silk and Empire*, by Brenda King, was published by Manchester University Press.
3. Wardle 1887, p. 81.
4. Menon 2013, p. 16.
5. Bandyopadhyay 2009, p. 1.
6. Ibid.
7. King 2013, p. 21. SUTRA is a textile studies organisation founded by Amrita Mukerji in 2003.
8. Balfour-Paul 2013, p. 18.
9. Organised by Amrita Mukerji, founder and then president of SUTRA.
10. Bandyopadhyay 2009, p. 1.
11. Bannerjee 2014, p. 1.
12. Wardle 1887, p. 81.
13. *The British Raj in the Peak District* was available on BBC Radio 4 iPlayer for some considerable time after the festival.
14. I am grateful to Nicholas Gilmour, Lana Gilmour's son, for this fascinating information.
15. Leek embroideries were produced for Grahamstown, South Africa; Port Elizabeth, South Africa; and Khartoum in the Sudan.
16. Leek Press papers, 1892.
17. Hicks 2006, pp. 184–5. Surprisingly, Hicks uses a photograph of Elizabeth Wardle to analyse her 'personality.' She is described as 'stolid' and 'obsessed'. There is no evidence to support the repeated claim that she had a mental health problem or that she ran the London shop occasionally. There are too many other inaccuracies to list in 'The Ladies of Leek' section of Hicks' book, which is devoted to the Bayeux Tapestry facsimile.
18. Cluckie 2008, p. 88, states that Elizabeth Wardle established an embroidery school 'motivated by factors concerning matriarchy, materialism and the need to be needed'. On p. 95 the author persists with this theme, stating that Elizabeth Wardle's motives for starting an embroidery society related to her 'bringing up so many children, the need to be needed must have been inculcated'. On p. 97 Cluckie states that 'Elizabeth's connection with embroidery would have been typical of the era, initially a group of women stitching together, blossomed into religious fervour with the massive church building programme …'. On p. 86 she declares that the Wardles purported that the school was a philanthropic venture. There is no basis in fact for these statements, nor for others too numerous to list, relating to the Wardle family.
19. Important material regarding the needlewomen of Leek has recently come to light owing to the strenuous efforts of local Leek historian Cathryn Walton. Her book, *Hidden Lives: Leek's Extraordinary Embroiderers*, reveals a great deal about the women who produced the work. It has, though, proved remarkably difficult to find anything at all about the skilled male workers who made a vital contribution to the success of the Leek Embroidery Society. The thread makers, weavers, dyers, block cutters, block printers and braid and fringe producers remain anonymous to a man. See Figure 7.

BIBLIOGRAPHY

Anon. 'The Book of the Opening of the William Morris Labour Church'

Anon. 'Church Needlework and Altar Hangings'. *The Ecclesiologist*, no. III, May 1845, pp. 97–197

Anon. *Exhibition of Modern Embroidery* catalogue. Leek, 1881

Anon. 'Art Needlework'. *The Lady*, 9 February 1888

Anon. *The Ladies Field*, 2 October 1898

Aplin, J. *The Letters of Philip Webb, Vol. 3*. London: Routledge, 2015

Balfour-Paul, J. 'Only Connect'. *Marg: A Magazine of the Arts*, 65/2, December 2013, pp. 17–19

Bandyopadhyay, K. 'A Treasure Trove to Dye For'. *The Times of India*, 24 October 2009, p. 1

Bannerjee, S. 'A Silk Story to Dye For'. *Telegraph*, 22 February 2014, p. 1

Betjeman, J. *Best British Churches*. Collins: London, 1958

Betjeman, J. *Ghastly Good Taste*. London: Anthony Blond, 1970

Cecil, B. and Dasgupta, U. *Natural Dyes, Destination India*. Kolkata: SUTRA, in collaboration with the Botanical Survey of India, 2014

Cluckie, L. *The Rise and Fall of Art Needlework*. Bury St Edmunds: Arena Books, 2008

Day, L.F. *Art in Needlework*. London: B.T. Batsford Ltd, 1900

Duffy, E. *Saints, Sacrilege and Sedition*. London: Bloomsbury, 2012

Edwards, J. and Hart, I. *Rethinking the Interiore*. 1867–1896, Farnham: Ashgate, 2010

Elletson, H. *William Morris Society Newsletter*. Autumn 2011

Fisher, M. *Staffordshire and the Gothic Revival*. Ashbourne: Landmark Publishing, 2006

Gere, C. *Artistic Circles: Design and Decoration in the Aesthetic Movement*. London, V&A Publishing, 2010

Goodall, M. *Friends of the William Morris Gallery Newsletter*. Autumn 2017

Hall, M. *George Frederic Bodley and the Later Gothic Revival in Britain and America*. New Haven and London: Yale University Press, 2014

Harrison, M. 'Church Decoration and Stained Glass', in L. Parry (ed.), *William Morris*. London: Philip Wilson Publishers (in association with the Victorian and Albert Museum), 1996, pp. 106–35

Harvey, H. and Press, J. *William Morris: Design and Enterprise in Victorian Britain*. Manchester and New York: Manchester University Press, 1993

Hicks, C. *The Bayeux Tapestry: the Life Story of a Masterpiece*. London: Chatto and Windus, 2006

Higgin, L. *The Royal School of Needlework, Handbook of Embroidery*. London: Royal School of Needlework, 1880

Higgin, L. 'The Revival of Decorative Needlework'. *Art Journal*, April–May 1886a, pp. 122–6

Higgin, L. 'The Revival of Decorative Needlework'. *Art Journal*, April–May 1886b, pp. 139–44

Hulse, L. 'Introduction', in L. Higgin, *The Royal School of Needlework, Handbook of Embroidery*. London: Royal School of Needlework, 2010, pp. 1–36

Inder, P. and Aldis, M. *Susanna's Carpet? An Historical Investigation*. Deepings Court Publications, 1998

Jacques, A. *The Wardle Story*. Leek: Churnet Valley Books, 1996

Kelvin, N. (ed.) *The Collected Letters of William Morris*. Princeton: Princeton University Press, 1984

King, B.M. *Silk and Empire*. Manchester: Manchester University Press, hardback 2005, paperback 2009a

King, B.M. *Dye, Print, Stitch: Textiles by Thomas and Elizabeth Wardle*. Published by the author, 2009b

King, B.M. 'Recalculating Colour: Thomas Wardle's Remarkable Dye Experiments'. *Colours of Nature: Dyes from the Indian Subcontinent, Marg: A Magazine of the Arts*, 65/2, December 2013, pp. 20–27

King, B. and Spring, M. *Knowing Design: An Interdisciplinary Approach to Understanding the Design Process in a National/Regional Context*. The 10th International Forum on Design Management Research and Education, Frankfurt, 16–18 November 2000

King, B. and Spring, M. 'The Design Process in its Regional/National Context: A Knowledge Management Approach'. *The Design Journal*, 4/3, 2001, pp. 4–19

Lister, J., Marsh, J. *et al.* (eds), *May Morris: Arts and Crafts Designer*. London: Thames and Hudson, 2017

MacCarthy, F. *William Morris: A Life for Our Time*. London: Faber and Faber, 1994

MacGowan, D. *The Strange Affair of Madeleine Smith*. Edinburgh: Mercat Press, 2007

Mackail, J.W. *The Life of William Morris*. New York: Dover Publications, 1899

Marsh, J. and Sharp, F.C. (eds) *The Collected Letters of Jane Morris*. Woodbridge: Boydell and Brewer, 2013

Masters, E.T. *The Gentlewoman's Book of Art Needlework*. London: Henry and Co., 1892

Menon, K.G. 'Foreword'. *Marg: A Magazine of the Arts*, 65/2, December 2013, p. 16

Miller, L. 'From the Papers'. *William Morris Society Newsletter*. Spring 2012

Monnas, L. *Merchants, Princes and Painters*. New Haven and London: Yale University Press, 2008

Morris, B. *Liberty Design*. New Jersey: Chartwell Books, 1989

Morris, M. *Decorative Needlework*. London: Joseph Hughes and Co., 1893

Morris, W. 'Of the Origins of Ornamental Art'. *Manchester Guardian*, 27 September 1886, p. 6

Mukerji, A. 'Introduction', in *Natural Dyes, Destination India*. Kolkata: SUTRA, Textile Studies, 2014, pp. 4–7

Parkes, K. 'The Leek Embroidery Society'. *The Studio*, 1/4, 1893, pp. 136–40

Parry, L. (ed.) *William Morris*. London: Philip Wilson Publishers, 1996

Parry, L. *William Morris Textiles*. London: V&A Publishing, 2013

Patten, B. and Barry, J. *The Rediscovery of Ritual: Embroidery and Architecture in the Nineteenth Century*. Slide pack. Manchester: Manchester Metropolitan University, 1996

Ruskin, J. *The Seven Lamps of Architecture: of Beauty, of Life, of Memory, of Obedience, of Power, of Sanctity, of Truth*. London: Smith, Elder and Co., 1849

Saint, A. *Richard Norman Shaw*. New Haven and London: Yale University Press, 2010

Schoeser, M. *English Church Embroidery 1833–1953*. London: Watts and Co. Ltd, 1998

Sedding, J.D. 'Design', in *Arts and Crafts Essays*. London: Rivington, Percival and Co., 1893, p. 405–13

Snell, P.M. '"The Priest of Form". John Dando Sedding (1838–91) and the Language of Late Victorian Architecture'. Unpublished Ph.D. thesis, Manchester University, 2006

Stamp, G. *An Architect of Promise: George Gilbert Scott Junior (1839–1897) and the Late Gothic Revival*. Donington: Shaun Tyas, 2002

Wainwright, C. 'The Architect and the Decorative Arts' (exhibition review). *The Victorian Web*, 1981, http://victorianweb.org/art/architecture/cw.html (accessed 9 August 2013)

Walker, L. 'Women and Church Art', in T. Sladen and A. Saint (eds), *Churches 1870–1914*. London: The Victorian Society, 2011, pp. 121–43

Walton, C. *Hidden Lives: Leek's Extraordinary Embroiderers*. 2014. Available from the author: wcathryn@hotmail.com

Wardle, G.Y. *The Morris Exhibit at the Foreign Fair, Boston*. Boston: Roberts Brothers, 1883

Wardle, T. *Handbook of the Collection Illustrative of the Wild Silks of India in the South Kensington Museum, with a Catalogue of the Collection and Numerous Illustrations*. London: Eyre and Spottiswood, 1881, sold at the South Kensington Museum

Wardle, T. Catalogue *The Silk Section*. Manchester, 1887

Wardle, T. 'Cheddleton Parish Magazine', 20th April 1890

Watkinson, R. 'Morris's Beginnings in Embroidery'. *Journal of William Morris Studies*, 8/1, Autumn 1988, pp. 25–8

Watkinson, R. 'Living Dyeing: Morris, Merton and the Wardles'. *Journal of the William Morris Society*, Autumn 1997, pp. 20–25

Wilson, H. *In Memoriam*. London: B.T. Batsford Ltd, 1892

FURTHER READING

Anon. *Making History: 300 Years of Antiquaries in Britain*. London: Society of Antiquaries, 2008

Anson, P.F. *Fashions in Church Furnishings: 1840–1940*. London: Studio Vista, 1965

Armstrong, B. and Armstrong, W. *The Arts and Crafts Movement in the North West of England. A Handbook*. Wetherby: Oblong Creative Ltd, 2005

Arts and Crafts Essays (by members of the Arts and Crafts Exhibition Society). Bristol: Thoemmes Press, 1996

Ball, P. *Bright Earth: The Invention of Colour*. London: Vintage Books, 2008a

Ball, P. *Universe of Stone*. London: Bodley Head, 2008b

Briggs, A. (ed.) *William Morris: Selected Writings and Designs*. Harmondsworth: Penguin, 1962

Browne, C., Davies, G. and Michael, M.A. (eds) *English Medieval Embroidery*. New Haven and London: Yale University Press, 2016

Bruce, J. Collingwood. *The Bayeux Tapestry Elucidated*. London: J.R. Smith, 1856

Calloway, S. (ed.) *The House of Liberty: Masters of Style and Decoration*. London: Thames and Hudson, 1992

Cumming, E. and Kaplan, W. *The Arts and Crafts Movement*. London: Thames and Hudson, 1991

Daniels, R. and Brandwood, G. *Ruskin and Architecture*. London: Spire Books, 2003

Dean, B. *Ecclesiastical Embroidery*. London: B.T. Batsford Ltd, 1958

Dolby, A. *Church Embroidery*. London: Chapman and Hall, 1867

Dore, H. *William Morris*. London: Chancellor Press, 2003

Hammond, C. 'Anglican Lurch'. *TLS*, 12 August 2016

Hands, H.M. *Church Needlework, a Manual of Practical Instruction*. 4th edition. London: The Faith Press Ltd, 1929

Hart, I. *Arts and Crafts Objects*. Manchester: Manchester University Press, 2012

Haweis, Rev. H.R. 'The Art Movement: Church Art and The Church Congress'. *Magazine of Art*, 1898, pp. 132–5

Hill, R. (ed.) *Victorians Revalued*. London: The Victorian Society, 2010

Hockney, D. and Gayford, M. *A History of Pictures*. London: Thames and Hudson, 2016

Hyde, M. *Britain's Lost Churches*. London: Aurum, 2016

Johnstone, P. *High Fashion in the Church*. Leeds: Maney, 2002

Jones, O. *The Grammar of Ornament*. Reprint. London: Parkgate Books, 1997

King, B.M. 'Full Circle: India–Leek–India'. *Journal for Weavers, Spinners and Dyers*, 237, Spring 2011, pp. 16–19

King, B.M. 'Collecting India: the Wardle Collection of Indian Silks and its Changing Role'. *Text*, 39, 2011–12, pp. 24–8

King, B.M. 'Thomas Wardle's Specimens of Fabrics Dyed With Indian dyes', in *Natural Dyes, Destination India*. Kolkata: SUTRA, in collaboration with the Botanical Survey of India, February 2014a, pp. 14–19

King, B.M. 'Whose Responsibility?' *Embroidery: The Textile Art Magazine*, November 2014b, pp. 50–52

King, B.M. *Ecclesiastical Textiles: A Heritage at Risk*. Textile Society, Ecclesiastical Textiles Study Day, London, March 2015a

King, B.M. 'Recalculating Colour: Thomas Wardle and India's Dyestuffs'. *Text*, 42, 2015b, p. 23–5

King, B.M. *Textiles and the Parish Church*. Online module for a Postgraduate Diploma in the History, Heritage and Fabric of the English Parish Church. York: Centre for the Study of Christianity and Culture, Department of History, University of York, 2015c

MacCarthy, F. *The Last Pre-Raphaelite*. London: Faber and Faber, 2011

Making History: 300 Years of Antiquaries in Britain. London: Society of Antiquaries, London 2008

Monnas, L. *Renaissance Velvets*. London: V&A Publishing, 2012

Morris, B. *Victorian Embroidery: An Authoritative Guide*. London: Herbert Jenkins, 1962

Morris, W. *Art and Beauty of Earth*. Chiswick Press, 1898

Naylor, G. *The Arts and Crafts Movement*. London: Trefoil Publications, 1971

Naylor, G. *William Morris by Himself*. London: Time Warner Books, 2004

Parry, L. *William Morris Textiles*. London: Weidenfeld and Nicolson, 1983

Parry, L. *Textiles of the Arts and Crafts Movement*. London: Thames and Hudson, 1988

Parry, L. *The Victoria and Albert Museum's Textile Collection: British Textiles from 1850 to 1900*. London: Victoria and Albert Museum, 1993

The Reformers' Year Book, 'Introduction'. London: The Labour Record Office, 1901

Rhodes, F. and Rhodes, P. 'Medieval Embroidered "Water Flowers"'. *Textile History*, 47/2, 13 September 2016, pp. 243–8

Ruskin, J. *The Stones of Venice*. London: Smith, Elder and Co., 1851–3

Schoeser, M. and Rufey, C. *English and American Textiles*. London: Thames and Hudson, London, 1989

Sennett, R. *The Craftsman*. London: Allen Lane, 2008

Service, A. *Edwardian Architecture and its Origins*. London: The Architectural Press, 1975

Sladen, T. and Saint, A. (eds) *Churches 1870–1914*. London: The Victorian Society, 2011

Staniland, K. *Medieval Craftsmen: Embroiderers*. London: British Museum Press, 1991 (7th impression, 2006)

Stavenow-Hidemark, E. *Sub-Rosa: Når skonheten om fran England*. Stockholm: Nordiska Museets, 1991

Trubner, P.K. *Trubner's Oriental Series*. London: Trench, Trubner and Co., 1893

Wainwright, O. 'Master Draughtsman's Work on Display at the RA'. *Guardian*, 31 May 2014, p. 17

Wardle, E. *Guide to the Bayeux Tapestry*. Bemrose and Sons, London; and Derby, 1886

Wardle, G.Y. *Memorials of William Morris*. London: British Library, 1897, Add MSS 45350

Wardle, T. *Report on the Dyes and Tans of India, Calcutta*. Printed by the Superintendent of Government Printing, India, 1887

Wardle, T. 'History and Growing Utilisation of Tussur Silk', a paper read at the Royal Society of Arts, London, 14 May 1891. W. Trounce, London

Williamson, P. (ed.) *The Medieval Treasury*. London: Victoria and Albert Museum, 1986

INDEX

Page numbers in *italics* refer to figures/caption text; plate numbers are in **bold**.

Milton Keynes UK
Ingram Content Group UK Ltd.
UKHW021502111023
430369UK00002B/40